Presidential Privilege and the Freedom of Information Act

New Perspectives on the American Presidency
Series Editors: Michael Patrick Cullinane and Sylvia Ellis,
University of Roehampton

Published titles
*Constructing Presidential Legacy: How We Remember the
American President*
Edited by Michael Patrick Cullinane and Sylvia Ellis

Presidential Privilege and the Freedom of Information Act
Kevin M. Baron

Forthcoming titles
Obama v. Trump: The Politics of Rollback
Clodagh Harrington and Alex Waddan

Series website: <https://edinburghuniversitypress.com/new-
perspectives-on-the-american-presidency.html>

PRESIDENTIAL PRIVILEGE AND THE FREEDOM OF INFORMATION ACT

Kevin M. Baron

EDINBURGH
University Press

To Serena and Alice with Love

Edinburgh University Press is one of the leading university presses in the UK. We publish academic books and journals in our selected subject areas across the humanities and social sciences, combining cutting-edge scholarship with high editorial and production values to produce academic works of lasting importance. For more information visit our website: edinburghuniversitypress.com

© Kevin M. Baron, 2019, 2020

Edinburgh University Press Ltd
The Tun – Holyrood Road
12(2f) Jackson's Entry
Edinburgh EH8 8PJ

First published in hardback by Edinburgh University Press 2019

Typeset in 11/13 Sabon by
Servis Filmsetting Ltd, Stockport, Cheshire
and printed and bound by CPI Group (UK) Ltd,
Croydon, CR0 4YY

A CIP record for this book is available from the British Library

ISBN 978 1 4744 4244 2 (hardback)
ISBN 978 1 4744 4245 9 (paperback)
ISBN 978 1 4744 4246 6 (webready PDF)
ISBN 978 1 4744 4247 3 (epub)

The right of Kevin M. Baron to be identified as the author of this work has been asserted in accordance with the Copyright, Designs and Patents Act 1988, and the Copyright and Related Rights Regulations 2003 (SI No. 2498).

Contents

Preface: Should the information be free?

In the first two months of 2018, former White House political advisor and Trump campaign manager Steve Bannon testified before the House Intelligence Committee, where he invoked executive privilege to refuse answering questions.[1] President Trump provided written justification to Congress authorizing the use of executive privilege, asserting that the president needed the ability to have confidence in his staff, therefore shielding his colleague from making private conversations public and giving him the ability to refuse answering questions during congressional testimony. The reasoning Trump provided to protect Bannon's testimony is consistent with the practice of postwar presidents. A month earlier, during testimony before the same committee, Bannon invoked executive privilege by refusing to answer questions. At the time Congress considered holding Bannon in contempt for his refusal, but never officially took steps to do so. Bannon was subpoenaed as part of Congress's investigation into Russian interference during the 2016 election, and Bannon managed Trump's campaign before working in the White House. While both Republican and Democratic members of the committee were irritated over Bannon's unwillingness to answer questions, Congress has thus far allowed Trump's invocation of executive privilege to stand.

The current investigations into Russian interference in the 2016 election, from both Congress and the Justice Department, raise specific questions about the use of executive privilege by the

---

[1] Manu Raju, Jeremy Herb, and Kara Scannell, "Bannon stonewalls House panel after WH advised him to invoke executive privilege," CNN, February 15, 2018. Available online: <https://www.cnn.com/2018/02/14/politics/bannon-contempt-hearing/index.html> (last accessed February 18, 2018).

Trump administration. First, while Trump remains consistent with past precedent on use of executive privilege, the question becomes whether it can be invoked to shield information or testimony during the campaign period, prior to Trump being elected president. Can the current president invoke executive privilege to cover a time when he was not president? That question has not been addressed before from a legal perspective, and the political ramifications are more striking in bringing continued accusations of wrongdoing and collusion during the campaign. Second, while Trump is following the same guidelines on executive privilege as his predecessors, the Supreme Court decision in *US v. Nixon* from 1974 determined specifically that executive privilege cannot be used by the president in cases of criminal intent. The question now being whether there was collusion between Trump's campaign and Russia or other foreign entities, which at the time of this writing, twenty-three indictments have been issued by the special investigator, Robert Mueller, to members of Trump's campaign staff and Russian nationals. While Trump himself continues to deny these allegations, his authorizing former staff members to invoke executive privilege raises concerns, particularly within a politically charged environment. Executive privilege is a political grey area, and the current investigations into the Trump administration have brought past concerns back to the fore. Setting aside legal arguments, the question becomes whether Congress will politically hold Trump and his administration officials accountable in pushing back, or checking the power of executive privilege as they have done in the past.

Control of information has been a vibrant factor of politics since the colonial period. Issues like freedom of information, government secrecy, and executive privilege have dominated politics in the post-World War II era, and continue into the contemporary period. On January 21, 2009 on his first full day as president, President Barack Obama issued two memos focused on transparency and public access to government records. In the first memo, Obama followed through on a campaign promise of "creating an unprecedented level of openness in government."[2]

---

[2] Barack Obama: "Memorandum on Transparency and Open Government,"

His argument was that transparency leads to public trust, which increases participation and collaboration, thus strengthening democracy. In part, Obama's memo served as a political push-back against the George W. Bush administration, which had been popularly accused of being overly secretive. The second memo Obama issued focused on the Freedom of Information Act (FOIA), which reversed several Bush administration policy positions, such as establishing a clear presumption of disclosure reaffirming openness and transparency under FOIA as the norm.[3] The political argument Obama established was that open government and accountability leading to citizen oversight strengthened democracy to the benefit of everyone.

However, by the end of the Obama administration, accusations of being the least transparent administration and setting records for withholding the largest number of FOIA requests, more than the previous Bush administration, were rampant.[4] Widespread complaints forced Congress to act by passing the FOIA Improvement Act of 2016 (Public Law No. 144-185) to fix numerous procedural and administrative problems. The bill passed the Senate by unanimous consent and the House by a voice vote, which is almost unheard of in the modern hyperpartisan Congress. Beyond these measures, Obama targeted those

January 21, 2009. Available online at <https://www.archives.gov/files/cui/documents/2009-WH-memo-on-transparency-and-open-government.pdf> (last accessed November 10, 2018).

[3] Barack Obama: "Memorandum on the Freedom of Information Act," January 21, 2009. Available online at Gerhard Peters and John Woolley, *The American Presidency Project*, <https://www.presidency.ucsb.edu/documents/memorandum-the-freedom-information-act> (last accessed November 10, 2018).

[4] Alex Howard, "How should history measure the Obama administration's record on transparency?" Sunlight Foundation, September 2, 2016. Available online: <https://sunlightfoundation.com/2016/09/02/how-should-history-measure-the-obama-administrations-record-on-transparency/> (last accessed November 10, 2018); and Ted Bridis, "Obama administration sets new record for withholding FOIA requests," Associated Press, March 18, 2015. Available online: <http://www.pbs.org/newshour/rundown/obama-administration-sets-new-record-withholding-foia-requests/> (last accessed November 10, 2018).

leaking secret or classified information under the Espionage Act more than any other modern president, a model President Trump seems to be following with his Justice Department in tow.[5] The amendment to FOIA is the most recent change, but FOIA has been amended multiple times since being implemented in 1967. The Obama administration, while seeking increased transparency and openness in government, seems to have fallen into a pattern established long before he came into office. The same pattern of increased secrecy has extended to the Trump administration, which has been plagued by leaks of secret, classified, and inside information, prompting Attorney General Jeff Sessions and the Justice Department to increase investigations into leaks threefold.[6]

Contemporary US politics is a politically charged environment, where partisan politics dominates debates and accusations of fake news, political spin, and the use of propaganda have become commonplace. Underlying the current politics is a long history of contention between the citizenry and government over access to information. Debates from the colonial period helped enshrine the protections of the free press in the First Amendment, and comments from the Founders on the need for an informed citizenry. Less defined in the Constitution is the relation between the executive and legislative branches over access to information, in particular when it comes to congressional oversight functions, or in situations where the president claims a need for secrecy out of national security concerns. It is this institutional power ambiguity that led to the modern use of executive privilege and the subsequent congressional pushback.

Public access to government information has always been a

---

[5] Jon Greenberg, "CNN's Tapper: Obama has used Espionage Act more than all previous administrations." PunditFact, January 10, 2014. Available online: <http://www.politifact.com/punditfact/statements/2014/jan/10/jake-tapper/cnns-tapper-obama-has-used-espionage-act-more-all-/> (last accessed November 10, 2018).

[6] Charlie Savage and Eileen Sullivan, "Leak Investigations Triple Under Trump, Sessions Says," *New York Times*, August 4, 2017. Available online: <https://www.nytimes.com/2017/08/04/us/politics/jeff-sessions-trump-leaks-attorney-general.html> (last accessed November 10, 2018).

tenuous issue for those in American government, in particular for the executive branch. Going back to the mid eighteenth century, Benjamin Franklin is cited acknowledging a balance between "essential liberty" and safety.[7] This quote is often recited in a contemporary context by citizens angry over excessive government secrecy, or the National Security Agency (NSA) wiretapping program and metadata collection, or even by those exiled for leaking classified information, like Edward Snowden or Julian Assange. For those angry citizens, the quote serves to demonstrate an overbearing government infringing upon individual rights.[8] Yet regardless of Franklin's intent, the legacy of the quote has survived to create a contemporary conundrum for the modern era in trying to find a balance between the government need for security and the individual's need for liberty. However, determining the proper balance of liberty and security will always be tenuous as the balance can only be defined within the context of the moment in which it is being debated. Political change will shift the balance point, such as it did during the Cold War or post-9/11. Regardless, government officials will always make claims of needed security, which stands in contrast to the governed, who seek liberty. Context matters, as the politics of the moment impact the policy decisions made by those in office or in power, which has long-term impacts on society. The president will always claim secrecy out of a need for national security within the public interest. It becomes incumbent on the other branches, Congress and the courts, to check the use of that power as needed, or when it seems out of balance within the political climate.

However, this debate is not new, and in fact is part of a much larger discussion that stretches back to the colonial and founding period. An American tradition of a free press and open access to government records was derived from the English roots of the

---

[7] The quote is "Those who would give up essential Liberty, to purchase a little temporary Safety, deserve neither Liberty nor Safety."

[8] Benjamin Wittes, "Against a Crude Balance: Platform Security and the Hostile Symbiosis between Liberty and Security," Brookings Institution Report, September 21, 2011. Available online: <https://www.brookings.edu/research/against-a-crude-balance-platform-security-and-the-hostile-symbiosis-between-liberty-and-security/> (last accessed November 10, 2018).

colonists, much as a response to unyielding secrecy. During the seventeenth and eighteenth centuries in England, the press was barred from reporting on any activities of parliament and was severely punished if they did, where punishment could result in death.[9] Many colonial governments shared a similar perception that government business was in no way a public matter. Governor Berkeley of Virginia best sums up this position in a 1671 correspondence where he stated,

> I thank God, we have no free schools nor printing; and I hope we shall not have these hundred years; for learning has brought disobedience and heresy and sects into the world; and printing has divulged them, and libels against the government. God keep us from both.[10]

While it would seem that the governing class within the colonies preferred an uneducated and ill-informed citizenry, many of the colonists began to revolt at such conditions. A 1689 uprising led by John Coode protested the Maryland government for passing a law that would punish "all speeches, practices, and attempts relating to his lordship and government, that shall be thought mutinous and seditious."[11] Punishments for violating this law were "whipping, branding, boring through the tongue, fines, imprisonment, banishment or death." Numerous examples like this shape the history of colonial America, although the crackdown and subjugation of newspapers during this period sowed the seeds of its own destruction. As colonial America came closer and closer to rebellion in what we now know as the American Revolution, the idea of an informed citizenry became seen as vital in the efforts to push back against what was viewed as an oppressive English regime.

In 1765, a young John Adams published an anonymous essay in the *Boston Gazette* arguing that an informed citizenry was the most effective defense against tyranny. Adams stated,

> Whenever general Knowledge and sensibility have prevailed among the People, Arbitrary Government and every kind of oppression have

---

[9] Foerstel, *Freedom of Information*, 1999.
[10] Ibid.
[11] Ibid. p. 2.

lessened and disappeared in Proportion. . . . The people have a right, an indisputable, inalienable, indefensible divine right to that most dreaded and envied kind of knowledge, I mean the characters and conduct of their rulers. . . . The preservation of the means of knowledge among the lowest ranks, is of more importance than all the property of all the rich men in the country.[12]

The sentiment expressed by Adams would continue to grow among the colonists at this time, driven not just by the need to inform people of what was quickly being understood as an illegitimate governing regime across the pond, but also as a means of informing citizens about actions that could benefit the growth of a better form of self-government. In 1774, the Continental Congress passed the Quebec Declaration, which among a listing of grievances towards the British Crown and rights afforded the colonies through natural law, included a specific statement on the necessity of a free press. The declaration states,

The last right we shall mention regards the freedom of the press. The importance of this consists, besides the advancement of truth, science, morality, and arts in general, in its diffusion of liberal sentiments on the administration of government its ready communication of thoughts between subjects, and its consequential promotion of union among them, whereby oppressive officers are shamed or intimidated into more honorable and just modes of conducting affairs.

The colonial perspective on the value of a free press became paramount as the means to disseminate information about the oppressive governing regime in order to make a case for creating a new government. The core of the argument being that citizens have a right to be informed of government action, as an informed citizenry would serve as the basis of self-government. However, those Framers who would assert the need for such openness also suffered from hypocrisy. Representative David King (D-UT), in a House floor speech to support passage of FOIA in 1966, stated:

The deliberations that produced the Constitution of the United States were closed. Early meetings of the US Senate were not regularly opened to members of the public until February 1794. Some 177

[12] Ibid. p. 3.

years ago, the House of Representatives heatedly debated and finally tabled a motion that would have excluded members of the press from its sessions. It was the beginning of the nineteenth century before representatives of the press were formally granted admission to the Chambers of the Senate and the House of Representatives.[13]

Clearly, while the natural rights of men were wielded against the savage usurpations of the British Crown towards the colonists, the colonists themselves in both establishing a new government and through the implementation struggled with allowing complete and unfettered open access. Much as contemporary politics struggles to find a balance between the need for secrecy and public access, this debate began during the founding as the demands of politics and governing smashed into the ideals of open government.

Federalist and Anti-Federalist debates over what would become a bill of rights engaged around the issue of a free press, and the inherent or implied right of public access to information. The Anti-Federalist argument was expressed through the Letters of Brutus argued forcefully from the position of natural law and natural rights, in particular in Brutus II. Herbert Storing notes that one of the major areas of liberty for the Anti-Federalists was liberty of the press.[14] The focus of Brutus II centers on the classic liberal argument of natural rights and natural law. Brutus is utilizing the Federalist argument to contend that certain liberties exist in natural law that are afforded to all men, and that the new government cannot infringe upon those rights. The Anti-Federalist position was asserting the need for specific protections of liberty, based on natural rights, of which a free press and therefore access to information was considered essential and must be specifically expressed through a bill of rights.

The final outcome of this debate provided the Bill of Rights in which the First Amendment protects both liberties of speech and press. However, the practice of protecting such liberties from government quickly became a murky debate, as with the Alien and Sedition Acts of 1798. These laws provided the president

[13] Congressional Record. 1966. 89th Cong., 2nd sess., vol. 112, p. 13643.
[14] Storing, *Complete Anti-Federalist*, 1981.

with broad authority to imprison, fine, or punish any individual, including any member of the press, for speaking out against the government.[15] In following suit from their English forebears, the laws criminalized making false statements or criticizing the government. While President John Adams and the Federalists claimed the laws were needed for national security, the politics of the moment lent them to be condemned as violating the First Amendment.

The Alien and Sedition Acts marked another iteration in the continuing debate between governing and information control, setting a precedent establishing executive power over these matters that would be utilized time and time again. The Espionage Act of 1917, passed as the US entered into World War I, revived the ideas of seditious libel, which included the passage of an amendment to the Espionage Act a year later, referred to as the Sedition Act of 1918. By 1919, a trio of Supreme Court decisions handed down centered on the Espionage Act, all of which upheld the law including the punishments as constitutional and not in violation of First Amendment protections. In the 1925 decision in *Gitlow v. New York*, the Court upheld the prosecution of an individual for distributing left-wing pamphlets; the Court did, however, recognize the applicability of the First Amendment to the states through the liberty provision of the Fourteenth Amendment's due process clause.[16] The decision in *Gitlow* marked a shift in legal precedent that would establish First Amendment protections for individuals and the press, which would become part of the arguments the press asserted several decades later of the implied "right to know" in the First Amendment.

The roots of the current politics surrounding the issue of freedom of information become evident as grounded in colonial debates at the founding. Then as now these debates gain momentum as a response to perceived government abuses and secrecy. The ability to understand and contextualize this history provides the backdrop to understanding how the Freedom of Information Act came to exist, and the debates surrounding its legislative

---

[15] Foerstel, *Freedom of Information*, p. 8.
[16] Ibid. p. 9.

Acknowledgements

Writing a project of this magnitude, one finds oneself indebted to many for their support and assistance. The origins of this research date back to when I was in graduate school, so thank you to my mentors Larry Dodd, Rich Conley, Beth Rosenson, Zach Selden, and Sean Adams, as well as to my colleagues Keith Lee, Sebastian Sclofsky, and the Doddian Working Group, who listened to endless hours of my talking about FOIA. I owe a big debt of gratitude to the crew at the Bob Graham Center for Public Service, and the Department of Political Science at the University of Florida. I wish to thank all of the discussants and colleagues who have commented on this work at various stages through multiple presentations at the annual meetings of the American Political Science Association, the Midwest Political Science Association, the Southern Political Science Association, and the American Politics Group of the PSA. And a special thanks to T. J. Pyche for his willingness to be a research assistant with the newspaper dataset collection.

All of the archival research meant spending substantial time in reading rooms across the country, only made possible with assistance from many. The archival data on LBJ was made possible through a grant from the Lyndon Baines Johnson Foundation for research at the LBJ Presidential Library, and a grant from the Gerald R. Ford Presidential Foundation for research at the Gerald R. Ford Presidential Library. Thank you for the hospitality shown to me from the folks at the Richard M. Nixon Presidential Library, thank you to Thomas Eisinger and the staff at the Center for Legislative Archives at the National Archives in Washington, DC. Thank you to Sheila O'Neill at the John E. Moss Archives at Cal State Sacramento. And thank you to Mike Crespin and the wonderful staff at the Carl Albert Center

Acknowledgements

at the University of Oklahoma. Thank you to the archivists and staff at the Harry S. Truman, Dwight D. Eisenhower, and John F. Kennedy Presidential Libraries for creating numerous digital online archives available for researchers, allowing access to documents without having to travel.

A large thank you is owed to David Lonergan, Jen Daly, Rebecca Mackenzie, Camilla Rockwood, and the fine folks at Edinburgh University Press. A giant, warm, heartfelt thank you to Sylvia Ellis and Michael Cullinane for their endless support and guidance on this project; I hope your gamble on me has paid off. You have truly been a pleasure to work with and have put together a wonderful series on the American presidency that I am proud to be a part of. I would also like to thank all of the anonymous reviewers who provided helpful feedback at various stages of this project.

Huge personal thanks are owed to my parents, Bryon and Suzy Baron, for their continued belief in and support of my educational and academic efforts. To my daughter Alice, thank you for believing in me, and continue to follow your dreams—I love you. Last, but certainly not least, to my darling wife and partner, Serena, we began a journey together a long time ago, and you continue to make the ride worthwhile. I can never thank you enough for being you—thank you and I love you.

List of abbreviations

APA   Administrative Procedures Act of 1946
APME   Associated Press Managing Editors Association
ASNE   American Society of Newspaper Editors
BOB   Bureau of the Budget
CLDC   Continuing Legislative Development Cycle
DNC   Democratic National Committee
DOD   Department of Defense
DOJ   Department of Justice
EP   Executive Privilege
EO   Executive Order
FOGI   House Foreign Operations and Government
        Information Subcommittee
FOI   Freedom of Information
FOIA   Freedom of Information Act
HUAC   House Un-American Activities Committee
NSA   National Security Agency
OIS   Office of Strategic Information
RNC   Republican National Committee
SDX   Sigma Delta Chi
UN   United Nations

1

Introduction

An informed public makes the difference between mob rule and democratic government. If the pertinent and necessary information on governmental activities is denied to the public, the result is a weakening of the democratic process and the ultimate atrophy of our form of government.

—William L. Dawson, Chair, House Committee on
Government Operations, 1955

The information is free, if you can get it

Late in the morning on July 4, 1966, President Lyndon B. Johnson would reluctantly sign the Freedom of Information Act (FOIA) from his Texas White House. With no signing ceremony or fanfare Johnson signed the bill just a few hours before it would have been pocket vetoed and knowing full well that Congress lacked the votes to override a standard veto. Like all of his postwar predecessors, LBJ was not supportive of any legislation that would interfere with the president's ability to determine what information would be made public, especially if that information were to undermine national security interests. So why would LBJ sign the bill, and perhaps more importantly, why would a unified Democratic Congress seek to push a bill undermining presidential power over government information with their own president in office? These questions underlie this research, and in seeking to answer them, will lead us to better understand the contentious relationship between the president and Congress when it comes to the politics of policy, in particular, transformative policy that reshapes institutional power.

However, when examining the development of FOIA it becomes clear that it was not just LBJ who opposed opening up

1

executive information to Congress and the public. Increased government secrecy became entrenched within the executive branch following World War II, creating political space for the president and members of the administration, to act with little regard for congressional access and bolder assertions of executive privilege. Control over information is a tool of power, and one that has come to define the modern presidency. Within a separated system of shared power there exist a lot of grey areas, with a large one being executive privilege and access to information, particularly during the early postwar period prior to the end of the Nixon administration. The politics of secrecy and public access to government information functions within the confines of an institutional power that is dynamic in nature, fluctuating between the executive and legislative branches across time.

Excessive presidential control of information and rampant use of executive privilege to deny Congress access to information or testimony became institutionalized within Congress in the spring of 1955 with the formation of the Special Subcommittee on Government Information in the House of Representatives, chaired by Representative John E. Moss (D-CA). Known as the Moss Subcommittee, it was given jurisdiction to provide oversight and

> to study the operation of the agencies and officials in the executive branch of the government at all levels with the view to determining the efficiency and economy of such operation in the field of information both intragovernmental and extra governmental. With this guiding purpose your subcommittee will ascertain the trend in availability of government information and will scrutinize the information practices of executive agencies and officials in the light of their propriety, fitness, and legality.[1]

Firmly within the politics of the issue, the creation of the Moss Subcommittee provided the first congressional check on growing

---

[1] Letter from William L. Dawson to John Moss establishing the Special Subcommittee on Government Information, in Preface of Subcommittee Hearing Opening Statement, 1955. Folder: Hearings (1955–1956)—Correspondence re: plans and preparation [October 1955–February 1956], Box No. M-5, Center for Legislative Archives, National Archives, Washington, DC.

presidential power to control information flows within the unfolding Cold War era. As this research will show, beginning with Truman in 1946 through Ford in 1976, each administration used national security concerns to justify a stranglehold on executive branch information, and beginning with Eisenhower, the institutionalization in the president's use of executive privilege. Congress would respond in kind, by using tools of oversight and policy to counter claims of presidential power.

The political factors impacting the policymaking process creates a grey area of inter-branch power forming two distinct perspectives. The first perspective is that of the president, encompassing both the individual who has influence and input on the policy agenda, and the institution as the whole of all the agencies, offices, and personnel that comprise the executive branch.[2] The second perspective is that of Congress, which provides an individual viewpoint whereby certain members seek influence on specific issues or policies while constrained by rules and norms.[3] These individuals are often referred to in the literature as entrepreneurial, although there are different types, as I will show later. The institution of Congress as a whole, or at least within each house, directly engages with the executive branch within the policy process and on issues of ill-defined constitutional power. While Congress has historically sought avenues of limiting executive power through procedural means, shifting circumstances create new instances to debate ongoing power issues that have either remained unresolved or need to be reviewed anew.[4]

Therefore, policy itself can serve as a tool to better delineate the lines of power. When it comes to influence within the legislative process, the president and Congress each seek to shape the development period, control the voting period, regulate the implementation, and then circle back to seeking influence of the oversight and amendment period. As opposed to taking a

---

[2] Edwards, *At the Margins*, 1990; Burke, *The Institutional Presidency*, 2000; Beckmann, *Pushing the Agenda*, 2010.

[3] Oleszek, *Congressional Procedures*, 1978; Schickler, *Disjointed Pluralism*, 2001; Baumgartner and Jones, *Agendas and Instability*, 2009.

[4] Brass and Ginsberg, "Congress Evolving in the Face of Complexity," 2014.

presidency-centered approach or a Congress-centered approach, this research examines Constitutional power struggles as a constant, dynamic, and continual process, much like an ongoing game of chess. Two players seek short- and long-term strategies of success that place them in control at times and on defense at times, utilizing different tools at hand, all while being constrained by the rules of the game. While the chess analogy has been used before to describe this process and the political functionality inherent within, chess does provide a basic frame from which to begin. Neither the president nor Congress is in complete control, and while each attempts to dominate the other, they simultaneously rely on each other in order to accomplish their desired outcomes. It is possible for the politics of inherent Constitutional power, or intra-branch conflict, to change the rules of the game in response to certain moves.

Utilizing a single case, FOIA, offers the ability to examine these dynamics in depth, taking a look at the political development of one policy issue intertwined within the ongoing struggle between branches. The politics surrounding the development of FOIA offers several important factors requiring our attention. The first is that FOIA is an example of transformative policy. For my purposes here, transformative is defined as policy that alters the politics and functionality of governing institutions. As Brass and Ginsberg note, institutionalized transparency can come through policy by targeting process in the executive branch. When Congress alters executive processes, they can subtly or dramatically alter the functionality and capability of the executive branch. Institutionally, FOIA transformed the executive branch bureaucratically by establishing the need for an office in each department to handle requests, along with agency lawyers to address appeals. Due to the legal mechanism within the legislation allowing for federal lawsuits based on request denials, judicial branch functionality was altered as well. As we will see, the legal mechanism was one of the most contentious issues of the original bill, with the resulting compromise providing for nine categorical exemptions to public records requests. While not directly impacted as Congress chose to exempt themselves, the oversight function of Congress was transformed through establishing new committee jurisdiction, as well as offering members of Congress and their staff the ability to make requests under FOIA themselves.

As transformative policy, FOIA altered more than institutional roles; it also altered the politics within and between branches. This research centers on the political interactions between Congress and the president. FOIA became a policy tool in the midst of a contentious debate over issues of government secrecy, executive privilege, and public access to records. The Democratic Congress institutionalized the issue in the Moss Subcommittee as a direct response to the Eisenhower administration's clampdown on information to Congress, particularly through executive privilege and the creation of the Office of Strategic Information (OSI). Eisenhower's establishment of executive privilege acted as a game-changing move that prompted a congressional reaction, each branch using the issue to gain political footing with the public in seeking to influence the power debate. This debate is still ongoing in the contemporary period, where access to information remains paramount and executive privilege is potentially resurgent with the Trump administration.

FOIA provides a fascinating example for another reason, being that it is a counter-narrative to more traditional literature in this area. Much of the presidential literature on policymaking centers on the role of the president, with the narrative being given from the president's perspective on how this individual or those within the administration seek to influence policy against Congress. Much of the congressional literature generally treats the president and administration actors as marginal by focusing on the institutional perspective on policymaking within Congress, including the role of individual members. While it is understandable that these literatures focus the way they do, FOIA offers a policy that was specifically conceived by Congress as a check on presidential power. Yet LBJ signed it into law, where FOIA offers an example of how Congress is able to impose policy upon a president, specifically how Congress can use policy as a means of checking presidential power. Beyond the institutional power dynamics, FOIA is a case where a Democratic-controlled Congress foisted legislation on a Democratic president to reduce usage of executive privilege and wrest some control of government information from the president's strong grip. Understanding the politics behind the development and implementation of FOIA gives us a new perspective on the intricacies of the relationship between the president and Congress during the lawmaking process.

The continuing legislative development cycle

To analyze legislative development, we must begin to look at the processes, functions, behavior, and politics from a new viewpoint. Therefore, I have developed an analytical model to provide a narrow focus that is empirically valid, while remaining general enough for theoretical development and relevance when applied to other political policy issues. The model is termed the Continuing Legislative Development Cycle (CLDC), which requires understanding the policymaking process as one that functions across a continuing long-term time horizon. Issue saliency leading to legislative development is best understood as fluid, a process that functions across multiple administrations and congresses.

Charles O. Jones refers to a continuing agenda, where the US system provides an ongoing and often shifting legislative process that presidents will enter and exit, attempting to influence the agenda with their own priorities, while simultaneously endeavoring to tackle the ongoing legislative priorities of Congress that began before the president came into office and remain ongoing.[5] At times agenda issue items will align between the president and Congress, while many specific policy issues will remain a priority for only one. Political claims of electoral mandates, public opinion, and crises also can have an impact on the policy agenda, although both Jones and Edwards note the circumstantial and contextual nature of presidential influence. Taking these factors into consideration, the CLDC is one that functions both across time and within time, whereby issue evolution and policy innovation on a specific issue will mark a critical juncture in the process

---

[5] Jones, *Presidency in a Separated System*, 1994, pp. 164–5.

that leads from development through to votes on policy.[6] While scholars like Kingdon and Polsby provide a perspective on how policy innovation happens over time, my focus moves beyond agenda formation to one of political process and function.[7] The CLDC concentrates on blending policy innovation and development with the politics of the legislative process, which includes the debate, bargaining, and coalition formation within Congress and between Congress and the president. This process is one that happens across time, meaning a long-term historical perspective, as well as within time, meaning the influence and constraints of the politics of any moment under examination. The CLDC will develop as being continual and constant, but functional within the politics of the moment in which a policy is being considered. By analyzing legislative development in this manner, it becomes clear how policy becomes a relevant factor that impacts institutional change.

Logically, each policy agenda item forms a singular iterative game, even if that idea takes the form of multiple bills, which then allow the evolution of an issue within the policy development process to be examined through the actions of individual actors within an institutional setting across time. Jones asserts lawmaking as iterative and alterative, denoting a repeated cycle whereby in each iteration a bill is altered substantively making the process meaningful in order to achieve an outcome that benefits society.[8] Legislative politics is constrained through institutions, which can provide clarity to analyze the iterative and evolutionary nature of a single issue. The CLDC provides the space and context to examine a single issue as it moves through development, permitting analysis of multiple factors from various perspectives that influence and alter the issue and policy as it develops. Using the CLDC, we analyze the politics of FOIA development through a historical period marked by the Cold War, executive privilege, and partisan politics, illustrating how a single policy issue over

---

[6] Carmines and Stimson, *Issue Evolution*, 1989; Kingdon, *Agendas and Public Policies*, 1984; Baumgartner and Jones, *Agendas and Instability*, 2009.

[7] Polsby, *Political Innovation*, 1984.

[8] Jones, *Presidency in a Separated System*, 1994, p. 184.

time evolves in direct response to changing political conditions. The CLDC provides the sequence and iteration through a narrow lens on a single issue to better understand the contextual nature of the politics of policy development.

To provide context to demonstrate the functionality of the CLDC, FOIA is used as an explanatory case. Legislative development follows a progression of sequencing specific moments and actions showing the confluence of issues that ultimately resulted in the FOIA law. The CLDC perspective is grounded within Pierson's theoretical development of using historical analysis to explain social phenomena across time with factors "such as path dependence, critical junctures, sequencing, events, duration, timing, and unintended consequences" in examining issue evolution and policy development.[9] American Political Development (APD) scholars like Pierson, Orren, and Skowronek argue the complexities of institutional politics based within path dependent courses marked by moments of congruous relationships leading to action that brings about an inevitable reaction.[10] Whether it is path dependent with causal chains as argued by Pierson, or intercurrence as asserted by Orren and Skowronek, the importance of a deep historical understanding that brings the contextual elements of political development surrounding an issue is a necessity for making sense of social and political phenomena in the contemporary world. To understand the current issues of government secrecy and public information, executive privilege, whistleblowers, Wikileaks and the like, we must first delve into the past to examine how FOIA came to exist in the first place.

Briefly, we can examine the notions of sequencing across time bringing about the action-reaction nature of the politics of policymaking as influenced by institutional power struggles. The issue of government secrecy and freedom of information goes back further than the 1960s, to the immediate aftermath of World War II with the rise of the Cold War, the Red Scare and McCarthyism, and the Korean War, where a national security

---

[9] Pierson, *Politics in Time*, 2004, pp. 5–6.
[10] Orren and Skowronek, *Search for American Political Development*, 2004.

menace in the form of communism was perceived as a threat at home and abroad. In a 1947 speech, President Harry Truman argued for a reorientation of American foreign policy to offer assistance to preserve democratic regimes in opposition to communism and the growing Soviet threat. This ideological shift in policy became known as the Truman Doctrine and would provide sufficient concerns for a paradigm shift in behavior within the executive branch. Administration officials therefore sought action to severely limit information being provided to the press and members of Congress. By the late 1940s, many in the press, including press groups like Sigma Delta Chi and the American Society of Newspaper Editors (ASNE), had formed freedom of information committees that began to advocate against enhanced government secrecy.[11] In these efforts, ASNE employed Harold Cross, lead counsel for the *New York Herald Tribune*, to produce a report. The report was published in 1953 as a book titled *A People's Right to Know* and provided a legal account on government secrecy and access to information.[12] The Cross report was foundational in providing details on public records laws already enacted at the state level, which could be used as models for legislative action at the national level. Press advocacy groups like ASNE used the report to lobby Congress to enact a national public records law.

During this period, while ASNE and other members of the press took a more assertive role as an interest group on the issue, the Eisenhower administration formed the OSI within the

---

[11] One of the founding issues of importance to the United Nations (UN) in 1946 was freedom of information, an issue that would be debated through early sessions, culminating in a 1948 conference in Switzerland. Much of the UN focus on this issue was on propaganda and the need for a free and independent press, much as we think of First Amendment press rights in the US. Historical newspaper archives show considerable press attention during the late 1940s to the issue of freedom of information, but within the UN context. While the UN debates are left out of this research as it had little impact on domestic US politics, it does provide some ammunition for members of the US press to begin to use the UN debate as a stepping stone in arguing for a law to provide public access to government information.

[12] Cross, *Right to Know*, 1953.

Commerce Department in November of 1954.[13] The justification was to create a central office within the executive branch that could screen information and work with the business community to ensure that unclassified strategic data would not be made available to foreign nations that would use the information against the interests of the US. The policies of OSI spread across all executive agencies, especially the Department of Defense (DOD), helping to establish a culture of secrecy among agencies when dealing with the press or Congress seeking specific information. In spring 1955, Secretary of Defense Charles Wilson issued a directive to government officials and defense contractors that they must limit any public information activities, and that any information from the Defense Department to be made public must first meet security requirements and make a "constructive contribution" to the Defense Department's efforts.[14] These administrative actions were encouraged by Eisenhower's assertion of the president's constitutional power of executive privilege under the "take care" clause. Congress and the press began to refer to this and other such directives as the "paper curtain" from which the American people were being denied their constitutional right to access public records.[15]

With a Democratic takeover of Congress following the 1954 midterm elections, moving from unified Republican control to divided government, the political opportunity came for Congress to act on checking the Eisenhower administration's invocation of executive privilege as having a negative impact on oversight capabilities. The response from Congress was to create a special subcommittee under the Government Operations Committee to research and focus on the issue. Sophomore representative John Moss (D-CA) was picked to chair the Special Subcommittee on Government Information, as he had proven himself politically

---

[13] Department Order No. 157, Department of Commerce, November 1, 1954. Freedom of Information Act—Legislative Background—Legislative Proposals, 1955–1957 [Folder 1 of 2], Box No. M-186, Center for Legislative Archives, National Archives, Washington, DC.

[14] Foerstel, *Freedom of Information*, p. 20.

[15] Archibald, "Early Years of FOIA," 1993.

astute on this issue, along with developing strong ties with House leadership.

The issue of freedom of information was institutionalized in the House, providing Congress with a starting point for oversight and policymaking, marking another critical juncture in the evolution of the issue.[16] This juncture demarcates a political turning point in the CLDC, where the institutionalization of the issue begins the policy development process. The final version of FOIA would be signed by LBJ on July 4, 1966, providing a nearly twelve-year span that took the issue from institutionalization to law. To the point of passage, and setting aside the implementation, oversight, and amendment portion that I will delve into with Richard M. Nixon and Gerald Ford, the CLDC perspective offers the means of examining a specific issue evolution across time to provide the context of the functionality of politics and policy development.

The CLDC offers an enhanced APD perspective and provides a foundation to analyze issue and policy development at any time. To understand the politics of legislative development and the dynamic nature of intra-institutional power between the president and Congress during the policymaking process, it is necessary to delve deep into the weeds by isolating a single issue from which we can extrapolate more general theories or perspectives in research. Using the CLDC as an analytical tool, the temporal and contextual details of political development bring to light factors that contribute to political and institutional change otherwise overlooked.

It is incumbent upon political science to provide coherent explanations of shifts within politics that lead to reforms, and the impacts—both intentional and unintentional—those reforms have on our politics, on our governing institutions, and within society. Larry Dodd stated,

---

[16] Shortly after the House formed the Moss Subcommittee, the Senate Judiciary Committee formed a Senate Constitutional Rights Subcommittee under the leadership of Chairman Thomas Hennings (D-MO) to investigate issues of executive privilege and government information. As will be shown, this subcommittee served as the Senate counterpart to the Moss Subcommittee in the House, and a continuing indication of the growing saliency of the issue.

The goal for political science, I believe, is not to discover and predict a recurring consistency in the structure, substance, and logic of political behavior but to clarify the processes whereby political actors create, operate within, dissolve, and recreate new and unforeseeable political worlds. The goal of the political scientist, in essence, is to understand the form, variability, and contingencies of political change, not to predict a content that is unforeseeable and a constancy that is nonexistent in a long-term and substantive sense.[17]

Once we seek to understand political change, the questions of how change happens moves to the fore. We must develop analytical models of explanation that offer empirical insight, while being flexible enough to focus narrowly and broad enough to incorporate multiple perspectives in providing comprehensive understanding. The CLDC is consistent with previous literature in creating such a model to allow a policy idea or issue, one which is transformative in nature, to be viewed through several different lenses that stand alone in perspective, yet function together as each influences the politics of the others.

Political change and issue evolution through social learning

To analyze the politics of policy development, we must turn our attention to the factors at play within the cycle. The CLDC allows a narrow focus on a single issue within a political environment, so then nested within the cycle are the factors that influence and shape the political debates that drive policymaking. Scholarship and literature in the social sciences, and political scientists in particular, have been debating correlation and causal arrows when it comes to influence for a very long time. Generally speaking, the debate centers on whether politics or policy is influenced by society (the public) or elites (political actors or elected officials), where the question is which way the causal arrow flows, or who influences whom. The debate centers on whether the public influences elite behavior, which correlates to policy outcomes; or whether elites influence public opinion, whereby public opinion

---

[17] Dodd, *Thinking About Congress*, 2012, p. 205.

is used to influence policy outcomes.[18] In my opinion, a causal arrow is too narrow to understand development and influence, as an arrow flows in only one direction. Society will make demands on political actors in seeking to influence policy outcomes or responses to meet their demands. Political actors will seek to influence society by convincing the public of the benefits of their particular policy solutions due to the political benefits provided by positive public opinion. Instead of thinking that influence only flows one way, as a linear action from societal demands to political elites (or vice versa) to policy outcome, we must shift our thinking of influence to one that flows in both directions simultaneously and continuously.

Pierson's path dependency argument relies on positive feedback loops that serve to reinforce decision-making on issues over time. In the same manner, information flows that serve to influence decision-making on policy function through a continual feedback process between society and elites. Society forms one loop that is interconnected to political actors that form a second loop. Information flows constantly back and forth between each loop, so there is always a continual signaling flow of information from each to the other and back again. As Pierson's positive feedback loops serve as self-reinforcement mechanisms, the flow of information that serves to inform and seeks to influence society and politics forms an interconnected double feedback loop. An interconnected double feedback loop is continual and functions constantly in conveying information between actors, both internal and external. The easiest way to make sense of this function within the CLDC is through a social learning perspective that provides context for how information flows between actors, and how it is processed and utilized to achieve an outcome.

Social learning provides a means to understand how information acts as the glue that connects the loops between the public and elites, and is the political foundation of legislative development.

---

[18] This is, of course, an extreme oversimplification of very complex social issues. My purpose here is not to dwell on the ongoing causal arrow of influence debate within social science, but to springboard beyond this debate to one where influence is far more fluid and constant on all sides.

For analytical purposes, the CLDC functions as a system, but we must give attention to the subsystems that give life to the system as a whole. In this case, social learning is how we understand the interactions of shifting societal demands upon government with the politics of issue evolution leading to policy development. A social learning lens opens the door to see how the real and perceived threats from communism following World War II led to the rise of the modern American security state, as exemplified by presidential control over public information that was so dramatic, it created a new mindset or cognitive swing within the executive branch. This paradigm shift, referred to here as a Cold War Paradigm, was defined by administration control of information flows to Congress and the press, and subsequently the public. The Cold War Paradigm marked a shift in cognitive political response by the White House, breaking with the previous period and establishing the critical juncture for the FOIA issue.

Social learning provides a way to understand such a change in thinking, driven by new information, and how that change creates an action-reaction political response. Dodd uses a social learning perspective to understand the genesis of the Republican Revolution of 1994, noting how paradigm shifts driven by altering societal conditions in a post-industrial era, or social crises, and outmoded political thinking lead to the construction of new governing paradigms through a social learning process. Dodd states, "Each generation must develop a realistic understanding of how best to balance personal and collective well-being within its particular historical conditions."[19] As societal demands change or social crises occur, the political means of addressing this new situation is often lacking, leading to an exacerbation of the problem or political gridlock. These political means are now based on obsolete thinking, so the old ways of doing things no longer work, making that type of politics obsolete. New information is then utilized in the development of ideas to address new problems. It is the introduction and analysis of new information that brings about a marked change in thinking, through a process of social learning.

[19] Dodd, *Thinking About Congress*, 2012, p. 303.

To provide a more precise definition of social learning, I borrow from Peter Hall, who stated,

> Learning is conventionally said to occur when individuals assimilate new information, including that based on past experience, and apply it to their subsequent actions. Therefore, we can define social learning as a deliberate attempt to adjust the goals or techniques of policy in response to past experience and new information. Learning is indicated when policy changes as the result of such a process.[20]

Hall's definition provides the understanding that new policy is influenced by past policies, which allow the learning process to be pushed forward by key individual actors who possess issue expertise or political power, or both. The combination of understanding the inability of past policy or actions to address current demands combines with the input of new information to bring about a shift in thinking, whereby the learning process is detectable through a policy outcome arrived at by a change in politics.

Solving collective action problems by bringing individuals and institutions together is what policy seeks to do within a politically charged environment. As the process unfolds across time within the CLDC, social learning is demonstrated through alternating actions that achieve a political outcome, showing that learning is marked as being iterative over time.[21] Fikret Berkes states, "With iterative feedback between the learner and the environment, the learner changes the environment and these changes in turn affect the learner."[22] The social learning process focuses on problem solving across time where individuals introduce, analyze, and use new information that alters the environment, which in turn alters the political debate. Within the CLDC, the social learning process unfolds over time, with the interconnected double feedback loop pushing new information between all actors involved in a particular issue, in this case FOIA development, in seeking a policy outcome. For Hall, social learning demarcates the end of outdated thinking for policy development, but for my purposes, I

---

[20] Hall, "Policy Paradigms," 1993, p. 278.
[21] Berkes, "Evolution of Co-Management," 2009.
[22] Ibid. p. 1696.

am examining the beginning and development of a new cognitive mindset that is built on the creation of a new politics, born from the failure of previous thinking.

Dodd and Hall use the scientific paradigm framework established by Thomas Kuhn as an analogy to understand a paradigmatic shift as resultant from a social learning process.[23] Hall develops a model of three orders of learning, with first- and second-order learning being where the instruments and settings of policy will change through new information learning, but the overall goals remain the same. Third-order learning is relevant here, whereby the policy instruments, settings, and goals change through the introduction of new information. This leads to a paradigmatic shift in the Kuhnian sense, as third-order change is reflective of a disjointed process associated with a break in the general continuities of the policy process.[24] In Pierson's terms, a third-order change or Kuhnian paradigm shift is a critical juncture. Dodd found a paradigm shift driven by unaddressed societal problems of post-industrial America fueled by the inability of the dominant majority party in Congress to develop policy to address these problems. This led to the takeover of Congress by the Republican Party for the first time in forty years, which brought about political reforms of the institution of Congress itself in the mid-1990s. Hall found a policy paradigm shift through sociological and power dynamic shifts leading to changes in British macroeconomic policy in the 1970s and 1980s.

A Kuhnian policy paradigm shift is generally marked first by failure—failure of politics to address current societal demands, failure of past policy actions, failure of outdated thinking. Contextually and situationally, a paradigm shift is recognized through political changes that occurred forcibly due to previous failure, inaction, or crisis that altered the environment. The CLDC for the development of FOIA begins with the paradigm shift demarcated by the dramatic alteration of executive branch policy following the end of World War II. The situation at that

---

[23] Kuhn, *Scientific Revolutions*, 1970.
[24] Hall, "Policy Paradigms," 1993, p. 279.

time was one of new perceived threats requiring increased security measures surrounding the public release of information. The Cold War Paradigm mindset became institutionalized in the executive branch, creating a new politics of the era, setting a path for future struggles between the president and Congress. Hall's third-order shift is apparent in the FOIA development debates as society and government grappled with how to balance security concerns with democratic governance, established on a system of checks and balances requiring information for oversight. Oversight of administration actions, either from Congress or the public through the press, depends upon receiving new information, processing and using the information to signal positioning on issues. As the White House cut off those channels of information, the Cold War Paradigm established a new system of action-reaction-reaction between the president and Congress. Across time, multiple iterations of actions and responses taken by the president and Congress provide the framework to view the politics of policy development. The Cold War Paradigm operates within the CLDC, which begins with the Kuhnian shift, marking the end of the previous era, and the beginning of a new era that develops over time.

Measurement and empirical support for the model

The next logical question is how to measure and provide empirical support for this model. There are three main factors addressed in the following chapters that offer empirical support for the narrative of FOIA development. The first illustrates the functionality of social learning to explain the action-reaction nature of intra-branch political power struggles. The second offers insight into the first loop where societal demands surrounding the issue of government secrecy and public records change over time, from having very little attention to being of greater importance. This establishes issue saliency, and will demonstrate how public demands seek to influence political actors and policy. The third will illustrate the politics of the moment throughout the CLDC, by examining how individual political actors within Congress and the administration drive policy forward while responding to constraints and motivations offered from the public, allies, and opponents. Each factor is driven by new information, but individuals acting on the issue interpret and utilize that information differently, leading to the iterative action-reaction nature of politics.

Keeping with Hall's definition, we can recognize that a social learning process happened through the passage and implementation of FOIA. It then becomes possible to work backwards to mark the policy paradigm shift as beginning in the late 1940s, as the Cold War political climate escalated. Within the period under consideration, 1946–76, executive privilege is utilized to measure the social learning process. Intricately embedded within the legislative development of FOIA, executive privilege quickly became a unilateral tool for presidents to deny information to Congress. Presidents and scholars alike have claimed executive privilege as a constitutional power, harkening back to examples from the Washington administration.[25] However, while the concept may have been debated from the beginning, the term executive privilege as it is currently defined was coined by the Eisenhower administration and rose quickly to become widely used by administration officials to deny information to Congress and the press. Mark Rozell defines executive privilege as "the right of the President and high-level executive branch officers to withhold information from Congress, the courts, and ultimately the public."[26] Included in his definition, Rozell offers two circumstances in which executive privilege can be used: for national security reasons, and for protecting White House deliberations when in the public interest as defined by the Supreme Court in *US v. Nixon*. Setting aside the debates on the constitutionality of executive privilege, my interest here is to demonstrate the political implications that arose from its usage, showing how Congress would learn from administration claims of executive privilege to respond in various manners, including by the development of policy. Executive privilege is a tool of power, one

---

[25] Fisher, *Politics of Executive Privilege*, 2004; Rozell, *Executive Privilege*, 2010.

[26] Rozell, "Executive Privilege and the Modern Presidents," 1999.

the president gave himself, leaving it incumbent upon Congress or the courts to challenge that power. My purpose here is to understand the politics of this power struggle, as the interactions between branches within the Cold War Paradigm define the politics of the moment, as executive privilege is an inherent power that creates a learning process for both the president and Congress.

As executive privilege is not explicit in the Constitution, yet informs political discourse, an institutional power grey area is created between branches. The overuse of the claim by administration actors led to a constitutional power crisis as Congress was being stifled in its oversight ability, leading to the growth of executive power at a loss to Congress. It is important to note that during this period Congress was quite cognizant of the realities posed by the changed global environment and the reality of authentic national security concerns. As we will see, members of Congress also responded to the Cold War Paradigm environment, as demonstrated through the passage of bills like the Internal Security Act of 1950, and perhaps more telling, the actions of the House Un-American Activities Committee and the rise to prominence of Senator Joseph McCarthy. As the debate surrounding the policy development of FOIA unfolded, Congress learned from the White House's overuse of executive privilege, thereby choosing to (re)act as a check on executive power to prevent the creation of a culture of secrecy leading to a complete shutdown of access. This reasoning, as Fisher notes, was established through the exemptions included in FOIA to account for legitimate claims of national security concerns and executive privilege.

Rozell contends that executive privilege does have constitutional foundations for the president to keep certain information secret, but the solution to executive privilege is one born out of power struggles between Congress and the president. The power dilemma established by executive privilege is the grey area I referred to, and while Rozell offers a legal and constitutional justification, I assert that the political argument is more meaningful. The political power stalemates caused by executive privilege assertions within a separated system of shared power, as Fisher contends, are often broken by political decision making. In this way, Congress will assert power through various means at its disposal, or the executive branch will make a calculated political decision based on the cost-benefit analysis of continued usage. While debates of executive privilege tend to be couched in legal or constitutional terms, both Fisher and Rozell note that instances of executive privilege use are contextual and largely dictated by the politics of the moment. The context of the political considerations becomes a meaningful framework through which to understand the politics of the power dynamics between Congress and the president. The contextual aspect of executive privilege as provided by Rozell and Fisher becomes useful, as the power grey area is demonstrated by the president's ability to wage claims of executive privilege as he sees fit, which can grow in scope until checked by Congress or the courts. Institutional power can be malleable and change over time, which we will see is the case here.

Executive privilege becomes the learning mechanism that drives social learning as a direct response to the Cold War Paradigm shift. Only by the president's continued and growing use of executive privilege across multiple administrations does Congress learn and respond to the impacts such claims have on their own constitutional responsibilities, which have political ramifications. During this period the president learns that use of executive privilege is acceptable only until it is not, meaning that Congress or the courts must provide a direct check on executive power. At that point, the president has the ability to simply alter the use of executive privilege and continue its use until such time that a check is provided again. Congress learns that the denial of information by the administration through executive privilege claims builds a wall to prevent members from fulfilling their oversight function or constituent service, which comes at a political cost. Social learning happens as members of Congress process information on the president's use of executive privilege, then develop strategic responses to overcome these claims through policy development, which simultaneously provides a political benefit.

The second factor operating within the CLDC to be examined is issue saliency with the public. This is the first loop of the interconnected double feedback loop, as the public will signal to elected leaders their positions, often through the press. Understanding how societal demands evolve over time to influence policy development is crucial to issue saliency. Tracing how an issue evolves into one of prominence with the public provides insight into the political responses crafted to address them. For example, Dodd illustrates how shifts within the US to a postindustrial society created an institution (Congress) incapable of meeting the personal power needs of career-oriented members, while maintaining its ability to function as a legislative body. Nelson Polsby demonstrated how the modernization of society and technological innovation, like the invention of air conditioning, changed the politics of the South and the country, setting in motion demographic shifts leading to institutional and policy change. Joseph Cooper and David Brady use a diachronic analysis of environmental factors to examine how industrialization and career politicians proved unable to adapt to changing societal conditions, leading to the implosion of the strong party system and the end of congressional government. Julian Zelizer discusses how failures of Progressive Era reforms when placed in the context of post-World War II politics, which included increased union power and the Civil Rights movement, created an institutional crisis leading to the congressional reforms of the 1970s.[27] Larry Bartels's research into the issue of income inequality traces how impacts brought about from changing economic conditions, including individual income and wages, changes the politics of certain groups within society over time, which in turn then impacts the policies and politics of institutional actors.[28] The literature is rich with examples of the impacts of shifting societal demands on policy change. These examples also

---

[27] Polsby, *How Congress Evolves*, 2004; Cooper and Brady, "Diachronic Analysis," 1981; Zelizer, *On Capitol Hill*, 2004; Bartels, *Unequal Democracy*, 2008.

[28] A portion of the above literature discussion appeared in an earlier working paper: Kevin M. Baron, "The Information is Free," presented at the Midwest Political Science Association Annual Meeting, Chicago, IL, 2013.

demonstrate the strongly interconnected nature of society and politics, and how each influences the other.

In order to measure societal demand on a specific issue as it develops within the CLDC, issue saliency is defined through public attention. It is problematic to make broad assumptions about society as a whole, as within any single issue a division exists among the public across a continuum of positions; however, when examining an issue across time it becomes possible to see how positioning from the public can shift to show how an issue gains attention. Therefore we can see long-term trends as opposed to short-term flashes to show valid gains in attention. Scholars usually turn to polling or survey data in order to show these trends, positions and changes across time, but I cannot do that here. Quantitative data sources on issues of government secrecy, support for public records access, and executive power are non-existent or limited during the period under examination, 1946–76. There is no consistent statistical data that allows us to look at the public positioning across time. There are not even variables in datasets that come close as proxies on this particular issue.

There are a few snapshots of data on public opinion. A Gallup poll from July 1947 asked respondents, "Do you think our Government is giving the people all the important facts about world conditions today, or do you think the Government is holding back on a lot of important information which the people ought to have?"[29] The results found that 59 percent of respondents believed the government was holding back information, with only 18 percent thinking the government provided enough. A follow-up question in the same survey, asking respondents what type of further information they wanted from government, revealed 63 percent of respondents wanting more information related to Russia, communism, foreign policy and foreign affairs.[30] Another

---

[29] Gallup Organization, Gallup Poll, July 1947 (survey question). USGALLUP.082347.RK13A. Gallup Organization (producer). Storrs, CT: Roper Center for Public Opinion Research, iPOLL (distributor), accessed December 12, 2015.

[30] Gallup Organization, Gallup Poll (AIPO), July 1947 (survey question).

Gallup poll from June 1954 asked, "Government employees are not permitted to reveal secret or confidential information—even to members of Congress—without permission. Do you think this is a good rule or a poor one?"[31] Seventy-seven percent of respondents thought this was a good rule. Although a misleading aspect of this question is the wording of "secret or confidential information," which can skew the results, as it would be logical for respondents to believe that secret or confidential information would betray national security interests if made public. Additionally, Pew Research Center data, in conjunction with the American National Election Study (ANES), demonstrates that public trust in government during part of the period of FOIA development was high. In 1958 under Eisenhower, the national average was 73 percent, moving up to 77 percent in 1964; it then began a decline down to 65 percent in 1966 and 53 percent in 1972 when Nixon was reelected, dropping to 36 percent when Nixon resigned, and remaining there through Ford's tenure.[32] The decline in public trust during this period is indicative of numerous factors and cannot be applied specifically to the debate surrounding the development of FOIA; however, it is important to note, as it does impact politics.

The lack of quantitative data does not prevent sound analysis, but it means we must look to different measurements. Examining issue development across time points to one easy and significant factor to measure: press coverage. The press plays a unique role in FOIA development. First, the press is a two-way conduit, meaning it both provides information to the public and political elites, and reflects societal and elite demands on issues. Social

---

USGALLUP.401.QK13D. Gallup Organization (producer). Storrs, CT: Roper Center for Public Opinion Research, iPOLL (distributor), accessed December 12, 2015.

[31] Gallup Organization, Gallup Poll (AIPO), June 1954 (survey question). USGALLUP.54-532.Q08. Gallup Organization (producer). Storrs, CT: Roper Center for Public Opinion Research, iPOLL (distributor), accessed December 12, 2015.

[32] "Public Trust in Government: 1958–2015," Pew Research Center. Available online: <http://www.people-press.org/2015/11/23/public-trust-in-governme nt-1958-2015/> (last accessed November 10, 2018).

learning happens as new information is presented, processed, and used to take action on issues, so the press plays a crucial role in presenting information from both society and political actors to one another. The constant signaling and positioning informs ongoing debate and influences policy. Second, press attention logically demonstrates issue saliency. Increased press attention signals to the public and elites, who can then use the increased attention as justification for policy. Third, the issue of government secrecy, and executive privilege specifically, is significant to the press, as their own self-interest allowed many within the media to serve in an advocacy role within this debate. The development of FOIA is impacted by many in the press acting as an interest group to actively lobby for political action and policy change.

Using historical newspaper archives, I have been able to aggregate a dataset of press stories from 1946–76 that demonstrates a growth and sustained increase in press attention. Additionally, content analysis of these newspaper stories provides rich context into the debates of the moment, showing how positions were influenced and changed over time. Social learning is demonstrated through press stories as new information is presented, and then used for politics and policy development. This approach is supported by scholars like Mayhew, and Binder, who examined newspaper articles over a fifty-year period to argue that attention of an issue in the *New York Times* editorial pages illustrated issue saliency.[33] In this way, Binder was able to successfully argue that congressional agenda items were based around issue saliency from public attention vis-à-vis the press. My approach is that press attention is a proxy variable for societal demand, so that increased press attention on an issue builds saliency. If press attention grows over the period of time under examination, then the saliency of the issue grows reciprocally, allowing an argument that societal demand has shifted. As Peter Hall stated, "The press is both a mirror of public opinion and a magnifying glass for the issues that it takes

---

[33] Mayhew, *America's Congress*, 2000; Binder, *Stalemate*, 2003.

up."[34] Content analysis of news stories provides the empirical foundation from which to demonstrate social learning through issue development.

Taking my lead from Binder, I examine two prominent national newspapers that provided coverage of politics, the *New York Times* and the *Washington Post*. The historical archives of both newspapers offers a wealth of information that informed the debates between 1946 and 1976. The dataset of news stories I have compiled is based on four basic search terms—"government secrecy," "executive privilege," "freedom of information," and "John E. Moss"—in order to develop a view of how saliency grew over time, and for content analysis purposes.[35] In constructing the newspaper dataset, I included news stories, front page stories, special features, wire service stories, editorials, op-eds, and letters to the editor. This yielded a dataset of 3,303 newspaper mentions, rich with content that provides the context informing the debates over time. Issue saliency rose in conjunction with the amount of press coverage during this period, as demonstrated by Figure 1.1. The figure demonstrates rising press coverage across time, hitting specific peaks in coverage at moments prior to congressional action as response to presidential action. This reinforces those critical junctures within the CLDC, albeit with a slight lag effect for attention to translate to political action, but clearly illustrative of specific moments in time when these issues gained mass attention, as in 1973–4 during Watergate. The figure clearly shows that coverage grew and sustained a higher level of continued attention during this period. Press coverage in national newspapers fed the information flow to the public, providing fuel for societal demand. Press attention is the means by which society seeks to influence policy and politics, which simultaneously creates the

---

[34] Hall, "Policy Paradigms," 1993, p. 288.

[35] I chose John E. Moss as a search term due to the key role Moss played in the development of the issue and policy that would become FOIA. As we will see, there were other prominent congressional actors and administration officials who played a role in FOIA development, but I chose to focus attention on Moss as an example of how important an individual member of Congress can be to policy development and issue saliency.

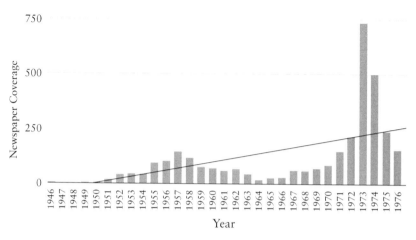

Figure 1.1: Total Freedom of Information Related Newspaper Coverage 1946–76

NOTE: N=3303. Coverage from the *New York Times* and *Washington Post* based on the search terms of "freedom of information," "executive privilege," "government secrecy," and "John E. Moss." Each item in the dataset was examined for relevance and relation to the issue of FOIA development.

flow of information to political elites that the issue is significant enough to be addressed.

The same reasoning to establish issue saliency can be applied to the Cold War Paradigm mindset. Using the same methodology, a newspaper archive search of different keywords ("communism," "communist," "subversive," and "McCarthyism") yielded a dataset of more than 381,000 hits across the same time period in the *New York Times* and *Washington Post*. The issues related to the Cold War were so dominant during this period that every other issue paled in comparison. However, for my purposes this data offers insight into the rise and continued reinforcement of the Cold War Paradigm. As the mindset frames the political and policy debates surrounding the development of FOIA and issues of executive privilege, it is clear in Figure 1.2 how dominant Cold War press coverage is versus FOIA coverage, as measured across the bottom of the figure. The same data as shown in Figure 1.1 seems practically nonexistent in comparison to the Cold War coverage as illustrated in Figure 1.2. The coverage grows in 1946

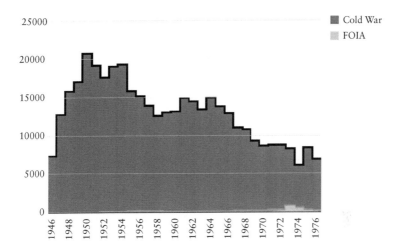

Figure 1.2: Total Cold War Newspaper Coverage 1946–76

NOTE: N=381,496. Coverage from the *New York Times* and *Washington Post* based on the search terms of "communism," "communist," "subversive," and "McCarthyism." Each item in the dataset was examined for relevance and relation to the issue of establishing the saliency and dominance of the Cold War Paradigm, and how that compares to the FOIA development data.

and increases before peaking in the McCarthy era of the early 1950s and eventually diminishing by the mid to late 1960s. The public saturation of the Cold War influences the politics surrounding FOIA development and feeds into the paradigm shift under Truman.

Newspapers provide a societal perspective, leaving the political perspective as the final factor of examination within the CLDC. To this task, extensive archival research was conducted at the LBJ, Nixon, and Ford Presidential Libraries, along with the John E. Moss Archive at California State University Sacramento, the Carl Albert Center at the University of Oklahoma, and the Center for Legislative Archives at the National Archives in Washington, DC. To fully appreciate and understand the politics driving legislative development within the CLDC, I find it meaningful to examine the role individual political actors play within the legislative process—in particular, how individuals in Congress or the executive branch are able to use their institutional power to influence process and policy. Scholars have demonstrated how the self-interest of individual behavior interacts within the power structure of a political institution, and how those interactions can lead to change in both the individual behavior and the institution.[36] A focal point to understand the motivations of politicians and government officials has been to understand their behavior as a quest for personal power; in other words, it is driven by self-interest. In the policymaking process, an individual actor in pursuit of their own self-interest will align with other individuals with similar interests or goals, where the actor can persuade or motivate those to form a coalition in support of a policy outcome leading to reform the status quo.[37]

Much of the congressional literature defines this type of individual behavior as entrepreneurial in one form or another, which is useful here. Scholars define the role of entrepreneurship in Congress in different ways, such as those members who differentiate themselves from others by providing policy expertise and development, or by being a political activist, or by being able to solve a collective action problem that also benefits their own personal goals through coordination and in providing resources.[38] Kingdon defines policy entrepreneurs as advocates who are willing to invest their resources of time, energy, reputation, and money in order to promote a position in return for some anticipated future gain.[39] Polsby goes further by describing entrepreneurs as those who serve as innovators of ideas, and utilize their ambition, position, expertise, and skill to drive an idea through the policy process to enactment.[40] Wawro identifies legislative entrepreneurs as rational actors who "bear much of the burden of the production of legislation. Members engage in legislative entrepreneurship when they invest time, staff, and other resources to acquire knowledge of particular policy areas,

---

[36] Fenno, *Congressmen in Committees*, 1973; Mayhew, *Electoral Connection*, 1974; Weingast, "Congressional Norms," 1979; Schickler, *Disjointed Pluralism*, 2001; Dodd, *Thinking About Congress*, 2012.

[37] Schickler, "Entrepreneurial Defenses," 2007.

[38] Uslaner, "Policy Entrepreneurs," 1978; Fowler, "Political Entrepreneurs," 1994; Fiorina and Shepsle, "Theories of Leadership," 1989.

[39] Kingdon, *Agendas and Public Policies*, 1984, p. 188.

[40] Polsby, *Political Innovation*, 1984, pp. 171–4.

draft legislation addressing issues in those areas and shepherd their proposals through the legislative process by building and maintaining coalitions," using a variety of activities they have at their disposal.[41]

Adam Sheingate emphasizes the policy entrepreneur as political innovator. Sheingate contends that as rules form the basis of institutions, these same rules structure the behavior of goal-oriented actors. Within a complex institutional structure, policy entrepreneurs push for innovation due to the heterogeneity, uncertainty, and ambiguity of complex institutions that "provide actors with resources for creative recombination and speculative opportunities to redefine the scope of institutional authority."[42] Schickler and Sheingate illustrate how policy innovation channeled through entrepreneurial efforts pushes against the institutional status quo, thus paving the way for reform and change. An entrepreneur is therefore able to capture and utilize institutional power as a tool to engage in activity that promotes such change.

Entrepreneurial activity within the legislative development process requires policy to be at the center. Schickler demonstrates how individuals within Congress form coalitions centered on specific issues at specific moments in time through a legislative package, or common carrier that serves the goals of a diffuse group of members, often to challenge the status quo. Wawro also describes the necessity of a legislative package as the core feature to which an entrepreneur will build coalition. Therefore, these common carriers can be understood as an action strategy to pursue through a policy item that serves the interests of individual members allowing for a large enough coalition to form to provide an outcome that serves the collective interest. Including the temporal factor of the CLDC, legislative items as individual bills within Congress can be introduced, debated, modified, killed, and reintroduced multiple times throughout the development process until a final version is passed, one that meets the goals of a majority in Congress, along with presidential approval.

Building upon the literature, I define entrepreneurs as political

---

[41] Wawro, "Legislative Entrepreneurship," 2000, pp. 2–3.
[42] Sheingate, "Terrain of the Political Entrepreneur," 2007, pp. 14–15.

actors who utilize their position, staff, resources, expertise, and ambition to develop policy and build coalitions to achieve political or policy outcomes. I add an additional factor, which is an ability to utilize information to their advantage. Through a social learning perspective, an entrepreneur can employ and exploit information in a strategic manner in order to influence the policy debate in favor of their desired goal. Within the CLDC, social learning becomes essential for political entrepreneurs to process and use new information to respond to and support their positioning on issues. The skill which I include as entrepreneurial is the ability of individuals to effectively sell their goals to other political actors or the public. A member of Congress like John Moss must be capable of convincing other members of Congress to engage in oversight and policy making to combat the issue of executive privilege, while convincing the public that the president is in the wrong for invoking such privilege. Using new information to message and sell the politics, and ultimately policy, is a skill needed by any political entrepreneur. This skill demonstrates the social learning process as it unfolds in the CLDC, showing how the second loop seeks to influence issue development over time. Through individual entrepreneurial actions like those of Moss, the learning process happens through the CLDC that drives policy development as it responds to changes while seeking to alter the status quo—in this case, the status quo created by the politics of the Cold War Paradigm.

The rest of the book will proceed chronologically from President Truman through President Ford, with each chapter focusing on one administration. The narrative surrounding the development of FOIA is intertwined with the rise and use of executive privilege in modern presidential administrations. Over a thirty-year period, FOIA development and implementation offers insight into how issues evolve institutionally, and how politics influences behavior. Beginning with Truman, I show how the threat of communism created the Cold War Paradigm mindset that solidified the modern presidency into a position of enhanced secrecy, while Congress reinforced Truman's position, ultimately leading to a showdown over public access. Eisenhower entrenched government secrecy and control over information more than perhaps any modern president, but when faced with a Democratic Congress, a politically viable issue became institutionalized. Eisenhower's expanded use of executive privilege solidified administration control over information to Congress as an inherent Constitutional power. The political dynamics under Kennedy shifted with unified Democratic control of government, but by then the issue had too much momentum, with congressional Republicans finding fertile attacks on the new president. The Johnson administration desperately fought to prevent FOIA from becoming law, but ultimately relented and fell back on old Eisenhower-era talking points once the bill became law and was implemented. FOIA under Nixon led to renewed control of information within the executive branch. Nixon's reinvigoration of secrecy policies and executive privilege forced Congress to seek reforms and amend FOIA, which passed under Ford and was influenced by the politics of Ford's pardon of Nixon. The context for the CLDC and the factors operating within are led by presidential actions, beginning with Truman and the Cold War Paradigm that altered politics. The demand for secrecy that emerged from national security concerns drove administration policy, leading to extra-constitutional power claims of a privilege that allowed the president to deny information and testimony to Congress. As political factors changed and new information was presented, Congress would begin to push back on executive claims of power, thus paving the way for the issue of freedom of information to lead to policy, altering politics and institutions.

2

Truman and the shift to a Cold War Paradigm mindset

Communism maintains that social wrongs can be corrected only by violence. Democracy has proved that social justice can be achieved through peaceful change. Communism holds that the world is so deeply divided into opposing classes that war is inevitable. Democracy holds that free nations can settle differences justly and maintain lasting peace. ... I state these differences, not to draw issues of belief as such, but because the actions resulting from the Communist philosophy are a threat to the efforts of free nations to bring about world recovery and lasting peace.

— Harry S. Truman, Inaugural Address, January 20, 1949

The institutionalization of the Cold War and the Truman Doctrine

On March 12, 1947, President Truman addressed a special joint session of Congress expressing a grave concern over the need to support Greece and Turkey, focused mainly on Greece's civil war with its own communist party. With Great Britain lending support to both countries, Truman faced a need to support the democratic governments against a rising communist insurgency supported by the Soviet Union. Truman told Congress, "The very existence of the Greek state is today threatened by the terrorist activities of several thousand armed men, led by Communists, who defy the government's authority at a number of points, particularly along the northern boundaries."[1] He would continue by asserting

---

[1] Harry S. Truman: "Special Message to the Congress on Greece and Turkey: The Truman Doctrine," March 12, 1947. Available online at *The American Presidency Project*, <https://www.presidency.ucsb.edu/documents/special-message-the-congress-greece-and-turkey-the-truman-doctrine> (last accessed November 10, 2018).

that, "There is no other country to which democratic Greece can turn." While the main point of his speech was to convince Congress of the need to provide American support for Greece and Turkey monetarily and militarily, the speech would mark a specific shift in American foreign policy from a positon of non-intervention to one of actively offering support to nations fighting against communist interference and influence; a strategy of containment, now known as the Truman Doctrine. Truman's speech sent a signal to all democratic nations that the US would be willing to offer political, military, or economic support to oppose communist or authoritarian influences globally. The shift in American foreign policy signaled a dramatic change, placing the US in direct contention with the Soviet Union to prevent the spread of communism globally and set the precedent for what would become standard foreign policy for the course of the Cold War.

The postwar period beginning in 1946 is the starting point, setting aside the prewar and wartime periods. While there are traces of influence dating back before World War II, like the creation of the House Un-American Activities Committee (HUAC) in 1938, the immediate postwar period redefined foreign and domestic policies of the executive and legislative branches. Therefore, the postwar period is distinct as marking a political shift during the Truman administration, where we can pinpoint moments that taken together create a paradigm shift in mindset. Through the lens of history, we are able to look back to see how the issues of government secrecy, executive privilege, and access to public records intertwined and became institutionalized through cognizant actions and responses taken by Truman, and then perpetuated under Eisenhower and their successors. The Truman administration demarcates the initial critical juncture within the CLDC as the paradigm shift establishing the mindset that will lead to the politics and debates surrounding executive privilege and public records. Unlike a single event like 9/11, which defines a clear juncture, the CLDC provides us room to view a string of events over a short period of time that taken together create a juncture, and in this case a paradigm shift in thinking that was rapidly followed by political and policy change beginning with Truman.

However, it was not just Truman administration officials that brought about this paradigm shift. While Truman proved to be significant in his actions within the executive branch in demonstrating that the goals and framework of policymaking had significantly shifted, Congress played a large role as well. The House Un-American Activities Committee, Senator Joseph McCarthy, and Congress's support of the Truman Doctrine showed alignment in government on these issues. It was not until Congress passed the Internal Security Act of 1950, also known as the McCarran Act, that the division between branches over access to information arose, which helped lead to Congress overriding Truman's veto on that bill.[2] As we will see, Congress was active during this period in institutionalizing the fear of communism and altering the political climate, structures, and goals in conjunction with Truman, by continually beating the drum of anti-communism. As the Truman Doctrine took a huge step in altering foreign policy, domestically Congress and the administration worked in lockstep during most of this period to permanently alter the political goals and policy framework that strengthened the president's position to control information, justified by the subversive and dangerous elements lurking within the public and government.

If we look back to Figure 1.1, we can see the late 1940s has very little coverage of the issues related to secrecy, executive privilege, or freedom of information. The first peak did not come until a decade later. While we will see how the issue was simmering just below the surface on many policy and political debates, during the institutionalization of the Cold War Paradigm shift these issues were not politically salient enough to overcome the more viable domestic threats of communists working in government, a problem that the administration sought to root out with the help of Congress. Examining Figure 2.1, we can see that press coverage of issues related to communism, subversive activity, and McCarthyism were dominant, completely saturating the American consciousness. The amount of coverage numbered in the thousands in 1946, moving past 10,000 by 1947 and topping

---

[2] Schrecker, *Age of McCarthyism*, 1994, pp. 193–5.

34

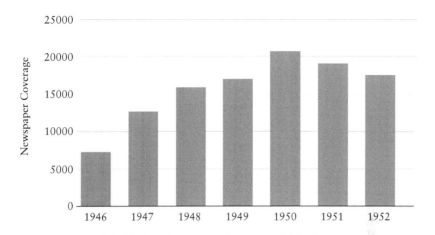

Figure 2.1: Total Cold War Newspaper Coverage 1946–52

NOTE: N=110,126. The data comes from the *New York Times* and *Washington Post* historical archives. The search terms were specified to "communism," "communist," "subversive," and "McCarthyism." The purpose here was to demonstrate the proliferation of the issues in the public sphere by highlighting how the Cold War mindset, including concerns over domestic communist threats, were prevalent during the Truman administration, providing fodder and support for positions taken by the administration and Congress.

20,000 by 1950. The daily barrage and signaling from the press and political elites during this period drove the paradigm shift by creating the real and perceived evil menace of communism. From 1946 to the end of the Truman administration, there were more than 110,000 newspaper mentions in the *New York Times* and *Washington Post* alone. With such a massive amount of attention, coupled with the actions being taken by Congress and within the Truman administration, it becomes clear how the new Cold War Paradigm had become institutionalized within government, altering politics and policy along with it.

The rest of this chapter will provide the foundation and narrative of the institutionalization of the new Cold War mindset. The Truman administration sets the stage for the development of FOIA by altering the politics, policy, and functionality of how the executive branch handled public records and the flow of information. Congress assisted in making this change permanent by responding in kind to the administration's actions on communist threats. It must be pointed out that for my purposes here, while the foreign threat of communism from the Soviet Union and others on the global stage plays an important role, my focus will be on domestic policy and issues unfolding within the US and from within government. By examining the domestic threats of communism from within, this chapter will demonstrate how new information led to a dramatic alteration of politics and policy that created the foundation of executive control over public information. The critical juncture established by the Truman years, 1946–52, was not one single event, but a series of events that spawned actions leading to reactions, which will show how the new Cold War Paradigm became institutionalized within US politics.

Executive orders, loyalty oaths, and subversive activities

By the fall of 1945, Truman was already discovering that Soviet threats at home were just as damaging, if not more so. On November 8, 1945, J. Edgar Hoover sent a letter to Brigadier General Henry Hawkins Vaughan, who was Truman's military aid at the time. In the letter, Hoover discusses an ongoing FBI investigation that has revealed a confidential source who has indicated that a number of people within the US government have been furnishing data and information to persons outside the government, and that these persons have been providing the information to Soviet espionage agents.[3] More than a dozen individuals from various agencies are named in the letter. Hoover clearly states, however, that he is not yet certain that any of these individuals were aware that the information they were providing

---

[3] J. Edgar Hoover to Harry H. Vaughn, November 8, 1945. Truman Papers, President's Secretary's Files. "S." Available online: <https://www.truman-library.org/whistlestop/study_collections/loyaltyprogram/documents/index.php?documentid=17-10&pagenumber=1> (last accessed November 10, 2018). NOTE: While 1945 is technically outside the date range being examined, I felt it necessary to include this one letter to exemplify how the domestic Soviet threat had permeated the Truman administration from the early days following the end of World War II, and how the FBI was monitoring government workers.

was part of a Soviet espionage ring, and that his investigation was continuing. Hoover ends the letter by noting his belief that the president would be interested in these preliminary results.

Several months later, in February 1946, another letter and report made its way to Truman via the Treasury Department. Fred Vinson, Secretary of the Treasury, had received a letter and report from Hoover concerning a Treasury official, Henry Dexter White, who had been nominated by Truman as one of two delegates to the International Monetary Fund.[4] The letter from Hoover and the FBI report reveal that White and ten other Treasury Department employees, or people related to those individuals, were working as part of an underground Soviet espionage ring operating within Washington, DC. The report details how White and others were copying or photographing information to pass along to Soviet spies. White's nomination created a serious political hazard for Truman, in particular as he was nominated to a position that would be focused on international finance, and as the Soviet Union had not yet ratified the Bretton Woods agreement. The report, as part of a continuing FBI investigation demonstrated the troubling realization to Truman of the real dangers posed to the US from Soviet espionage and interference. The new information being presented to Truman and members of his administration of subversive activity from within federal agencies confirmed the threat, and thus a need for action. The CLDC begins, and the Truman administration shows the initial stages of social learning.

By the fall of 1946, Truman felt it time to act against growing Soviet threats from within government itself. On 25 November 1946, Truman issued Executive Order (EO) 9806, titled "Establishing the President's Temporary Commission on Employee Loyalty."[5] The commission was established to develop

---

[4] Memo, Fred M. Vinson to Harry S. Truman, with FBI attachment, February 6, 1946. Truman Papers, President's Secretary's Files. "W." Available online: <https://www.trumanlibrary.org/whistlestop/study_collections/loyaltyprog ram/documents/index.php?documentid=17-12&pagenumber=3> (last accessed November 10, 2018).

[5] Harry S. Truman: "Executive Order 9806—Establishing the President's Temporary Commission on Employee Loyalty," November 25, 1946.

standards and rules relating to investigations into the background of government employees, and how to remove or disqualify any disloyal or subversive person. While Truman never referred to communists in the EO, the order clearly establishes a concern over subversive elements working within the federal government. For example, Section 3a of the order directs the commission to determine,

> Whether existing security procedures in the executive branch of the Government furnish adequate protection against the employment or continuance in employment of disloyal or subversive persons and what agency or agencies should be charged with prescribing and supervising security procedures.

The language provided within the EO establishes Truman's intent, which was to clean house. At this point, based in part on Hoover's investigations and on congressional action, concern about disloyal individuals working within the government had become impossible to ignore. Truman had congressional support for his EO. In 1945, Congress passed a resolution authorizing the House Civil Service Committee to conduct studies into the practices and policies for government employment, with respect to employee loyalty in particular.[6] A special subcommittee was created to conduct an investigation and issue a report. The subcommittee report to the full Civil Service Committee stated that "it is of vital importance to our country that those employed in all departments of federal service be of high integrity and unquestioned loyalty to our government." The report went on to say:

> Adequate protective measures must be adopted to see that persons of

Available online at *The American Presidency Project*: <https://www. presidency.ucsb.edu/documents/executive-order-9806-establishing-the-pres idents-temporary-commission-employee-loyalty> (last accessed November 10, 2018).

[6] Report of the President's Temporary Commission on Employee Loyalty, November 26, 1946. Truman Papers, Official File. OF 252-1: Presidents Temporary Commission on Employee Loyalty. Available online: <https:// www.trumanlibrary.org/whistlestop/study_collections/loyaltyprogram/ documents/index.php?documentid=4-1&pagenumber=1> (last accessed November 10, 2018).

questioned loyalty are not permitted to enter into the federal service. These protective measures should, of course, be absolutely fair and impartial, but doubts must, in the nature of things, be resolved in favor of the government.

The subcommittee went on to recommend the establishment of an interdepartmental commission to continue to investigate existing laws, security measures, and standards for federal employees, as well as to make recommendations for future legislation and policies that would be relevant. Truman would issue EO 9806 shortly thereafter.

It is important to acknowledge that both the administration and Congress were acting in concert on these issues. The Civil Service Subcommittee report is clear in its language that even the slightest threat or doubt should end any individuals' rights to federal employment. While language was given to discuss that procedures and practices be "fair and impartial" the intent spoke volumes to any government employee that any doubts of loyalty came with a zero tolerance policy. Truman and Congress's lockstep movements in targeting the federal workforce demonstrate how much the Cold War Paradigm shift had become solidified through the process of social learning. What becomes most stark in driving the paradigm shift and setting up the modern use of executive privilege to keep government information secret is the threat from within—that those working for the government or living within US communities were Soviet spies or communist sympathizers.

Less than four months after creating a temporary commission to investigate employee loyalty, Truman would give his speech to a joint session of Congress on the importance of supporting Greece and Turkey against internal and external communist threats. As described above, this speech formed the basis of the Truman Doctrine, altering American foreign policy to one of containment against communism generally, and a Soviet threat specifically. The complete change in policy course, along with the altered political landscape, supports the paradigm shift in thinking to the Cold War Paradigm that created the modern American security state, demanding a need to be ready to tackle any communist threat that arises.

Within a few weeks from the speech, Truman would issue another executive order, 9835, titled "Prescribing Procedures for the Administration of an Employees Loyalty Program in the Executive Branch of the Government."[7] This EO made permanent the temporary commission that had been created by his order of the previous year. The threat of communist infiltration within the ranks of the federal government had become a perceived reality and one that needed to be quashed immediately in the strongest of terms as a threat to democracy itself. The EO states,

> WHEREAS it is of vital importance that persons employed in the Federal service be of complete and unswerving loyalty to the United States; and WHEREAS, although the loyalty of by far the overwhelming majority of all Government employees is beyond question, the presence within the Government service of any disloyal or subversive person constitutes a threat to our democratic processes; and WHEREAS maximum protection must be afforded the United States against infiltration of disloyal persons into the ranks of its employees, and equal protection from unfounded accusations of disloyalty must be afforded the loyal employees of the Government.

Institutionalizing the threats faced by communism, the Truman administration's fiat via executive order to remove subversive persons from federal employment sent a clear message to the public that the dangers were real. The order established a set of rules, standards, procedures, and security measures when it came to hiring new federal employees and screening current ones. In working together, Truman with the support of Congress offered a unified anti-communist message that was not just focused on government employees, although they did make for an easy target, but on ending any communist influence within the US permanently. The Truman Doctrine established containment of Soviet influence abroad while creating a fervent crusade to stamp

---

[7] Harry S. Truman: "Executive Order 9835—Prescribing Procedures for the Administration of an Employees Loyalty Program in the Executive Branch of the Government," March 21, 1947. Available online at *The American Presidency Project*: <https://www.presidency.ucsb.edu/documents/executive-order-9835-prescribing-procedures-for-the-administration-employees-loyalty> (last accessed November 10, 2018).

out any and all domestic communist elements within democratic society. The Cold War mindset had become fully institutionalized with Truman's assertions of domestic communist threats as being the greatest danger to American democracy, values, and society. Whether the threats were real or perceived did not matter, the paradigm shift so dramatically altered domestic politics leaving the Truman administration and Congress no choice but to fully buy into the new Cold War and its smothering effect on governance.

Nowhere were these perceived threats made clearer than in J. Edgar Hoover's testimony before the House Un-American Activities Committee (HUAC) on March 26, 1947, just days after Truman issued EO 9835. Hoover rarely appeared before Congress, so his testimony was widely reported on, and he used this opportunity to press the FBI's legal assault on communism within the US. In particular, Hoover's testimony targeted various labor organizations, the film industry, and government agencies as repositories of communist party activity, setting the stage for the McCarthy era.[8] In his testimony, Hoover stated that the communist movement in the US "stands for the destruction of our American form of government; it stands for the destruction of American democracy; it stands for the destruction of free enterprise; and it stands for the creation of a 'Soviet of the United States' and ultimate world revolution."[9] Hoover's message would reverberate through the halls of Congress, the administration, and the public in general, reinforcing the move to the Cold War paradigm.

The dangers and warnings expressed by Truman, Hoover, and others were made real in 1948 when prominent State Department official Alger Hiss and several others were accused of having belonged to the Communist Party by confessed ex-communist witness Whittaker Chambers during a HUAC hearing.[10] My purpose here is not to delve into the details of the Hiss case or the intricacies of the HUAC hearings during this period. However, the

---

[8] Schrecker, *Age of McCarthyism*, 1994, p. 113.
[9] Ibid. p. 114.
[10] Ibid. p. 121.

Hiss case is significant in that it emphasizes the domestic threat of communism from inside government. Truman's executive orders, Hoover's investigations and testimony, and Congress's hearings and investigations demonstrate the construction of the new security state and the institutionalization of the Cold War Paradigm mindset. By having a prominent individual from within the State Department be accused of communist ties, and later convicted of perjury as related to this accusation, the incident provided clear evidence to justify the actions being taken by the Truman administration and Congress. Alger Hiss now illustrated the need for increased security measures to protect national security and American democracy.

Nearly one year after issuing EO 9835, Truman sent a directive to all executive branch officers and employees regarding any and all reports, papers, files, and records created as part of his loyalty program under the EO. The directive specified that out of national security concerns and for the welfare of the country, and in keeping with FBI procedure and precedent, all materials dealing with employee loyalty would remain confidential and only certain executive branch officials would have access.[11] Truman stated,

> Any subpoena or demand or request for information, reports, or files of the nature described, received from sources other than those persons in the executive branch of the Government who are entitled thereto by reason of their official duties, shall respectfully be declined, on the basis of this directive, and the subpoena or demand or other request shall be referred to the Office of the President for such response as the President may determine to be in the public interest in the particular case. There shall be no relaxation of the provisions of this directive except with my express authority.

Truman makes clear in the directive—based on the lessons learned from cases like Hiss's, as well as on his doctrine of communist containment—that the president has the power to withhold information from any requestor, including Congress, if he

[11] Memorandum from Harry S. Truman, March 13, 1948. Folder: Executive Privilege—Congressional Reference, Folder 2, Staff Member Office Files—Buzhardt, Box 15. Richard M. Nixon Presidential Library.

believes it to be in the public interest. This directive establishes an early justification for what will become known as executive privilege.

The ongoing anti-communist campaign coming from the Truman administration, coupled with the Hiss example, provided plenty of space for politics to step in and the political parties were happy to fill that space. In the Democratic and Republican party platforms for the 1944 presidential cycle there was no mention of communism; however, the party platforms of 1948 tell a completely different story. The Democratic Party Platform in 1948 explicitly states,

> We condemn Communism and other forms of totalitarianism and their destructive activity overseas and at home. We shall continue to build firm defenses against Communism by strengthening the economic and social structure of our own democracy. We reiterate our pledge to expose and prosecute treasonable activities of anti-democratic and un-American organizations which would sap our strength, paralyze our will to defend ourselves, and destroy our unity, inciting race against race, class against class, and the people against free institutions.[12]

Without mincing words, the Democratic Party itself helped establish the real and perceived communist menace facing the US. The platform that year would include support for the Truman Doctrine, the importance of supporting allies fighting communism's influence anywhere in the world, and in stopping the aggressive infiltrations of communism at home. The rise and prominence of communism's place within the party platform demonstrates how solidified the Cold War mindset had become. However, it was not just the Democrats seeking to insert their political proclivities into the public space in support of the Cold War Paradigm. The Republican Party also committed to stringent anti-communism policies in their 1948 platform, by stating,

---

[12] Democratic Party Platforms: "Democratic Party Platform of 1948," July 12, 1948. Available online at *The American Presidency Project*: <https://www.presidency.ucsb.edu/documents/1948-democratic-party-platform> (last accessed November 10, 2018).

> We pledge a vigorous enforcement of existing laws against Communists and enactment of such new legislation as may be necessary to expose the treasonable activities of Communists and defeat their objective of establishing here a godless dictatorship controlled from abroad.[13]

The platform would continue to note the importance of the "rooting out of Communism wherever found." The social learning process unfolding within the CLDC illustrates the shift in politics as a response to the Cold War mindset, and the political parties' position on the issues of the day offer evidence through the platforms demonstrating societal and political change.

Truman would continue with his anti-communist campaign following the election as well. We have already seen his unilateral position through executive orders such as 9835 which established a loyalty program for government employees, but Truman would continue to push against a communist menace in his inauguration address. In tackling the issue head-on early in his speech, Truman stated,

> In the pursuit of these aims, the United States and other like-minded nations find themselves directly opposed by a regime with contrary aims and a totally different concept of life. That regime adheres to a false philosophy which purports to offer freedom, security, and greater opportunity to mankind. Misled by that philosophy, many peoples have sacrificed their liberties only to learn to their sorrow that deceit and mockery, poverty and tyranny, are their reward. That false philosophy is communism. . . . I state these differences, not to draw issues of belief as such, but because the actions resulting from the Communist philosophy are a threat to the efforts of free nations to bring about world recovery and lasting peace.[14]

Truman's inaugural address, along with the party platforms, demonstrates the institutionalization of the Cold War Paradigm

---

[13] Republican Party Platforms: "Republican Party Platform of 1948," June 21, 1948. Available online at *The American Presidency Project*: <https://www.presidency.ucsb.edu/documents/republican-party-platform-1948> (last accessed November 10, 2018).

[14] Harry S. Truman: "Inaugural Address," January 20, 1949. Available online at *The American Presidency Project*: <https://www.presidency.ucsb.edu/documents/inaugural-address-4> (last accessed November 10, 2018).

and how the hysteria around communism had taken hold of the politics of the time. The election of 1948 would keep Truman as president as well as sweeping in Democratic Party control of both houses of Congress, establishing unified government under the Democrats. While Truman and Congress all seemed to be in lockstep on anti-communist measures, social learning allows for politics to evolve in time as well, which would come to dominate the space surrounding these issues.

No better example of the altered political environment could be found than the growing prominence of Republican Senator Joseph McCarthy (WI) and his populist accusatory rhetoric, already reaching a fever pitch by this time. In February 1950, during a speech to the Women's Republican Club of Wheeling, West Virginia, McCarthy famously claimed to have a list with the names of more than 200 subversive State Department officials.[15] McCarthy's fiery rhetoric mercilessly attacked Truman as purposefully harboring these individuals within government, and added, "When a great democracy is destroyed, it will not be because of the enemies from without, but rather because of the enemies from within."[16] McCarthy's use of populist language and fearmongering helped the senator achieve a level of fame, as demonstrated by this period being known for "McCarthyism" as a catch-all term encompassing the anti-communist sentiment within government and among the American public. However, McCarthy's speech and accusations serve as a turning point, not in the Cold War mindset, but in the CLDC, marking a juncture where the politics between Truman and Congress had begun to break apart. While both the administration and Congress were actively seeking to root out domestic communist influences at home, partisan politics had regained its footing so that members could stake out new territory within the Cold War mindset that moved beyond what Truman had in mind. The juncture

[15] Ellen Schrecker (1994) provides evidence to show that while McCarthy claimed over 200 during his speech, when he entered a version of this speech into the Congressional Record on February 20, 1950, he claimed to know of only 57 subversives working within the State Department.

[16] Schrecker, *Age of McCarthyism*, 1994, p. 211.

demonstrates the point where the administration's concern over public information became significant, while Congress moved toward wanting to utilize more public information. The rift that begins to form here on information between Truman and Congress establishes the foundation upon which FOIA development and use of executive privilege will grow.

When anti-communist hysteria goes too far: A turning point

The growing tension between Truman and Congress became typified in the debate over the McCarran Act in 1950. Truman had been active in communicating with Congress over his concerns on issues like the growing influence of communist propaganda and what the US should be doing to overcome such misinformation campaigns as threats to national security.[17] Congress at this time had been working on anti-communist legislation to target subversive activities across multiple areas of government and American life. The main bill that had been slowly developing within Congress was sponsored by HUAC Republican Reps. Richard Nixon (CA) and Karl Mundt (SD). The bill, known as the Internal Security Act, gained attention and momentum when Senate Judiciary Chair Pat McCarran (D-NV) supported the measure in response to the start of the Korean War.[18] The Internal Security Act, now known as the McCarran Act, contained broad-sweeping anti-communist measures—many of which were not supported by Truman, in part due to the legislation mandating that government information be made public, which Truman believed would harm national security by giving the Soviets sensitive information that could be used against the US. Congress passed the bill in September 1950 over Truman's objections, sending the bill to his desk and his veto

---

[17] Harry S. Truman: "Letter to the Speaker on the Need for an Expanded Truth Campaign to Combat Communism," July 13, 1950. Available online at *The American Presidency Project*: <https://www.presidency.ucsb.edu/documents/letter-the-speaker-the-need-for-expanded-truth-campaign-combat-communism> (last accessed November 10, 2018).

[18] Schrecker, *Age of McCarthyism*, 1994, p. 192.

pen. Congress overrode Truman's veto several days later by a large margin. In his extensive veto message to Congress, Truman gave a list of provisions within the bill he found objectionable, stating, "Legislation with these consequences is not necessary to meet the real dangers which communism presents to our free society. Those dangers are serious, and must be met. But this bill would hinder us, not help us, in meeting them."[19] The first example Truman uses to explain his position focuses specifically on making government information public, to which he warns of the real danger. He states,

> One provision alone of this bill is enough to demonstrate how far it misses the real target. Section 5 would require the Secretary of Defense to "proclaim" and "have published in the Federal Register" a public catalogue of defense plants, laboratories, and all other facilities vital to our national defense—no matter how secret. I cannot imagine any document a hostile foreign government would desire more. Spies and saboteurs would willingly spend years of effort seeking to find out the information that this bill would require the Government to hand them on a silver platter. There are many provisions of this bill which impel me to return it without my approval, but this one would be enough by itself. It is inconceivable to me that a majority of the Congress could expect the Commander-in-Chief of the armed forces of the United States to approve such a flagrant violation of proper security safeguards.

Within the CLDC as the Cold War Paradigm has been institutionalized, this provision illustrates the coming power struggle between the executive and legislative branches over access to public information. Truman clearly articulates his concerns over making public information that would offer support to spies and enemies. The unfolding social learning process within the CLDC gives insight into Truman's use of his veto pen to prevent an overzealous Congress from offering support to the enemy. The legislative battle over the McCarran Act demonstrates that

---

[19] Harry S. Truman: "Veto of the Internal Security Bill," September 22, 1950. Available online at *The American Presidency Project*: <https://www.presidency.ucsb.edu/documents/veto-the-internal-security-bill> (last accessed November 10, 2018).

Truman had found an end-point to the Cold War Paradigm with the recognition that Congress's fervency over anti-communist policies had begun to trample upon the democratic values these policies were supposed to protect. Toward the end of his veto message, Truman states:

> I do not undertake lightly the responsibility of differing with the majority in both Houses of Congress who have voted for this bill. We are all Americans; we all wish to safeguard and preserve our constitutional liberties against internal and external enemies. But I cannot approve this legislation, which instead of accomplishing its avowed purpose would actually interfere with our liberties and help the communists against whom the bill was aimed.
>
> This is a time when we must marshall all our resources and all the moral strength of our free system in self-defense against the threat of communist aggression. We will fail in this, and we will destroy all that we seek to preserve, if we sacrifice the liberties of our citizens in a misguided attempt to achieve national security.
>
> There is no reason why we should fail. Our country has been through dangerous times before, without losing our liberties to external attack or internal hysteria. Each of us, in Government and out, has a share in guarding our liberties. Each of us must search his own conscience to find whether he is doing all that can be done to preserve and strengthen them.

My intention is not to delve deep into the details of either the McCarran Act or the legislative veto battle between Truman and Congress, but to establish the significance of this exchange situation for two reasons. The first being that the McCarran Act is the first major anti-communist policy to become law, which offers a clear example of the social learning process through the CLDC. As the Cold War mindset becomes institutionalized, the real and perceived threats of communism as demonstrated through Truman and Hoover's actions shows how new information is processed and utilized through the construction of policy, in this case the McCarran Act, and how the learning process happens as the politics of the Cold War Paradigm recurrently form. The legislation itself demonstrates the learning process, according to Hall, but we can also see the learning process unfold with Truman's veto of the bill. For Truman, the bill took the anti-communist hysteria within the country too far, just as McCarthy would eventually be diminished as American society and government sought to find a balance between liberty and security. Secondly, we can see through this exchange that the issue of public information begins to move apart the positioning of the administration and Congress. This split signifies the upcoming power struggle that will be underlying the entire development period of FOIA and follow the law through implementation, oversight, and amendment. The different political perspectives from each end of Pennsylvania Avenue come through: Truman believes that in trying to defend the country from communist threats, Congress is actually endangering the country by forcing executive information into the open. The politics that continue to unfold between the executive and legislative branches over public information and what will become executive privilege are now influenced by the president's concern that congressional politics can be detrimental to security, thus learning to tighten control over information. The inter-branch power struggle is now fully formed as the president is fearful that Congress itself will unwittingly aid the enemy, and Congress responds to increased secrecy by seeking more access.

The increased attention the Truman administration began to give to government information solidified the concern for control within the executive branch, regardless of congressional apprehension. The Administrative Procedures Act of 1946 contained a section addressing public access to government records that was vague in its language, providing a narrow definition that was capitalized on by the president and executive branch actors.[20] This ambiguity in the law gave Truman the ability to deny access to government information for national security reasons, as defined in whatever manner he chose. In September 1951, Truman issued Executive Order 10290, "Prescribing Regulations Establishing

---

[20] Again, the purpose here is not to delve into the specifics of the Administrative Procedures Act (APA) of 1946 other than to note that it was the current law dictating presidential records and conduct of executive branch information. This law will resurface again during the FOIA development debates, and ultimately, FOIA as a law is an amendment to the APA.

Minimum Standards for the Classification, Transmission, and Handling, by Departments and Agencies of the Executive Branch, of Official Information Which Requires Safeguarding in the Interest of the Security of the United States."[21] As the title of the EO would suggest, Truman unilaterally established a hierarchy and classification system for government information, such as "Top Secret," "Restricted," or "Classified," as well as the procedures and security clearances required for access to and storage of such information. In the absence of a clear law or mandate from Congress, and after the concerns Truman expressed during the veto debate over the McCarran Act, this new order provided the administration with clear guidance and control over information.

Many members of the press did not respond favorably to Truman's new EO, as the order would have a direct impact on the ability of the press to gain access to government information. Prominent media organizations like the American Society of Newspaper Editors (ASNE) had formed freedom of information committees to examine the growing concerns over increased government control. In an editorial following Truman's EO, James S. Pope, chair of ASNE's freedom of information committee, stated: "It is impossible for our committee to challenge a genuine effort to protect military security. However, we do not believe that the President's order will protect security as much as it will smother legitimate information about the operation of government."[22] Pope makes the argument that ambiguity in the order will lead to confusion over what information should be kept secret or classified as it represents a security threat if made public. The vague wording, coupled with the inability of most agency employees to comprehend the technical nature of the information, will lead to a system where most, if not all, government information is

---

[21] Staff Memorandum No. 82-1-60, "Constitutional and Legal Aspects of S.2190," November 29, 1951. Folder: Executive Orders 10501 and 10901— [1951–1959; Folder 1 of 2], Government Operations Subcommittee on Foreign Operations and Government Information BOX M-14, Center for Legislative Archives, National Archives, Washington, DC.

[22] *Christian Science Monitor*, "Truman Restriction on News Rapped by Kentucky Editor," September 26, 1951, p. 17. Accessed via *ProQuest Historical Newspapers*, December 15, 2015.

considered classified or secret. He also notes the difficulty in having no means to appeal an agency decision classifying information, except by convincing the same officials who classified the information to begin with. Truman responded to these attacks by accusing the press of intending to "carp and criticize" instead of being helpful.[23] He argued that many members of the press were invited to contribute input to the crafting of his executive order, but this invitation had been rebuffed, and the order was now met with complaining instead of constructive feedback. These public squabbles between Truman and the press would continue throughout the remainder of his term as president, but there were no additional unilateral or legislative actions addressing the issues.

Conclusion

The starting point in the development of FOIA is grounded in the Truman administration for two reasons. The first is the Cold War Paradigm shift that creates not just a new mindset to understand the evolving actions of the world and the need for a new American security state, but creates a new politics along with it. As demonstrated throughout this chapter, Truman ushered in a stark shift that meets Hall's definition of Third-Order learning as the immediate postwar era under Truman was disjointed from the previous era's politics and policies. With the end of the war, Truman was able to establish new policies and politics centered on the fight against communism and the containment of the Soviet Union. The CLDC begins in 1946 with the Truman administration, and through the social learning lens, we are able to see how the administration orchestrated dramatic policy changes, specifically leading to the restriction of government information being made public, all out of concerns over domestic and foreign communist threats. The power of the Cold War had become institutionalized and would continue to influence policy

---

[23] *Washington Post*, "Editors Apparently Want to 'Carp and Criticize,' Truman Writes," December 19, 1951, p. 18. Accessed via *ProQuest Historical Newspapers*, September 24, 2015.

and politics for the next forty years. It was the actions of the Truman administration with an equally zealous Congress that institutionalized the new politics of the Cold War Paradigm.

The second reason became clear during the latter half of the Truman administration. While the administration had plenty of help and support from Congress, their relationship began to break apart, driven in part by the differing political demands faced by each branch. The demands on the executive branch were exemplified in Truman's response to the new Cold War mindset—that threats posed by communist elements at home and abroad required the need for greater control over information. The fight over the McCarran Act illustrated Truman's position on preventing government information from being made public if it could pose a threat to national security. Down Pennsylvania Avenue, however, Congress was faced with differing political concerns, as partisan politics would bring about those legislators, like McCarthy, willing to take extreme positions on secrecy and public information issues. Congress as a whole was beginning to find itself in the position of needing to challenge these new restrictive administration policies, even though executive restrictions were a reaction to congressional politics. However, in the absence of congressional action to address executive branch controls on information at this time, Truman was able to fill that vacuum with unilateral action through executive orders to redefine the gaps in policy to his advantage. The actions from Truman, along with Congress's intransigence to address public records, especially for oversight purposes, produced tensions between Congress and the president that would continue to grow, thus paving the way for FOIA development.

In the next chapter, our attention turns to the Eisenhower administration and how the new politics developed under Truman help to bring about the creation of the Office of Strategic Information, the institutionalization of executive privilege, and the creation of the Moss Subcommittee on Government Information. Over a short period of time, the politics of the Cold War Paradigm push Eisenhower to clamp down on public information in such a fierce manner that it forces Congress to learn how to overcome administration policies through oversight and legislation. The CLDC continues with new junctures, but what begins to emerge is a clear path of policy evolution, as Eisenhower leans heavily on Truman in establishing national security policies on public information and his use of executive privilege.

3

Eisenhower's executive privilege and the public interest

I have stated this time and again: I believe that every investigating committee of the Congress, every auditing office like the GAO, should always have an opportunity to see official records if the security of our country is not involved.

—Dwight D. Eisenhower, press conference, 5 November 1958

May 17, 1954 was a noted day for two very different reasons. The first reason saw Supreme Court Chief Justice Earl Warren deliver the unanimous decision in the landmark *Brown v. Board of Education* ruling, striking down the separate but equal reasoning to justify segregation in the schools.[1] The second and less known reason was a letter President Dwight Eisenhower sent to Secretary of Defense Charles Wilson, directing him to withhold information from the Senate Committee on Government Operations as a means of protecting internal executive branch deliberations and documents.[2] Eisenhower grounded his assertions as essential to maintain the separation of power between the executive and legislative branches of government, therefore making a direct claim that the president held a constitutional power to withhold information "whenever he found that what was sought was confidential or its disclosure would be incompatible with the public interest or jeopardize the safety of the nation."

---

[1] "The Present Limits of 'Executive Privilege.'" Congressional Record. 1973. 93rd Cong., 1st sess., vol. 119, pp. 10079–10083.

[2] Dwight D. Eisenhower: "Letter to the Secretary of Defense Directing Him To Withhold Certain Information from the Senate Committee on Government Operations," May 17, 1954. Available online at *The American Presidency Project*, <https://www.presidency.ucsb.edu/documents/letter-the-secretary-defense-directing-him-withhold-certain-information-from-the-senate> (last accessed November 10, 2018).

In this communication, Eisenhower never used the term "executive privilege." However, he attached a memorandum from Attorney General Herbert Brownell, Jr., which offered a long historical summation of how past presidents, all the way back to Washington, had utilized the separation of powers doctrine to justify assertions that the powers held by one branch cannot be imposed upon by another branch. Brownell asserted that in the public interest and for national security reasons, executive branch actors must at times refrain from making information available to the public or Congress—a precedent long established and provided by the Constitution. Brownell states in the memo:

> For over 150 years . . . our Presidents have established, by precedent, that they and members of their Cabinet and other heads of executive departments have an undoubted privilege and discretion to keep confidential, in the public interest, papers and information which require secrecy. American history abounds in countless illustrations of the refusal, on occasion, by the President and heads of departments to furnish papers to Congress, or its committees, for reasons of public policy. The messages of our past Presidents reveal that almost every one of them found it necessary to inform Congress of his constitutional duty to execute the office of President, and, in furtherance of that duty, to withhold information and papers for the public good.[3]

Brownell continued in his memo to note the importance of the separation of powers in carving out space for presidents to assert the necessary authority to protect the public interest by keeping information secret:

> Courts have uniformly held that the President and the heads of departments have an uncontrolled discretion to withhold the information and papers in the public interest; they will not interfere with the exercise of that discretion. Congress has not the power, as one of the three great branches of Government, to subject the Executive Branch to its will any more than the Executive Branch may impose its unrestrained will upon the Congress.[4]

---

[3] Ibid.

[4] Memorandum to President Eisenhower from Attorney General. Papers of John F. Kennedy. Presidential Papers. White House Staff Files of Lee C. White. General File, 1954–1964. Executive privilege, 17 May 1954–21

The arguments articulated by Eisenhower and Brownell establish the justification for the modern usage of executive privilege, grounding it within an institutional framework as a necessary outcome of the separation of powers doctrine. Again, while neither Eisenhower nor Brownell use the actual term, the directive of both memos was clear: that the president and all members of the executive branch have the Constitutional authority to deny information to Congress. The Congressional Research Service notes in a 1973 report that past administrations had used similar claims to deny information to the public or the press, but this was the first time an administration had specifically made a Constitutional claim of power to withhold government information from Congress.[5] Additionally, the two memos articulated that this power was given to all members of the executive branch—not just the president specifically, but any department or agency head or employee.

As the CLDC continues into the Eisenhower administration, the Brownell memo offers an example of a learned response to previous incidents. Within the memo, Brownell cites previous administrations' actions in denying information to Congress, and the Truman administration provides numerous examples for Brownell to build his argument upon. Brownell states, "During the Truman Administration also the President adhered to the traditional Executive view that the President's discretion must govern the surrender of Executive files."[6] The memo lists ten examples between 1948 and 1952 where Truman or members of his administration denied information, records, testimony, or papers to congressional committees, most out of national security concerns. One such example cited was from February 22, 1950, noting Senate Resolution 231, which directed a Senate subcommittee to acquire State Department loyalty files. The memo states

August 1961.

[5] "The Present Limits of 'Executive Privilege.'" Congressional Record. 1973. 93rd Cong., 1st sess., vol. 119, pp. 10079–10080.

[6] Memorandum to President Eisenhower from Attorney General. Papers of John F. Kennedy. Presidential Papers. White House Staff Files of Lee C. White. General File, 1954–1964. Executive privilege, 17 May 1954–21 August 1961. JFKWHSFLCW-005-004-p001. JFK Presidential Library.

that this resolution was met with the president's refusal, along with "vigorous opposition" from J. Edgar Hoover.[7] Politically, social learning unfolds within the CLDC as the Eisenhower administration needed the space in order to deny information to Congress, without running into the same conflicts as Truman. Executive privilege became the learned response for Eisenhower, justifying the dynamic and forceful memo from Brownell in making such sweeping assertions of executive power. By making the claim of an inferred constitutional power, Eisenhower places Congress in a politically tenuous position whereby in order to stop, prevent, or alter the use of executive privilege, they must specifically offer some kind of legislative check—a requirement which is made even more difficult when the administration refuses to turn over information vital to oversight on this issue.

This claim by Eisenhower led to one of the greatest power struggles between the executive and legislative branches—one that continues on today—which is whether the president does have the Constitutional authority to deny information to Congress. In fact, the onus for Eisenhower's directive to Wilson was specifically to keep sensitive information from Senator McCarthy during the Army-McCarthy hearings in the spring of 1954. Grounded in a power conflict with Congress, Eisenhower claimed the authority and established precedent for the now modern use of executive privilege, one that has shifted over time, but continues to endure. As I mentioned previously, the purpose here is not to revisit the argument on whether the president has the Constitutional authority for executive privilege (as scholars have devoted plenty of time to that),[8] but to examine how the politics of this power struggle is intertwined with the Cold War mindset and led to the development of FOIA. Inter-branch power struggles, as with executive privilege, are founded in Constitutional ambiguity and are political in nature, subjected to the context of the moment. Across time, past struggles set the precedents upon which future struggles are built, but once Eisenhower asserts authority for an executive privilege, it becomes incumbent upon the other two

[7] Ibid.
[8] See Rozell 1999, 2010 and Fisher 2004.

branches to check that power or face expanded use. While the 1952 election ushered in a unified Republican government under Eisenhower, it was short-lived, and congressional Democrats learned quickly to challenge expanding secrecy.

The rest of this chapter will examine the political context of the Eisenhower administration's use of executive privilege in denying information to Congress, and how Congress would learn from these experiences in order to offer a response that challenged executive power. Information security became a paradox for Eisenhower, as the more government operations and actions were viewed through the lens of the Cold War mindset, the more the president comprehended that any public information was a threat to national security and must therefore be classified or denied. The fervency with which the Eisenhower administration acted in keeping information out of the hands of Congress, and to a lesser extent the press, became the basis for congressional actions responding directly to these issues. This chapter will detail the political conflicts surrounding the Eisenhower administration and Congress over executive privilege, leading to the institutionalization of freedom of information through the creation of the Moss Subcommittee in 1955.

Executive orders, the Office of Strategic Information, and John Moss

In having the support of the Republican Congress during the early years of his presidency, Eisenhower had breathing room to target specific actions relating to public information and keeping government records secret. While tensions with Congress had been on the rise with Truman, the new administration and Congress were back to working together, and once again focused on issues concerning national security. As Figure 1.1 has shown, press coverage surrounding the secrecy and access issues began to gain more attention, as the press became more impacted by the administration's position on keeping the press locked out. Simultaneously, as Figure 1.2 demonstrates, press coverage of issues surrounding the domestic Cold War threats remained high, but began to fall during the Eisenhower era. However, with the public saturation point persistently high in comparison to government secrecy coverage, this offered continued incentives and reinforcement for tighter information controls through the executive branch.

On 27 April 1953, Eisenhower issued Executive Order 10450, titled, "Security Requirements for Government Employment."[9] While the order repealed Truman's 1947 Executive Order 9835, Eisenhower was able to effectively reconfigure the bureaucratic structure within the administration to expand efforts aimed at subversive employees. By eliminating the loyalty commission that Truman created, Eisenhower established officers within every agency and department charged with creating and maintaining programs to ensure that employment was "consistent with the interests of the national security."[10] The new president was able to effectively decentralize power from the loyalty commission that oversaw the entire executive branch of government, to recentralize power within each and every department and agency, providing greater reach across the administration. The change from the loyalty commission, which was viewed as a temporary measure to satisfy public outcry and concerns over subversive employees within government, to EO 10450, which created a new bureaucratic structure within the executive branch to root out and prevent subversive elements from taking hold, demonstrates how Eisenhower institutionalized the Cold War Paradigm further. This new structure also created a hierarchical control system for Eisenhower, who sat at the top and was able to use this power as he saw fit.

Shortly thereafter, Eisenhower moved on to the accompanying part of the issue through Executive Order 10501, titled, "Safeguarding Official Information in the Interests of the Defense of the United States."[11] The opening language makes

---

[9] Dwight D. Eisenhower: "Executive Order 10450—Security Requirements for Government Employment," April 27, 1953. Available online at *The American Presidency Project*, <https://www.presidency.ucsb.edu/documents/executive-order-10450-security-requirements-for-government-employment> (last accessed November 10, 2018).

[10] Ibid.

[11] Dwight D. Eisenhower: "Executive Order 10501—Safeguarding Official

Eisenhower's case for the need to protect information in the national interest by stating,

> WHEREAS it is essential that the citizens of the United States be informed concerning the activities of their government; and WHEREAS the interests of national defense require the preservation of the ability of the United States to protect and defend itself against all hostile or destructive action by covert or overt means, including espionage as well as military action; and WHEREAS it is essential that certain official information affecting the national defense be protected uniformly against unauthorized disclosure.

The EO alters the bureaucratic structure within the executive branch to remake the classification structure of information and who, specifically, has the authority within the administration to make such claims. Eisenhower again demonstrated a high measure of control over the function and process by designating specific agencies and departments, as well as individuals within each, who have "original classification" control over information, and those who generally do not deal with sensitive information as having limited classification control "as designated by the President."[12] Through this EO, the president was able to recentralize power back into the executive office of the president, providing a new bureaucratic structure to manage information and giving the president complete control.

The EO was met by the press with mixed feelings, as many thought the changes established by Eisenhower were an improvement over the approach of his predecessor, and this new structure offered a more measured balance of public information to national security. Press associations like ASNE, who had formed

Information in the Interests of the Defense of the United States," November 5, 1953. Available online at *The American Presidency Project*, <https://www.presidency.ucsb.edu/documents/executive-order-10501-safeguarding-official-information-the-interests-the-defense-the> (last accessed November 10, 2018).

[12] Staff Memorandum No. 82-1-60, "Constitutional and Legal Aspects of S.2190," November 29, 1951. Folder: Executive Orders 10501 and 10901— [1951–1959; Folder 1 of 2], Government Operations Subcommittee on Foreign Operations and Government Information BOX M-14, Center for Legislative Archives, National Archives, Washington, DC.

a freedom of information committee, and individual editors offered some praise to Eisenhower for rolling back "Truman's rigid public information restrictions."[13] The *Washington Post* ran a front page story praising Eisenhower for taking action "to make it possible for our citizens to know more of what our government is doing."[14] However, the press was also cautious about insisting on the continued vigilance of the White House to ensure that public access and press freedoms were maintained in the face of new classification controls. The positive press attention was only fleeting, however, as the Cold War Paradigm established a need for secrecy that would push Eisenhower to seek greater control over information policies within the executive branch, which would bring a learned response from Congress, aided by the press.

The Republican Party's electoral victories from 1952 placed them in unified government control. However, one House seat that was lost by the Republicans in that election was picked up by a Democratic businessman from Sacramento, California, named John Moss. As a freshman member of the minority in the 83rd Congress (1953–5), Moss took his committee placements as assigned and worked on the House Post Office and Civil Service Committee, which would quickly set him up for direct confrontation with the administration over policies established through executive orders. In January of 1954, Congress was holding investigations and hearings on Eisenhower's firing of more than 2,800 federal employees, all of whom were deemed as national security threats from the administration under EO 10450.[15] From his seat on the Civil Service Committee, Moss requested the records from the Civil Service Commission providing all the

---

[13] *New York Times*, "A.P. Editors Laud News Rule Change," November 8, 1953, p. 78. Accessed via *ProQuest Historical Newspapers*, October 10, 2015.

[14] *The Washington Post*, "Disputed Truman News Curbs Are Eased by Eisenhower," November 7, 1953, p. 1. Accessed via *ProQuest Historical Newspapers*, September 15, 2015.

[15] *The Washington Post*, "Explanation of 'Risk' Data Put to Ike," January 27, 1954, p. 2. Accessed via *ProQuest Historical Newspapers*, September 24, 2015.

information related to the firings for oversight purposes, and was flatly denied.[16] With little interest from his Republican colleagues in control of the committee, Moss had no power to respond to the administration in any meaningful way. This incident left an impression on Moss, and would help guide his future actions. Many in Congress, however, were growing anxious that such an incident was now typical of the administration, and while the administration later cited concerns like drunkenness, homosexuality, and over-talkativeness as reasons for the firings, Moss and his colleagues did not believe these reasons amounted to threats to national security.

Shortly after the executive privilege memos and just about the time the Senate censured Joseph McCarthy, severely curbing the activities of HUAC and slowing the frenzied pace of communist accusations, Eisenhower took a massive step in seeking to centralize more control over information by creating the Office of Strategic Information (OSI) within the Commerce Department in November 1954.[17] The office was established by request of the National Security Council and justified under EO 10501, with R. Karl Honaman, a former director of publications for Bell National Labs, named as director. OSI would remain in place within the Commerce Department for only three years, but would quickly become the focus of congressional rebuke. Eisenhower justified the establishment of OSI in order to coordinate "the international flow of unclassified scientific and technical information," with the "voluntary cooperation" of the press and Congress.[18] Honaman would testify before Congress to offer justification of OSI by stating, "Too much information has been released which is of no benefit to the American public, but which

---

[16] Lemov, *People's Warrior*, 2011, p. 48.

[17] Staff Memorandum, August 2, 1965. Folder: Staff Memos [1963–1965] Box No. M-21, Center for Legislative Archives, National Archives, Washington, DC; Statement from Congressman John E. Moss, March 30, 1965. Folder: Freedom of Information Miscellaneous [1965–1966] Box No. M-25, Center for Legislative Archives, National Archives, Washington, DC.

[18] Staff Memorandum to John Moss from Sam Archibald and Jack Howard, October 28, 1960. Folder: Moss—Speakers Bureau [1960–1961], Box No. M-7, Center for Legislative Archives, National Archives, Washington, DC.

is of tremendous value to our opponents."[19] The press hit hard on the administration, calling OSI "the most serious threat to freedom of information that has developed in the Eisenhower Administration."[20]

While the justification from the administration was based on ensuring foreign adversaries could not attain vital technology or scientific information that could be used against the US, Congress saw the actions of OSI as a consolidation of power to keep information from being made public. A congressional report prepared for Moss with background information on OSI stated, "The agency immediately began to force other agencies—particularly defense department agencies—to cut down on the flow of information, not only abroad but also within the United States."[21] Eisenhower had successfully centralized power and control of government information to Congress and the public by effectively using unilateral powers like executive orders and claims of executive privilege. By cutting out or ignoring congressional input on these administration policies, which suffocated the flow of information to Congress, Eisenhower had created what some in the press referred to as a "paper curtain" on government secrecy.[22] However, the consolidation of this much power within the executive branch had finally hit its zenith, and as we will see through social learning, Congress would finally begin to take actions in countering these expansions of executive power.

The election of 1954 swept the Democrats back into control of both houses of Congress, leaving Eisenhower facing a traditional divided government and losing any partisan cover he had been getting from Congress during his first two years. With

---

[19] Interim Subcommittee Report, "Department of Commerce." Folder: Reports, Material for [Folder 2 of 3; 1955–1958], Box No. M-9, Center for Legislative Archives, National Archives, Washington, DC.

[20] *New York Times*, "Editors Score Curb on Business Data," December 3, 1954, p. 34. Accessed via *ProQuest Historical Newspapers*, October 11, 2015.

[21] Staff Memorandum to John Moss from Sam Archibald and Jack Howard, October 28, 1960. Folder: Moss—Speakers Bureau [1960–1961], Box No. M-7, Center for Legislative Archives, National Archives, Washington, DC.

[22] Archibald, "Early Years of FOIA," 1993.

the Democrats moving back into control, Moss sought to gain a more prestigious committee placement, with his eye on the Government Operations Committee. On November 18, 1954, Moss met with soon-to-be Speaker Sam Rayburn and House Majority Leader John McCormack to discuss his committee placements.[23] Based on that conversation, Moss began to reach out to the House members who headed the delegations from each state, including his own of California, and to the committee chairs of the committees on which he wanted to serve. By January 1, 1955, Moss would send both Rayburn and McCormack a series of letters from these various members offering their support for Moss's desired committee placement, which was still focused on Government Operations.[24] In contacting dozens of more senior House members, including committee chairs and leadership, Moss demonstrated his ambition to move into a committee seat that would afford him a position of influence. Simultaneously, as a junior member, his outreach to consult and ask approval from senior members earned Moss a certain amount of respect from these members. Gaining the respect and notice of senior members and leadership would provide Moss with avenues of power as his career began to bloom. This ambitious activity would hasten Moss's ascent to becoming a power entrepreneur in Congress.

Being reassigned back to the Post Office and Civil Service Committee at the start of the 84th Congress left Moss motivated to see Speaker Rayburn to make a direct case for why he should be on the Government Operations Committee. In a brief exchange with Rayburn that was described as "not exactly" an argument, but an aggressive move for a junior member, Moss pleaded his case forcefully to the Speaker.[25] Moss received a call two days later informing him he had received his committee assignments and was to be on both the Commerce Committee

---

[23] Letter from John Moss to Sam Rayburn, November 19, 1954. Folder: 23, Box 85; Series 3. Subject Files, 1941–1978. John E. Moss Archive, California State University, Sacramento.

[24] Letter from John Moss to John McCormack, January 1, 1955. Folder: 23, Box 85; Series 3. Subject Files, 1941–1978. John E. Moss Archive, California State University, Sacramento.

[25] Lemov, *People's Warrior*, 2011, p. 46.

and the Government Operations Committee. The exchange had left Rayburn impressed by Moss's tenacity and willingness to challenge him directly, leading to the formation of a strong relationship. The argument and now budding relationship with Rayburn gave Moss the confidence on the committee to seek out action on Eisenhower's secrecy policies. The political winds had shifted on Eisenhower, and the Democratic Congress was seeking issues that would be salient to use against the administration. As the press had already been vocally opposed to the creation of OSI and in support of freedom of information, Moss recognized an easy policy area that would gain plenty of attention. Moss met with Rep. William Dawson (D-IL), Chair of the Government Operations Committee, to discuss strategies on tackling the issue. After meeting with House leadership, Dawson was given the go-ahead to form a special subcommittee to examine the issues of government secrecy and freedom of information, and to place Moss as the Chair. In the spring of 1955, the Special Subcommittee on Government Information was formed with Moss at the helm. In establishing the subcommittee, Dawson noted the charges against the administration by stating,

> Charges have been made that Government agencies have denied or withheld pertinent and timely information from those who are entitled to receive it. These charges include the denial of such information to the newspapers, to radio and television broadcasters, magazines, and other communication media, to trained and qualified research experts and to the Congress.[26]

The Moss Subcommittee began immediately by issuing a survey to each and every executive department and agency seeking details on the policies that guided public information and the classification authority of materials. The institutionalization of the issue of freedom of information would provide Congress, and

---

[26] Letter from William L. Dawson to John Moss establishing the Special Subcommittee on Government Information, in Preface of Subcommittee Hearing Opening Statement, 1955. Folder: Hearings (1955–1956)— Correspondence re: plans and preparation [October 1955–February 1956], Box No. M-5, Center for Legislative Archives, National Archives, Washington, DC.

Moss in particular, with a hammer to go after the administration's expanded policies on public information.

With the creation of the Moss Subcommittee, another important juncture has occurred within the CLDC. The importance of the subcommittee cannot be overstated. The politics of social learning that created the Cold War Paradigm and institutionalized executive policies that dominate control over information, when applied to Congress demonstrate a learning process that unfolded in direct response to the president. As Eisenhower pushed Congress further into a corner through his use of executive privilege and unilateral actions in denying information, Congress learned that a forceful response was needed, and the issue provided support from the most powerful built-in advocacy organization—the press. In forming the subcommittee, Congress created an avenue of oversight that could be wielded like a cudgel against the administration to provide a check on executive power. At the same time, the subcommittee would be able to provide research and support for legislation as needed. Moss described his subcommittee as taking the perspective "that Federal agencies don't have to spoon-feed the American public."[27] In this way, Congress offered a learned response to the overreach of Eisenhower, showing that the administration had finally crossed a line that Congress now needed to push back against.

One of the first major battles the Moss Subcommittee would undertake would be targeting OSI, an inter-branch power struggle that would last for three years, ultimately leading to the passage of an amendment to the Housekeeping Statute of 1789 (5 US Code 22) by Congress in order to clarify the executive's position on public records. If we look back to Figure 1.1 examining the rise in press coverage of these issues, we can see how the first peak appears during this period. OSI was institutionalized in the administration shortly after the election of 1954 when the Democrats won back control of Congress. The Moss Subcommittee was created the following spring, in part as a

---

[27] *The Washington Post*, "Moss Urges Restraint in News Curb," June 25, 1955, p. 4. Accessed via *ProQuest Historical Newspapers*, September 17, 2015.

direct response to the creation of OSI. Both of these moves had a dramatic impact on the press, where OSI infuriated editors and reduced access, and the Moss Subcommittee opened a congressional platform from which the press could seek influence. As the sides in the debate became more solidified, the press would increase attention and coverage, delivering a steady flow of information to the public on the problems of government secrecy. The number of press stories on government secrecy and freedom of information more than doubled from 1954 to 1955, and nearly quadrupled from 1954 to 1957. As public saturation began to grow through increased coverage, Congress took advantage of their built-in interest group by targeting the administration on the issue, thus giving the press more to cover.

A Senate hearing in March, led by Senators Hubert Humphrey (D-MN) and A.S. Mike Monroney (D-OK) examined secrecy and security policies in the Eisenhower administration, finding there was a "growing tendency" among agencies to withhold information despite the executive order from November 1953.[28] The administration's response to such congressional scolding was detailed in news stories describing Eisenhower's irritation with continued press exposure on Pentagon programs, leading Secretary Wilson to issue a "gag rule" memo tamping down on any information flowing to the press from the Defense Department (DOD).[29] Wilson issued a directive that "all information from the Pentagon must make a 'constructive contribution' to the mission of the Defense Department."[30] The directive was issued under the authority of EO 10501, which the Moss Subcommittee referred to as "based upon the reverse philosophy that all government information should be hidden except that

[28] *New York Times*, "2 Senators Attack Executive Secrecy," March 16, 1955, p. 30. Accessed via *ProQuest Historical Newspapers*, October 11, 2015.

[29] *New York Times*, "Pentagon's Press—III," April 15, 1955, p. 12. Accessed via *ProQuest Historical Newspapers*, October 11, 2015; *The Washington Post*, "Government News Curbs Protested," April 23, 1955: p. 1. Accessed via *ProQuest Historical Newspapers*, September 17, 2015.

[30] Staff Memorandum to John Moss from Sam Archibald and Jack Howard, October 28, 1960. Folder: Moss—Speakers Bureau [1960–1961], Box No. M-7, Center for Legislative Archives, National Archives, Washington, DC.

which the public and the Congress can prove a clear right to know."[31] The press response was one of outrage, stating that "it was up to the people, not the Government, to decide what is 'useful' or 'interesting' in the field of information."[32] As the Eisenhower administration continued to shut down information access Congress began to develop a strategy, or learned response, as channeled through the Moss Subcommittee.

In September 1955, Moss Subcommittee Chief of Staff Sam Archibald discussed ongoing coordination with James S. Pope, editor of the Louisville Courier-Journal and Chair of ASNE's Freedom of Information Committee, on how to influence public opinion and place increased pressure on the Eisenhower administration.[33] Pope detailed how numerous members of the press had been threatened by various agency officials with being completely cut off from sources if they supported or engaged with any efforts at reducing restrictions, which included working with the Moss Subcommittee. Both agreed that increased coordination on strategy was needed to build more support with the press and public, and to give the subcommittee increased support within Congress as well. Moss made a concerted effort in staffing his subcommittee with former members of the press, like Archibald, and would hold hearings that fall which opened with a friendly panel made up of members from various press associations like ASNE, Sigma Delta Chi (SDX), and the Associate Press Managing Editors Association (APME), all of whom had formed freedom of information committees.[34] During that first hearing, Moss

---

[31] Ibid.

[32] *The Washington Post*, "Defense Sets Up Terms For Giving Information," June 18, 1955, p. 2. Accessed via *ProQuest Historical Newspapers*, September 17, 2015.

[33] Letter to Sam Archibald from James S. Pope, September 15, 1955, and Letter to James S. Pope from Sam Archibald, September 30, 1955. Folder: Hearings (1955–1956)—Correspondence re: plans and preparation [June–October, 1955], Box No. M-5, Center for Legislative Archives, National Archives, Washington, DC.

[34] Letter from John Moss to Russell Wiggins, October 19, 1955. Folder: Hearings (1955–1956)—Correspondence re: plans and preparation [June–October, 1955], Box No. M-5, Center for Legislative Archives, National Archives, Washington, DC.

would directly target executive privilege and all of the actions Eisenhower had taken under his order, stating,

> Some of the regulations which the Subcommittee has reviewed indicate that virtually unlimited discretion, of questionable legal status, is sometimes passed down departmental hierarchies to subordinates. Also, there have been exaggerated claims of authority to withhold information based on a theory of "inherent" powers stemming from the presidency. There are indications that some officials in Washington today believe they have authority to exercise presidential powers without the President's authorization or his prior knowledge or even subsequent review of their acts. . . . I believe that a clear need for new legislation has been established.[35]

By the end of 1956, the subcommittee had held more than two dozen hearings that included participation from members of the press and media organizations, administration officials, and other members of Congress who had been officially denied information from the administration for either investigatory purposes or constituent services.[36]

The subcommittee utilized its mandate to target Eisenhower on all fronts, using a mixture of questionnaires, requests, and hearings for continued oversight, to educate the public through the press, as well as allowing Moss to build a reputation among his congressional colleagues as the go-to person whenever they were denied any information. The power Moss was able to wield from his subcommittee chair would continue to grow, providing him influence within Congress, where many different members from both the House and Senate offered praise to Moss and the work of his subcommittee.[37] Moss was developing relationships

---

[35] Chairman's Opening/Closing Statement, November 7, 1955. Folder: Hearings (1955–1956)—Correspondence re: plans and preparation [October 1955–February 1956], Box No. M-5, Center for Legislative Archives, National Archives, Washington, DC.

[36] Letter from Samuel J. Archibald to Paul Fisher, August 8, 1958. Folder: Freedom of Information Center [1958–1960], Box No. M-4, Center for Legislative Archives, National Archives, Washington, DC.

[37] Washington Newsletter from the Office of Congressman John J. McFall, February 6, 1957. Folder: Reports, Material for [Folder 1 of 3; 1955–1958], Box No. M-9, Center for Legislative Archives, National Archives, Washington, DC.

that would later prove beneficial as he began to push for legislative solutions. Early in the summer of 1955, staff on the subcommittee noted how House Judiciary Committee Chair Emanuel Celler had been having difficulty getting information from the Commerce Department. A handwritten note on the memo from Archibald stated that he would reach out the following week.[38] Very quickly, Moss and his subcommittee became invaluable for Congress, offering Moss celebrity status that included formal and informal power from within Capitol Hill, as well as power to use against the administration in frustrating their efforts at information control. The response to Eisenhower's policies on secrecy from Congress, now being directed through the Moss Subcommittee, demonstrates how the social learning process has unfolded, whereby actions from the administration bring about reactions from Congress.

The unfolding fight against OSI by 1956 was directly tied with the development and push from Moss for a legislative solution that would overcome Eisenhower's claims of executive privilege. Wilson's gag rule and OSI had finally pushed Congress to seek a legislative solution to clarify procedure and access for public records. Moss decided on a very public strategy, which would use the press to push both parties to make the issue of freedom of information part of their platforms in the upcoming election. By creating increased public pressure, Moss offered a legislative solution to the issues of secrecy and executive privilege that would specifically target OSI and the new bureaucratic infrastructure frustrating Congress and the press.[39] The Moss Subcommittee in conjunction with the Senate Committee on Constitutional Rights, chaired by Sen. Thomas Hennings, Jr. (D-MO), jointly called for legislation to amend the Housekeeping Statute of 1789, which

---

[38] Memorandum to Sam Archibald from J. Lacey Reynolds, July 29, 1955. Folder: Memoranda—Government Information Subcommittee [1955–1956], Box No. M-7, Center for Legislative Archives, National Archives, Washington, DC.

[39] *The Washington Post*, "Moss Favors 'Information' Party Planks," May 28, 1956, p. 2. Accessed via *ProQuest Historical Newspapers*, September 28, 2015.

had established record-keeping in the executive branch.[40] The statute allowed for federal departments and department heads, "to prescribe regulations, not inconsistent with the law, for the government of his department, the conduct of its officers and clerks, and the custody, use and preservation of the records, papers and property appertaining thereto."[41] During this period, Eisenhower and administration officials would frequently cite the Housekeeping Statute as grounds for executive privilege claims. Moss had realized that in order to target such claims and open congressional access around OSI, legislation targeting this statute was necessary.

The institutional power Moss held as chair of a special sub-committee with jurisdiction over the entire executive branch regarding information policies provided him a powerful platform to push back on the administration. However, it was not just the formal institutional power that proved beneficial; Moss was able to gain informal power through relationship and coalition building on both sides of the Capitol. By 1957, Moss had gained favor among his congressional colleagues, included the Speaker and House Majority Leader, committee chairs like Celler, and allies in the Senate such as Hennings.[42] Congress was realizing that Moss was not just a bulldog in attacking Eisenhower, but that he was making progress by applying pressure on agencies. While Congress continued to struggle to gain access to information being sought, members were taking comfort in asking Moss to contact administration officials on their behalf, serving to place departments and agencies on notice.

[40] *New York Times*, "Congress to Seek Curb on Secrecy," January 12, 1957, p. 11. Accessed via *ProQuest Historical Newspapers*, October 15, 2015.

[41] Foerstel, *Freedom of Information*, 1999, p. 33.

[42] There are numerous records in the archives that illustrate a steady call from bipartisan members of the House and Senate seeking help from the Moss Subcommittee in getting information from agencies. One such exchange included a note from Senator Robert Byrd, Chair of the Senate Armed Services Committee, asking for help to get information from DOD—Memorandum from Mitchell to John Moss, October 5, 1957. Folder: Moss, John E. [1955–1960], Box M-7, Center for Legislative Archives, National Archives, Washington, DC.

As congressional action and press outrage increased with Eisenhower's continued stonewalling on information, the inter-branch fight over OSI finally came to end in spring 1957 when Congress took action to defund the office completely. Rather than wait for the Moss and Hennings bill, the House Appropriations Committee seized their chance during the budget process, voting to remove all funding for OSI in Eisenhower's budget. Moss notes that his subcommittee had recommended to abolish OSI the previous year, and states,

> I compliment the Appropriations Committee for its action in deleting this item for an agency which in exhaustive hearings was unable to say what it was doing or what it hoped to do. It seemed to lack either policy or program.[43]

The House would vote a few days later on the appropriations bill that would outright kill OSI, putting an end to the short-lived office, which was announced as officially closed in June.[44] Moss and his press allies heralded the shuttering of OSI as a victory and a necessary step forward to addressing expansive presidential control on information. However, while closing OSI was by no means an end to the fight, progress was being made. As OSI closed, the Defense Department acknowledged and offered to change their restrictive press policies, which grew out of the 1954 executive privilege memo and Wilson's directives the following year.[45] The press had become more vocal, in particular, after being denied access to cover Eisenhower's inaugural oath-taking ceremony in 1957, which congressional Democrats blasted as "a gross neglect of essential functions of information."[46] Moss

---

[43] *The Washington Post*, "House Committee Votes to Abolish Disputed Commerce Dept. Agency," April 6, 1957, p. 2. Accessed via *ProQuest Historical Newspapers*, September 28, 2015.

[44] *The Christian Science Monitor*, "Weeks Says OSI To Be Abolished After Protests," June 28, 1957, p. 10. Accessed via *ProQuest Historical Newspapers*, December 16, 2015.

[45] *New York Times*, "Wilson to Rewrite US Secrecy Order," April 13, 1957, p. 6. Accessed via *ProQuest Historical Newspapers*, October 15, 2015.

[46] *New York Times*, "Congressmen Protest Inaugural News Ban," January 13, 1957, p. 4. Accessed via *ProQuest Historical Newspapers*, October 15, 2015.

redirected this momentum toward his legislation to amend the Housekeeping Statute to hopefully tear down Eisenhower's paper curtain.

Timed with the closing of OSI, Moss and Hennings jointly introduced their legislation to amend the Housekeeping Statute. The Moss Bill (H.R.2767), as it become known, was one simple line of text, which stated,

> This section does not authorize withholding information from the public or limiting the availability of records to the public.[47]

The *New York Times* ran a special feature on the legislation, citing the months of investigations and hearings conducted by the Moss Subcommittee and its counterpart in the Senate.[48] Moss is quoted in the story as saying,

> Federal agencies have seized on certain words and phrases in the law to keep information secret, not only from the public, but from Congress. This is a tortured interpretation of a law intended to make information available.

In covering the pending legislation, the *Washington Post* quotes Defense Secretary Wilson calling the draft legislation unconstitutional, as it "ignores or seeks to repeal the Constitutional separation of powers which nearly 170 years of experience has demonstrated to be one of the keystones supporting our great form of Government."[49] Wilson would assert in a widely distributed press release that "[t]he Subcommittee's implication that the Secretary of Defense has improperly established policies for denial of information to the Congress is contrary to the facts."[50]

---

[47] "Freedom of Information Act and Amendments of 1974 (P.L. 93-502)." Joint Committee Report, House Committee on Government Operations and Senate Committee on the Judiciary. Government Printing Office, Washington, DC, March 1975.

[48] *New York Times*, "Congress Asked to Curb Secrecy," April 25, 1957, p. 17. Accessed via *ProQuest Historical Newspapers*, October 15, 2015.

[49] *The Washington Post*, "Bill Would Free More Government Information," April 25, 1957, p. A17. Accessed via *ProQuest Historical Newspapers*, September 28, 2015.

[50] Press Release from Defense Secretary Wilson, April 24, 1957. Folder: Freedom of Information Act—Legislative Background—Legislative Proposals, 1955–1957

Moss responded by noting the legislation would remove barriers and "weak excuses to disregard the public's right to know."

Public rhetoric and broadsides notwithstanding, Moss had concerns over the effectiveness the bill would have on curbing executive privilege, when faced with EO 10501 and the Administrative Procedures Act (APA) of 1946.[51] The APA contained a section creating procedures for the administration when it came to organizing offices, creating public records, and providing access to those records. The language in the APA was ambiguous at best, allowing Eisenhower to continue in claiming executive privilege as superseding the APA for national security purposes. Discussions between Moss and members of his subcommittee staff including Archibald and John Mitchell, the subcommittee's chief counsel, continued through the rest of 1957 and into 1958, working closely with press associations to continue to publicize the bill in conjunction with ongoing subcommittee investigations and hearings.[52] It had become clear within the Moss Subcommittee that their legislative remedy to executive privilege would not have as great an impact as they hoped, but they knew it was a necessary first step. Additionally, Moss ran into one institutional hurdle in the process, which was that his subcommittee did not have jurisdiction over the APA. Jurisdiction and oversight of the APA in the House was held by the Judiciary Committee. On the Senate side, Hennings chaired a Judiciary Subcommittee that provided jurisdiction over both the APA and the Housekeeping Statute, but Moss was not as fortunate. The House committee system provided a procedural barrier for Moss, which is why his subcommittee was targeting the Housekeeping Statute in the first place. However, Moss continued to be dogged in his pursuit of passing the bill, while numerous cabinet agencies and the Bureau

[Folder 2 of 2], Box M-186. Center for Legislative Archives, National Archives, Washington, DC.

[51] Letter from John J. Mitchell to Harold L. Cross, September 30, 1958. Folder: Cross, Harold [1955–1959], Box No. 3. Center for Legislative Archives, National Archives, Washington, DC.

[52] Letter from John J. Mitchell to Harold L. Cross, June 6, 1958. Folder: Cross, Harold [1955–1959], Box No. 3. Center for Legislative Archives, National Archives, Washington, DC.

of the Budget (BOB) stood steadfast in opposition, claiming the bill was an unconstitutional power grab by Congress that would limit executive discretion.[53]

The persistence from Moss paid off in March 1958, when the House Government Operations Committee passed the Housekeeping Statute amendment.[54] The full House would pass the amendment by voice vote the following month, demonstrating unanimous congressional support on the issue as a message to Eisenhower.[55] Press coverage would cite concerns from Moss that passage was merely the first step in seeking to end overly burdensome policies restricting the flow of government information. The Senate would, without dissent, pass the bill in August, sending it to Eisenhower for his approval.[56] Attorney General William P. Rogers called the bill meaningless, noting that the Housekeeping Statute was "legislative recognition of the executive privilege," which provides the president the ability to withhold information as deemed necessary in the public's interest. Eisenhower would sign the bill, but issued a strongly worded signing statement reiterating the president's authority of executive privilege under the Constitution.[57]

In response to the passage of the Housekeeping Statute amendment in 1958, Eisenhower's statement rebuked the amendment's intent, reading in part,

[53] *New York Times*, "Cabinet Opposes Bill on US Data," July 21, 1957, p. 39. Accessed via *ProQuest Historical Newspapers*, October 15, 2015.

[54] *New York Times*, "House Unit Votes Information Bill," March 6, 1958, p. 14. Accessed via *ProQuest Historical Newspapers*, October 16, 2015.

[55] "Commentary on Information Aspects of 5 U.S.C. 22," Letter from Samuel J. Archibald to Paul Fisher, August 8, 1958. Folder: Freedom of Information Center [1958–1960], Box No. M-4, Center for Legislative Archives, National Archives, Washington, DC.

[56] *The Washington Post*, "Ike Gets Bill To Cut Secrecy," August 1, 1958, p. A14. Accessed via *ProQuest Historical Newspapers*, September 30, 2015.

[57] Dwight D. Eisenhower: "Statement by the President Upon Signing Bill Relating to the Authority of Federal Agencies To Withhold Information and Records," August 12, 1958. Available online at *The American Presidency Project*, <https://www.presidency.ucsb.edu/documents/statement-the-president-upon-signing-bill-relating-the-authority-federal-agencies-withhold> (last accessed November 10, 2018).

In its consideration of this legislation the Congress has recognized that the decision-making and investigative processes must be protected. It is also clear from the legislative history of the bill that it is not intended to, and indeed could not, alter the existing power of the head of an Executive department to keep appropriate information or papers confidential in the public interest. This power in the Executive Branch is inherent under the Constitution.[58]

Moss and Congress had believed that in removing the Housekeeping Statute from play, the administration would be forced to rely more heavily on preexisting laws to justify actions, which Congress thought gave them an advantage in oversight, removing the ability of administration officials and the president to continue their claims of secrecy. Archibald would comment,

> The Congress has now warned the Federal Executive officials that they—as the elected representatives of the pubic—are not going to stand quietly by while Federal Executive officials warp the power to decide what information the public shall, and shall not, have. . . . Not only did the public debate which resulted in enactment of the freedom of information law alert Congress to the current dangers of excessive secrecy, but the bill itself removed a blanket excuse Executive officials have been using to hide their activities from the people.[59]

However, Eisenhower's signing statement changed that perception. By asserting executive privilege the president created an end-run around the new law, leaving Congress in the same position they had been in prior to the amendment. In response to Eisenhower, Archibald commented,

> The President's statement dragged in an entirely unrelated issue, for the so-called "executive privilege" to keep information confidential is not mentioned in the freedom of information amendment to the "housekeeping" statute. By stating that the new law does not affect "executive privilege"—a valid claim since the law has absolutely

[58] Ibid.
[59] "Commentary on Information Aspects of 5 U.S.C. 22," Letter from Samuel J. Archibald to Paul Fisher, August 8, 1958. Folder: Freedom of Information Center [1958–1960], Box No. M-4, Center for Legislative Archives, National Archives, Washington, DC.

nothing to do with this particular issue—the administration contends that such a privilege does, in fact, exist. The presidential statement, which was prepared by the Department of Justice, even goes so far as to claim that the broad power of secrecy is "inherent under the Constitution" and seeps from the President down to the appointed heads of Executive Departments—departments and officials which are not even mentioned in the Constitution.

The administration's contention that there is a right above the law—and, indeed, above the Constitution—to hide the facts of government from the public and the Congress echoes authoritarian philosophies of a totalitarian government.[60]

The unfolding power struggle became stark as Congress sought to check executive power through legislative means, having learned from numerous examples of administration policies supporting secrecy, while the president was able to respond by learning that executive privilege had become the ultimate trump card to Congress that provided a blanket claim of constitutional protection. The closing of OSI and the passage of the Housekeeping Statute amendment provided another juncture within the CLDC, yet the issue continued to move forward. Congress now had to contend with Eisenhower's claim of an inherent constitutional power, demonstrating how the learning process unfolded for both the executive and legislative branches.

Following the passage of the Housekeeping Statute amendment, the Moss Subcommittee continued to pressure the administration over restrictive practices surrounding access to information. While Moss, along with other congressional allies like Senator Hennings, would continue to seek legislative solutions, executive privilege continued to be the elephant in the room suppressing efforts. Archibald notes in a memo to Moss in 1959 that,

Numerous examples of the abuse of "executive privilege" have been detailed in reports by the House Government Information Subcommittee and in reports and hearings of other Committees in Congress. Since passage of the 1958 freedom-of-information amendment to the "housekeeping" statute, agencies which had relied upon the statute as an authority for secrecy now fall back on the broad

---

60 Ibid.

claim of an "executive privilege" to hide their operations from the public and the Congress.[61]

Eisenhower was able to shut down congressional and public requests just as easily as he had prior to the Housekeeping amendment, learning that Congress was stifled due to the constitutional assertions inherent within the executive privilege doctrine. However, Moss was more determined than ever to find ways around this power conundrum in order to afford Congress a pathway to executive information at a time when assertions of privilege were more rampant than ever. A report in 1959 issued by the Moss Subcommittee does not mince words regarding the increased use of executive privilege, stating:

> When the Executive can select which laws shall and shall not be enforced; when this selective power is applied to laws providing information necessary for the legislative branch to carry out its constitutional duties; when the "executive privilege" to control information for the Congress flows down from the President throughout the executive bureaucracy, then the Government of this Nation ceases to be a representative democracy. Sweeping claims of an unrestrained "executive privilege" to control the facts of government are a step toward despotism.[62]

Seeking to keep up their pressure on the administration, Congress would take steps using any and all institutional means at their disposal. In spring 1959, the House passed the Hardy amendments to the Mutual Security Act of 1959, sponsored by Rep. Porter Hardy (D-VA) and based on research from the Moss Subcommittee. The amendment sought to undercut the use of executive privilege by requiring executive branch documents to be made available to Congress and the General Accounting Office. The problem with the amendment was, due to the Mutual Security Act being focused on foreign policy, it was only applicable to the operation and activities of the International Cooperation

---

[61] "The Growth of 'Executive Privilege'," Memo from Samuel J. Archibald to John Moss, September 28, 1959. Folder: Moss, John E. [1955–1960], Box No. M-7, Center for Legislative Archives, National Archives, Washington, DC.

[62] Ibid.

Administration. Regardless, Moss took to the floor of the House to state his support for the Hardy amendments and use it as a public victory illustrative of the growing coalition supporting the issue. Moss stated,

> Early in its study of Federal restrictions, the House Government Information Subcommittee uncovered repeated use of the "executive privilege" claim to hide the facts of government from the Congress and to keep the General Accounting Office from finding out how Federal agencies are spending the tax funds Congress appropriates. The shield of "executive privilege" has been held up against Congressional access to facts about the nation's missile program. It has been used to cover up financial operations in the Navy and even to hide scandals in high government offices.[63]

The continual back-and-forth action between the executive and legislative branches illustrates the social learning process unfolding through the CLDC. At this time, administration actions had brought about congressional reactions, leading the administration to react in ways that would provoke additional responses from Congress. The freedom of information issue would continue to evolve, demonstrating how congressional actors like Moss would learn the means of wielding institutional power against the administration in attempts to rebalance inter-branch power.

Responding to the increased pressure from Congress, Eisenhower was led to amend EO 10501 in May 1959 by issuing a new EO, 10816, which clarified which departments and agencies had authority to classify material under the previous order.[64] The ability of an agency to classify material provided the agency with the ability to deny that material to the public or Congress under executive privilege. While EO 10816 cut back

---

[63] Statement of Congressman John E. Moss, June 19, 1959. Folder 49, Box 338. John E. Moss Archive, California State University, Sacramento.

[64] Dwight D. Eisenhower: "Executive Order 10816—Amendment of Executive Order No. 10501 of November 5, 1953, Relating to Safeguarding Official Information in the Interests of the Defense of the United States," May 7, 1959. Available online at *The American Presidency Project*, <https://www.presidency.ucsb.edu/documents/executive-order-10816-amendment-executive-order-no-10501-november-5-1953-relating> (last accessed November 10, 2018).

on the number of agencies holding such power, the dynamics were not greatly changed by this action. Just prior to leaving office in January 1961, Eisenhower issued EO 10901, which again would amend EO 10501.[65] The new order further limited agency authority to classify information, providing a list of the specific agencies with such authority and those who held partial authority. Eisenhower's parting shot on the issue reduced agency ability to make executive privilege claims, but the reduction was minor, and he left office having presided over the expansion of presidential power while increasing tensions with Congress on access to information. These final EOs from Eisenhower also served to increase the centralization of executive privilege power into the Oval Office.

In recognizing the shortcomings of the Housekeeping amendment and the need for constant forward movement, Moss continued an aggressive strategy in the House through coalition building as well as gaining public momentum through his close ties with the press. A letter to Clark Mollenhoff, Pulitzer Prize-winning journalist for Cowles Publications, from Archibald discusses the future strategy of the Moss Subcommittee on creating new legislation and details future concerns on how to better utilize the subcommittee.[66] Archibald explains the reasoning for pursuing the Housekeeping amendment first as it was a positive strategy that could be more easily sold to the public. He notes the importance of pursuing any and all legislative paths for freedom of information during this period while momentum behind the bill is high, as he is fearful of momentum loss, and ultimately turning it into a losing issue if the Democrats take back control of the White House in 1960, due to what he calls "the First Law

---

[65] Dwight D. Eisenhower: "Executive Order 10901—Amendment of Executive Order 10501, Relating to Safeguarding Official Information in the Interests of the Defense of the United States," January 9, 1961. Available online at *The American Presidency Project*, <https://www.presidency.ucsb.edu/documents/executive-order-10901-amendment-executive-order-10501-relating-safeguarding-official> (last accessed November 10, 2018).

[66] Letter to Clark Mollenhoff from Sam Archibald, November 24, 1958. Folder: Freedom of Information Act—Legislative Background—Legislative Proposals, 1958–1959, Box M-186, National Archives, Washington, DC.

of Practical Politics." He goes on to explain this 'First Law' as being,

> A Congress controlled by one political party will accuse the executive controlled by the other political party of withholding information from the Congress and the public. The obvious corollary is that there will be fewer and less violent arguments about restrictions on information when the Congress and executive branch are controlled by the same political party. This may be because there is a greater flow of information or because there is less interest in uncovering skullduggery and boondoggling.

Archibald astutely points out the troubling political realities faced by Moss and the subcommittee moving forward on any new legislation. The assertive strategy Moss was taking would lose momentum and party support if a Democrat were elected as president. The recognition of these political realities at this time makes it clear why both Moss and Hennings pushed for more legislation under Eisenhower, but also why Moss would aggressively coalition build to gain allies in case the partisan control of government shifted. Constant exchanges between Moss and Archibald illustrate this strategy in real time during this period. In a memo to Moss in March 1959, Archibald mentions talking with Rep. Ken Hechler's (D-WV) office regarding a response from Hechler on an American Newspaper Guild (ANG) proposal for a public records law.[67] The response to Archibald notes that Hechler's reply will be to tell ANG to follow the lead of Congressman Moss. Later that year Moss would receive letters of praise from various members of the House and Senate, such as a letter from Senator Proxmire (D-WI) noting the important work the subcommittee had done in breaking the silence of the Army, which he had been fighting for information for more than nine years.[68] Another memo to Moss from Archibald in 1960

---

[67] Memorandum for the Record from Samuel J. Archibald, March 16, 1959. Folder: Freedom of Information Act—Legislative Background—Legislative Proposals, 1958–1959, Box M-186, National Archives, Washington, DC.

[68] Letter to John Moss from William Proxmire, September 5, 1959. Folder: Subcommittee Notices [1955–1960], Box M-10, National Archives, Washington, DC.

discussed a follow-up letter from Moss to the Army based on his intervention to get records for Rep. James O'Hara (D-MI) after he also had trouble.[69] With the power of his subcommittee chair, Moss developed strong ties with powerful allies across the Capitol while increasing status and policy expertise on these issues.[70] Understanding the shifting of the political winds allowed Moss to insulate himself and prepare for a change in partisan power resulting from the 1960 election.

Presidential power and congressional reprisal

The Eisenhower administration demonstrates how the Cold War Paradigm implemented under Truman became institutionalized with Eisenhower. The administration instituted numerous policies stemming from both existing law and unilateral action. While the executive orders drove agency procedures, the most impactful action Eisenhower took in office was the 1954 privilege memo. Social learning is a process that unfolds across time and while Eisenhower came into office following Truman's lead on secrecy of government information, he issued EO 10501 to clarify positioning and strengthen what he saw as weaknesses and vulnerabilities. Forced by congressional action due to the Army-McCarthy hearings in 1954, a direct outcome of the Cold War Paradigm shift, Eisenhower sought to avoid having any administration official provide information or testimony, which produced the modern inception of executive privilege. By grounding his claims as inherent constitutional powers, Eisenhower carved out a new space of power and touched off an inter-branch struggle that is still with us today. Executive privilege became the default mechanism for the administration as a response to any congressional action or press complaint. Even when faced with legislation specifically targeting the freedom of information

---

[69] Letter to John Moss from Sam Archibald, October 5, 1960. Folder: Moss, John E. [1955–1960], Box M-7, National Archives, Washington, DC.

[70] Memo to John Moss from William Proxmire, August 3, 1959. Folder: Subcommittee Notices [1955–1960], Box M-10, National Archives, Washington, DC.

issues, a defiant Eisenhower signed the bill and then claimed executive privilege allowed him to do what he wanted, a move his successors would follow. Eisenhower's signing statement claimed that by passing the Housekeeping amendment, Congress acknowledged the inherent Constitutional power of executive privilege, thereby adding another layer of support for the administration's actions in denying information to Congress.

The Eisenhower years also illustrate how members of Congress learned and responded to executive actions, in particular as those actions began to have increased impact on oversight efforts or constituent services. As the congressional overindulgence of McCarthyism began to wane, the steps taken by the administration created the need for a response from Congress. The creation of the Moss Subcommittee was the first major response delivered to put the administration on notice and utilize their powers of investigation and oversight. While members of Congress, including Moss, understood the need for some information to be kept classified, the extensive use of classification had gone too far. As Eisenhower took additional steps to control information flows with OSI, Congress learned that the best response would be legislative, as a bill could restrain executive overreach. Moss and members of Congress learned quickly following the passage of the Housekeeping amendment that that policy fix was insufficient, and therefore additional legislative actions were required, in particular with the claims of executive privilege as an inherent Constitutional power.

The other factor that plays into the learning process, and is exemplified through the CLDC, is the politics. After his first two years under unified Republican government, Eisenhower faced an opposition Congress seeking salient issues that played well within the public political realm. Moss struck gold by capitalizing on the freedom of information issue, giving congressional Democrats a significant and growing issue combined with the most powerful built-in advocacy group—the press. Together, owing to the leadership and entrepreneurial prowess of Moss, Congress positioned the issue front and center throughout the rest of Eisenhower's time in office. Simultaneously, Eisenhower found political relevance and support not just by opposing congressional Democratic efforts, but by continuing to insist that his actions were all influenced by the need for increased measures to protect national security and keep the public safe while Soviet containment remained a priority. There was political incentive from both the administration and Congress to pursue their interests surrounding the issue, each believing themselves to be vindicated by the public. By now turning to the Kennedy administration, we will see what happens as the political winds change and deliver the Democrats unified control of government.

4

Kennedy and the Democratic political considerations of compromise

As you know, it has been and will be the consistent policy of this Administration to cooperate fully with the Committee of the Congress with respect to the furnishing of information. But the unbroken precedent of the National Security Council is that its working papers and policy documents cannot be furnished to the Congress. As President Eisenhower put it in a letter dated January 22, 1958 to Senator Lyndon Johnson, "Never have the documents of this Council been furnished to the Congress."

—John F. Kennedy, letter to Senator John Stennis,
June 23, 1962

The election of 1960 dramatically altered the politics between Congress and the president, although it did not derail ongoing efforts to craft a public records law. The campaign season opened with Moss taking over as head of the Speakers Bureau for the Democratic National Committee (DNC), where he was in charge of coordinating campaign activities between members of Congress and the Kennedy/Johnson campaign.[1] Several weeks before the 1960 election, Moss provided Kennedy with a detailed report put together by his subcommittee on issues of government secrecy and executive privilege under Eisenhower. Moss was clear in his partisan position on the issue with Kennedy, admonishing the current administration in his role to help get more Democrats, including Kennedy, elected. The report states:

The past seven and one-half years have seen a growth of secrecy in the Federal Government unparalleled in American history. True, the excessive secrecy stems from the experience of two World Wars and

[1] Letter exchange between John Moss and Myer Feldman, October 28–November 1, 1960. Folder: Moss—Speakers Bureau [1960–1961], Box No. M-7, Center for Legislative Archives, National Archives, Washington, DC.

from the very bigness of the federal government. But the Eisenhower administration has used the excuse of military security and the argument of administrative efficiency to withhold the facts about governmental activities and to present, instead, a twisted view of the goodness of government and the rightness of Republicans.

This quote establishes the nature of the entire debate thus far and the problems facing Moss going forward. In one way, the issue is partisan in nature, and Moss had tremendous success in aggressively targeting the Eisenhower administration to counter their efforts at information control. In another way, the issue is institutional in nature, establishing a power struggle in which the executive branch claims inherent constitutional authority to withhold information for national security protections in the public interest, while Congress claims constitutional authority on investigation and oversight functions, demanding the ability to gain access to records. While the latter will help Moss going forward, the former will hinder efforts to develop legislative solutions to these issues, leaving Moss in a difficult political position.

The ascension of Moss to a DNC leadership position for the 1960 election, along with being made a Deputy Whip in the House, solidified his position of leadership and influence. Moss used this position to gain more attention for the freedom of information issue during the campaign. A press release from the DNC in early October 1960 refers to Moss as "[t]he California congressman who gained a nationwide reputation serving on the House of Representatives investigating committee," and includes a long list of speaking engagements for Moss in locations from New York to Utah.[2] Moss was in regular communication with members of Congress, offering specific examples from his subcommittee investigations that would be relevant for their constituents, which they could use while campaigning.[3] Moss was effective in working with the Kennedy campaign to have the issue

---

[2] Press Release, DNC Publicity Division, October 6, 1960. Folder: Moss—Speakers Bureau [1960–1961], Box No. M-7, Center for Legislative Archives, National Archives, Washington, DC.

[3] Letter to Senator Estes Kefauver from Jack Howard, September 27, 1960.

of government secrecy used as a campaign issue for the ticket. A memo to Moss from his staffer Jack Howard noted a conversation with Pierre Salinger that included a memo detailing secrecy issues with the Eisenhower administration and wanting a plank in the 1960 DNC platform on freedom of information. Howard mentions that Salinger was "very interested. Said would discuss with Kennedy. Said he would prefer to handle it at top level rather than thru Nat'l Committee. Said will contact me later for full talk on material to be developed & timing."[4] Moss's entrepreneurial prowess made him deft at influencing the campaign agenda through the DNC, directly with members of Congress, and directly with the Kennedy campaign as well.

The Democratic Party platform for 1960 offered a strong rebuke to the record of the Eisenhower administration and the Republican Party. As the Democrats were out of the White House, it was easier for them to take a defensive position in attacking administration policies, positions, and mistakes of the previous eight years. Both party platforms that year offered harsh condemnation of communism and the threat of global Soviet domination, along with virulent defenses of American values and freedoms—much of what would be expected in the platforms. However, the two parties differed on one policy area. While the Republican Party offered no mention of freedom of information, government secrecy, or any language on executive control over information, the Democratic Party platform included a small section under the header "Freedom of Information."[5] This section gives voice to the concerns Moss had continued to push from within Congress to the national party. It stated,

Folder: Moss—Speakers Bureau [1960–1961], Box No. M-7, Center for Legislative Archives, National Archives, Washington, DC.

[4] Memo to John Moss from Jack Howard, including reference memo. Folder: Moss—Speakers Bureau [1960–1961], Box No. M-7, Center for Legislative Archives, National Archives, Washington, DC.

[5] Democratic Party Platforms: "1960 Democratic Party Platform," July 11, 1960. Available online at *The American Presidency Project*, <https://www.presidency.ucsb.edu/documents/1960-democratic-party-platform> (last accessed November 10, 2018).

We reject the Republican contention that the workings of Government are the special private preserve of the Executive. The massive wall of secrecy erected between the Executive branch and the Congress as well as the citizen must be torn down. Information must flow freely, save in those areas in which the national security is involved.

The language provides a strong position on the issue, but includes a concession on national security to ensure that any future actions taken by a Democratic administration will be protected enough from claims of violating campaign pledges.

The success of Moss's entrepreneurial efforts in making freedom of information a national issue was undermined politically by Kennedy's election to the presidency. A unified Democratic government would force Moss to learn new strategies when taking on a president from his own party, whom he had actively campaigned to get elected. Marking another important juncture in the CLDC, the early 1960s provides insight into the changing political climate and how Moss and congressional Democrats would learn to alter strategies in seeking a bill to counter executive privilege. In demonstrating the learning process, congressional Republicans found themselves in the favorable position of defense, allowing them to attack a Democratic president for executive overreach on secrecy issues in the same manner that Moss had while Eisenhower occupied the White House. In fact, during the 1960 campaign House Republicans on the Government Operations Committee put forward a motion to disband the Moss Subcommittee, calling it "a waste of time and money" and stating that its only purpose "appears to be to harass the Administration and Republicans."[6] Campaign politics aside, Republican attacks on Moss preview the shifting partisan nature of the issue as government power changed parties, as well as illustrating the high profile Moss had now attained within Congress. While Kennedy's tenure as president was short, this chapter will detail several significant episodes, with one in particular that would change the executive privilege debate for every administration going forward.

[6] Copy of story transmitted by Associated Press, January 20, 1960. Folder: Subcommittee Notices [1956–1960], Box M-10, Center for Legislative Archives, National Archives, Washington, DC.

Democratic infighting: Directives, orders, and a clarification on executive privilege

Unified Democratic control should have been an ideal power position from which Moss could get legislation passed on freedom of information, believing that Kennedy would be far more transparent and open with public records. Not only had Moss worked closely with the Kennedy campaign, but Kennedy and Johnson had both supported his efforts from the Senate and voted in favor of the Housekeeping Statute amendment. Unfortunately, Moss instead found himself losing momentum on the issue and began to face pushback from his own party. Senator Hennings had died in September 1960, costing Moss one of his closest allies in the Senate, and Speaker Rayburn, his most powerful ally in the House, would die the following year. While Moss would regain Senate support with Hennings's replacement, Senator Edward Long (D-MO), who took over as Chair of the Judiciary Subcommittee with jurisdiction on government information, House leadership and most Democratic members were less interested, even fearful, of embarrassing the new president or derailing Kennedy's policy agenda. However, with House Democrats keeping the subcommittee in place, Moss maintained his position of power to press forward on the executive privilege and FOI issues, as long as he treaded carefully. Moss continued to coalition build through subcommittee work in assisting other members of Congress, like in helping Judiciary Committee Chair Celler with an executive privilege case his committee was working on as a leftover from the previous administration.[7] Moss believed he had an ally in the White House with Kennedy whom he could work with on the issues. Additionally, as Moss now had his reputation on the line in supporting and campaigning for Kennedy, politically he could not afford to be as aggressive in targeting Kennedy as he had been with Eisenhower. The political stakes had risen as the FOI issue

[7] Letter to Sam Archibald from Jacob Scher, January 25, 1961. Folder: Scher, Jacob [1955–1962], Box M-20, Center for Legislative Archives, National Archives, Washington, DC.

gained saliency, and had become a viable political football with which both parties could attack one another.

As Kennedy was readying to take the Oath of Office, Moss continued in pressing the outgoing Eisenhower administration on accessing records related to the funding for the Office of Inspector General and Comptroller General in the General Accounting Office (GAO).[8] In brief, passage of the Mutual Security Appropriation Act of 1961 provided funding for the Office of Inspector General and Comptroller, but was cut off by the Comptroller General based on his reading of a provision within the law that required funds to be withheld if the offices did not furnish all documents and papers to the GAO or any congressional committee if requested. The Comptroller General claimed funds for the offices were disallowed based on the president's actions in refusing to provide information to the House Government Operations Committee. However, the Attorney General offered a countering opinion that gave the administration the ability to fund the offices, claiming executive privilege. This incident demonstrates how Eisenhower overrode the decision of the Comptroller General and Congress by asserting that executive privilege claims were exempted from and overrode any law. A memo and report from mid-January 1961 sent to incoming BOB Chief David Bell from outgoing BOB general counsel Arthur Focke detailed the issues of executive privilege experienced under Eisenhower, and Focke warned Bell that on inauguration day the executive privilege issue "will come sharply into focus."[9]

The memo and report detail the growth and justification of executive privilege under Eisenhower, noting how the president defended its use through constitutional claims and in protecting the ability of administration officials to be fully candid in their commentary and work in ensuring the operations of the govern-

---

[8] Executive Privilege Memo from Arthur B. Focke to David E. Bell, January 8, 1961. Papers of John F. Kennedy. Presidential Papers. White House Staff Files of Lee C. White. General File, 1954–1964. Executive Privilege, 17 May 1954–21 August 1961.

[9] Ibid.

ment. To the incoming Kennedy officials, Focke summed up the situation in this way:

> The conflict over executive privilege has been in progress ever since the Constitution was adopted, and it is likely to be with us as long as the republic endures. Neither the Executive nor the Congress will ever yield on the basic principle, but the battles between them are generally waged with the tacit understanding that there will never be an end to the war. In the skirmishing, the agency heads and the employees of the Executive Branch take on the role of innocent bystanders and absorb the punishment. Because the initial requests from Congress are usually made to someone below the President in the Executive hierarchy, the issue frequently tends to become one between the chairman of a congressional committee and an agency head. One thing which has become clear in the past eight years is that no agency head can successfully contain the situation unless he is able to retreat to a previously prepared position where he will have the full backing of the President.[10]

The exchange illustrates how Kennedy's transition team was being informed on the issue of executive privilege use, along with a brief history on the heated exchanges between Eisenhower and Congress. The information presented here would influence the Kennedy administration in their future actions in dealing with Congress on these issues, and in how the president would use executive privilege.

The inter-branch battle of the Mutual Security Act appropriations set off a firestorm of activity from Congress. Moss and others began to press the Kennedy administration to release a series of records on the incident and other related issues going back to 1958 over the Killian and Gaither Panels that were set up to advise Eisenhower on Cold War strategies related to passive and active military actions.[11] The House Government Operations Committee seemed eager to press Kennedy on information that had been denied by Eisenhower in order to keep the political

---

[10] Ibid.

[11] White House Press Release of Letter from President Eisenhower to Lyndon Johnson, January 22, 1958. Papers of John F. Kennedy. Presidential Papers, National Security Files. Subjects. Executive privilege: General, 1955–1960.

focus on Eisenhower, but it would not last. By February 1961, Rep. Porter Hardy, Chair of the House Subcommittee on Foreign Operations and Monetary Affairs, formally requested records on aid operations in Latin America for an investigation.[12] The response from Secretary of State Dean Rusk and others within the administration was to tell the subcommittee that they would fully cooperate with their information requests, but would not be able to turn over any information as it interfered with the functioning of the agency's ability to make and conduct foreign policy. Rusk's response ended by stating:

> [L]et me assure you that responsible officials of the new administration have reviewed the documents heretofore withheld from you. They assure me that these documents were not withheld because they contained adverse information about the subjects of your investigation, but only on grounds related to the proper exercise of executive privilege.

The conversation from within the State Department was to ensure that Congress knew they wanted to cooperate, and there was no wrongdoing within the administration on the issues for which Congress was requesting information, but for reasons of executive privilege they were unwilling to provide any specific records to Congress. Agency officials believed this to be consistent with what the president would want. For Congress, it became clear that the Kennedy administration would follow the Eisenhower model of limited access to records, but would at least offer a smile while doing so.

In September 1961 Kennedy issued EO 10964, which amended Eisenhower's order 10501 from 1953.[13] This order would create administrative procedures for declassifying or downgrading

---

[12] Letter to Dean Rusk from Porter Hardy, February 28, 1961. Papers of John F. Kennedy. Presidential Papers. White House Staff Files of Lee C. White. General File, 1954–1964. Executive privilege, 17 May 1954–21 August 1961.

[13] John F. Kennedy: "Executive Order 10964—Amendment to Executive Order 10501—Safeguarding Official Information in the Interests of the Defense of the United States," September 20, 1961. Available online at *The American Presidency Project*, <https://www.presidency.ucsb.edu/documents/executive-order-10964-amendment-executive-order-10501-safeguarding-official-information> (last accessed November 10, 2018).

information if security concerns no longer required classification. Kennedy followed Eisenhower's lead by seeking to specify agency authority to use executive privilege in classifying information, and in providing for agency heads to more strongly control the classification or declassification procedures. Kennedy's order differed from Eisenhower by decentralizing information control from the Oval Office back to many of the agency heads. The Cold War mindset continued to dominate within the Kennedy administration as concerns over the situations in Cuba and Vietnam grew, and Congress began demanding more answers.[14] The administration sought a balanced approach with the order by still providing for executive privilege claims, while easing restrictions on declassification. However, congressional Republicans were quick to strike at the administration, as Democrats had done with Eisenhower. A Republican National Committee (RNC) press release from October 1961 stated:

> This administration has shown it couldn't care less. It is too busy bottling up hard news while spraying the press with artificial and leaked material. It is running a tandem censor-huckster operation at the highest Government levels. Generally complaints from the press are ignored, denied or tagged as falsehoods by the White House.[15]

In the new political landscape, congressional Republicans had learned how effective the Democratic attacks on Eisenhower had been, and they sought to tarnish Kennedy in the same manner. With increased pressure from the Republicans, congressional Democrats were even more concerned with protecting Kennedy. However, the president and members of the administration would continue to follow the Eisenhower-era positions on executive privilege, frequently citing national security concerns as reasons for denying information to Congress.

---

[14] Background Paper on Information Hearing, "Examples of tightened news control under Kennedy," March 5, 1963. Folder: Information Hearing [1963; Folder 1 of 2], Box M-15, Center for Legislative Archives, National Archives, Washington, DC.

[15] Letter exchange between John Moss and Myer Feldman, October 28–November 1, 1960. Folder: Moss—Speakers Bureau [1960–1961], Box No. M-7, Center for Legislative Archives, National Archives, Washington, DC.

Regardless of political considerations, Moss was steadfast in his determination to keep fighting. During 1961, his subcommittee began pressing the Kennedy administration for materials related to the National Security Council's (NSC) directives in using the military for Cold War activities, which dated back to the Eisenhower administration. Moss and Archibald sought access to documents that detailed specific military actions being taken by Kennedy and previous administrations in fighting the Cold War, but were continuously being denied. The conversations within the White House were focused on keeping Moss and any member of Congress from gaining access to these documents.[16] With the recent incidents in Cuba and the larger ongoing containment of the Soviet Union, Kennedy was not interested in providing anything related to these matters to Congress or the public. Both Moss and the Senate Foreign Relations Committee Chair, William Fulbright (D-AR), had uncovered and were investigating propaganda campaigns conducted by military personnel as directed by NSC policy. The campaigns "made use of extremely radical right-wing speakers and/or materials, with the probable net result of condemning foreign and domestic policies of the Administration in the public mind."[17] The intention was to disrupt activities and influence policy decisions of the Kennedy administration, and the NSC claimed executive privilege in denying any information on this program to Congress. Fulbright had found an NSC directive from 1958 that stated, "[I]t remains the policy of the United States Government to make use of military personnel and facilities to arouse the public to the menace of the cold war."[18] Through inquiries to the NSC and members of

[16] Memo to McGeorge Bundy from A.B., July 26, 1961. Papers of John F. Kennedy. Presidential Papers, National Security Files. Subjects. Executive Privilege: General, 1961.

[17] Memo, "Propaganda Activities of Military Personnel Directed at the Public." Papers of John F. Kennedy. Presidential Papers, National Security Files. Subjects. Executive Privilege: General, 1961. *The Washington Post*, "Study Asserts Military Rightists Raise Obstacles to Kennedy Program," July 21, 1961. Papers of John F. Kennedy. Presidential Papers, National Security Files. Subjects. Executive Privilege: General, 1961.

[18] Ibid.

the administration, Moss was told that under EO 10501 the NSC would review all material and determine whether the information was classified and needed to be safeguarded, or if it could be made available. Kennedy reaffirmed this position as provided through Eisenhower's order, thus giving the NSC authority in asserting claims of executive privilege.

With Republicans' aggressive attacks and Kennedy continuing to rebuff congressional Democrats' requests, politics demanded congressional action to push back on the administration's use of executive privilege. Being denied records from the NSC on their domestic propaganda campaign to utilize the military to influence public opinion in opposition to Kennedy was enough for Moss, but partisan politics demanded he use kid gloves. Kennedy continued to assert his support for a more open and less secretive government by noting how he supported the efforts of the Moss Subcommittee while he was in the Senate, even as his actions from the White House told a different story.[19] In February 1962, Kennedy sent a letter to Defense Secretary Robert McNamara directing him to withhold certain information from another Senate subcommittee investigation. Within a week, Moss wrote a letter to Kennedy expressing concerns over the directive to McNamara, comparing it to Eisenhower's directive from 1954.[20] Moss notes in his letter that through the ongoing investigations of his subcommittee, between 1955 and 1960, they found forty-four instances where executive privilege had been invoked by the administration to withhold information based on Eisenhower's 1954 letter. However, Moss decided to use a less aggressive strategy with Kennedy than he had with Eisenhower. Moss states,

[19] White House Press Release, April 19, 1961. Folder: American Society of Newspaper Editors [1960–1962; Folder 1 of 2], Box M-24, National Archives, Washington, DC; Letter exchange with John Moss and John Colburn, February 2, 1962. Folder: American Society of Newspaper Editors [1960–1962; Folder 1 of 2], Box M-24. Center for Legislative Archives, National Archives, Washington, DC.

[20] Letter from John Moss to John Kennedy, February 15, 1962. Folder: Executive Privilege [1962–March 1973; Folder 1 of 2], Box No. M-29, Center for Legislative Archives, National Archives, Washington, DC.

I am confident that you share my belief that your letter of February 8, 1962 to Secretary McNamara should not be seized upon by Executive Branch employees—many of them holding the same policy-making positions of responsibility they did under the Eisenhower Administration—as a new claim of authority to withhold information from the Congress and the public. A Subcommittee staff study indicates that during the year between the time you took office and February 8, 1962, the claim of an "executive privilege" to withhold government information was not used successfully once, compared to the dozens of times in previous years administrative employees held up "executive privilege" as a shield against public and Congressional access to information.[21]

Neglecting to bring up the NSC affair, while continuing to focus more on Eisenhower, or at least those within the bureaucracy that worked under Eisenhower, Moss baits Kennedy by asking him to clarify his position on the use of executive privilege as he intended in his letter to McNamara in the hope of preventing "the rash of restrictions on government information which followed the May 17, 1954 letter from President Eisenhower." With a deft touch, Moss maneuvered Kennedy into the need to clarify his position on the use of executive privilege, without an overt political attack.

A few weeks later, Kennedy sent a letter to Moss that shifted the debate on executive privilege forever. In his letter, Kennedy states that his directive to McNamara made clear that refusal of information to Congress would be made on a case by case basis, where "each case must be judged on its merits." Kennedy goes on to state,

> As you know, the Administration had gone to great lengths to achieve full cooperation with the Congress in making available to it all appropriate documents, correspondence and information. That is the basic policy of this administration, and it will continue to be so. Executive privilege can be invoked only by the president and will not be used without specific Presidential approval. Your own interest in assuring the widest public accessibility to governmental information is, of course, well known, and I can assure you this Administration

[21] Ibid.

will continue to cooperate with your subcommittee and the entire Congress in achieving this objective. [22]

The letter from Kennedy removed the ability of any agency head or cabinet secretary, or any other administration official, to make claims of executive privilege without specific approval from the president, overturning the agency-specific authority that had been granted through executive order and so heavily used under Eisenhower. Now, any invocation of executive privilege must have the express consent and authority of the president.

The position clarification offered to Moss from Kennedy marks another critical juncture within the CLDC and the policy development of FOIA. The exchange between Moss and Kennedy was politically savvy, providing a small victory for Congress in having the administration back away from blanket agency authority under executive privilege, while still giving Kennedy the power to withhold records as needed. Additionally, Kennedy, Moss, and congressional Democrats were spared a potentially embarrassing and public fight from within their own party. The politics surrounding the FOI issue continued to intensify, but the partisan considerations of unified government demanded the Moss Subcommittee work with the administration in seeking compromise solutions without publicly exposing intraparty animosity. Moss had now spent enough years investigating the issues through two administrations to have learned that the compromise with Kennedy on executive privilege was only a moderate gain, and that a stronger legislative solution was needed in order to check executive secrecy power.

From summer through fall in 1962, a series of exchanges between House Majority Leader Carl Albert and John Moss with V.M. "Red" Newton, Jr. from *The Tampa Tribune* and Chair of SDX's FOI Committee discussed the ongoing struggles surrounding the issues with the Kennedy Administration. In a late August letter to Newton, Majority Leader Albert sums up his fondness

[22] Letter from John Kennedy to John Moss, March 7, 1962. Folder: Executive Privilege [1962–March 1973; Folder 1 of 2], Box No. M-29, Center for Legislative Archives, National Archives, Washington, DC.

for Moss and the actions taken by his subcommittee, and notes the situation. He states,

> I agree with Mr. Moss' statement that the policies of this Administration have greatly improved the situation. But looking to the future, it is also true, as he comments, that we need legislation to ensure that the protection of full disclosure is afforded us as a matter of law, as well as of policy. I certainly will do whatever I can to assist in this endeavor.[23]

While Kennedy's policy change on the use of executive privilege had sent a positive signal to Congress, this exchange helps clarify how the congressional position was moving to a legislative remedy regardless, as Congress was seeking to hem in the administration, and future administrations, on these issues. Politically, Moss was being cautioned by House leadership, but at the same time, behind the scenes the conversation was more open to moving forward on legislation. Fortunately, Moss had previously served as a Deputy Whip under Carl Albert when he was Majority Whip under Speaker Rayburn. The close relationships Moss had established with House leadership, along with his dogged determination, kept him in a favorable position to utilize his power in coalition building on potential legislation.

Some mounting problems faced by Moss at this time came from resurgent congressional Republicans who were pursuing a similar strategy to the one Moss had used when Eisenhower was in the White House. The RNC press release from October 1961 had criticized the Kennedy administration for "censorship, favoritism, managing news, carelessness and attempting to use reporters as political propaganda conduits."[24] Congressional Republicans used floor speeches to attack the president. Senator Milward Simpson (R-WY) blasted the Kennedy administration

---

[23] Letter from Carl Albert to V. M. Newton, Jr., August 23, 1962. Folder: Government Operations—Freedom of Information, 1962. Box 51; Carl Albert Collection—Series 7: Legislative, 1934–1976. Carl Albert Center, University of Oklahoma.

[24] RNC Press Release, "Kennedy Runs Censor-Huckster News Shop," October 6, 1961. Folder: Party Platforms [1961–1964; Folder 2 of 2], Box M-27, National Archives, Washington, DC.

while citing a Sigma Delta Chi report on FOI. Senator Simpson stated,

> Every administration attempts to present itself in a favorable light, but the New Frontier has completely misused this logical prerogative with gestapo tactics, deliberate lies, as in the case of the TFX investigation, the Cuban crisis, and more currently, the situation in Vietnam.[25]

Simpson would continue by directly citing the report, which stated,

> Secretary of Defense Robert S. McNamara and his public relations director Arthur Sylvester, have created an oligarchy of control over the release of all news emanating from the Department of Defense and which led to its boast of "management of the news" in the Cuban crisis late in 1962. ... All the rest of the Federal Government falls back on the mushy claims of "confidential" and similar excuses in spreading the blanket of secrecy over the records of government.

The blistering attacks faced by the Kennedy administration from congressional Republicans were reminiscent of those leveled at Eisenhower by Moss, demonstrating how Republicans had learned how salient the line of attack on this issue had become. The political climate, while sticky for Moss, proved beneficial for his entrepreneurial efforts in developing policy.

The problem of executive control of government records had reached saturation politically and with the public. Figure 1.1 shows that press coverage had begun to dip. Both sides of the aisle were unhappy with Congress being left in the dark and denied records. While Kennedy pared back the use of executive privilege, it had little practical effect, and while Democrats and Republicans in Congress could agree on the validity of the issue, they were still too far apart politically. A February 1963 letter from Archibald to Paul Fisher, who created the Freedom of Information Center at the University of Missouri, notes some of the difficulty the subcommittee had been experiencing. Archibald

---

[25] Congressional Record—Senate, 1963, p. 19285. Folder: Sigma Delta Chi [1957–1964; Folder 1 of 2], Box M-20, Center for Legislative Archives, National Archives, Washington, DC.

laments the drop in press coverage on the issue, but asserts that under Eisenhower the press was the only way to reach top policy officials, and that route had verified results.[26] He does note how access had improved with the Kennedy administration, leading to some progress. Archibald also states,

> I get damn tired of people chipping their teeth about the Moss Committee not being as tough on the Kennedy Administration as it was on Eisenhower; at the same time, Moss and I catch Hell from some administration officials and from powerful Democrats in Congress for being too rough on the administration. When both sides in a controversy feel you are favoring the other side, you must be doing a pretty objective job.[27]

With Kennedy, Moss found himself in a political quagmire from which there was little room to move. Archibald's comments demonstrate how any activity the subcommittee was taking was either too rough on Kennedy for Democratic leadership or too timid for the Republicans. While investigations would quietly continue, Moss redirected the subcommittee's efforts toward coalition building around legislative development.

Coalition building proved a fruitful strategy for Moss, especially when faced with House leadership wanting him to focus efforts elsewhere so attention could remain on the New Frontier agenda. However, while efforts slowed in the House, the Senate became more energetic in its actions on the issue. Senator Long, having taken over Hennings's Judiciary Subcommittee, stepped immediately into the FOI issue and continued the subcommittee's work, providing Moss with a strong Senate ally. While Senate Republicans were critical of Kennedy on the secrecy issue, they were more open to working on legislation in a bipartisan manner than their House counterparts. With Long taking the lead, the Senate Judiciary Committee began a vigorous schedule of hearings and investigations with a legislative solution in mind.

[26] Letter from Sam Archibald to Paul Fisher, February 28, 1963. Folder: Freedom of Information Center (University of Missouri) [1958–1963], Box No. M-15, Center for Legislative Archives, National Archives, Washington, DC.

[27] Ibid.

The coalition in the Senate began to include Senators Everett Dirksen (R-IL), Sam Ervin (D-NC), Philip Hart (D-MI), and Eugene McCarthy (D-MN). During the 87th Congress (1961–3), seven different bills were introduced between the Senate and the House seeking a legislative solution through amending the APA.[28] Due to jurisdictional committee boundaries, the Senate FOI bill would amend the APA while Moss's FOI bill would amend the Housekeeping Statute. The increased activity in the Senate, however, gave Moss momentum to push legislation forward in the House. Through his subcommittee work, Moss had made allies in both the House and Senate by assisting other members when they had secrecy issues with the administration. This work now began to pay off, giving Moss a strong and growing coalition.

While legislative development activity increased in the both the House and Senate, none of the bills introduced at this time made it out of committee. This is indicative of the development cycle within the CLDC being one that is iterative in nature and altered through social learning. It had been more than seven years since the Moss Subcommittee was formed and the FOI issue institutionalized within Congress, and only one minor amendment bill had made it into law. Part of the issue had been that Congress had not sought legislative solutions until this time. Congress had learned that administration actions on secrecy were no longer able to be checked through oversight capacity alone. They had also learned that a minor bill like the Housekeeping amendment did nothing to overcome claims of executive privilege, where the president maintained claims of inherent constitutional authority.

---

[28] The bills introduced were: S.1887 (87th Congress) introduced by Senator Ervin; S.1567 (87th Congress) introduced by Senators Hart, Long, Proxmire; S.1907 (87th Congress) introduced by Senator Proxmire; S.3410 (87th Congress) introduced by Senators Dirksen, Carroll; in the House: H.R. 9926 (87th Congress) introduced by Representative Walter; and Moss reintroduced his freedom of information bill that had been introduced in the previous Congress (no bill number available currently). US Senate, Committee on the Judiciary, Subcommittee on Administrative Practice and Procedure. 1974. *Freedom of Information Act Sourcebook*. 93rd Congress, 2nd Session. Washington: US Government Printing Office.

Now Congress had learned that a more robust legislative solution that would target existing policy and claims could achieve their goal of limiting executive power on this issue. The 87th Congress saw the first major FOI bills being introduced, yet Moss and other supporters lacked enough support to move forward, in part due to a lack of political will among Democratic leadership. The learning process continued to unfold during this time, where bills failing to pass proved to be early iterations, as development on the issue would continue to evolve. The jurisdiction issues of the committees led to similar bills targeting different statutes, which would lead to procedural problems down the road for Moss, but allowed for the development process to continue as the policy evolved.

Early in the spring of 1963, the Moss Subcommittee was organizing a hearing to examine how news had been managed by the executive branch, particularly in light of what Archibald called the "Cuban Crisis."[29] Once again, Moss had learned that Kennedy's position on executive privilege did little to change access to government information, leaving Moss to focus on the final means of legislation as a fix. The hearing focused on the management and censorship of the news, which had been drawing increased criticism from the press and Congress surrounding issues with Cuba and the growing situation in Vietnam. Moss used this opportunity to bring together members of the press and the administration to draw attention to the problem and highlight potential legislative solutions already introduced in Congress. In background information provided prior to the hearing, Moss would note how control over the news had tightened under Kennedy, being even worse than Eisenhower.[30] While the use of executive privilege had declined from forty-four instances under Eisenhower to just one under Kennedy,

[29] Staff Memorandum from Sam Archibald, February 28, 1963. Folder: Information Hearing [1963; Folder 1 of 2], Box M-16, National Archives, Washington, DC.

[30] Staff Memorandum—I—Information Hearing, March 5, 1963. Folder: Information Hearing [1963; Folder 1 of 2], Box M-16, Center for Legislative Archives, National Archives, Washington, DC.

Moss notes how information had become more "tightly held" with Kennedy, including the increased coordination of all news releases through the Pentagon and DOD at the specific direction of the president. Subcommittee documents also discussed how the Kennedy administration would leak specific information to the press in order to use the coverage as propaganda to influence public opinion.

The debate over news censorship between Congress and the White House continued with Moss receiving a draft copy of the "Stand-By Voluntary Censorship Code" from the Office of Emergency Planning inside the Executive Office of the President, and a letter of explanation from Edward McDermott, Director of the Office of Emergency Planning.[31] Based on a similar code used during World War II, this new document was to go out to all broadcast and publication media detailing how to keep information of "value to our enemies" from being made public. Kennedy argued to Moss that the recent events with Cuba and the growing situation in Vietnam actually did constitute wartime, and therefore the president was authorizing the Office of Censorship within the Office of Emergency Planning to prepare for wartime censorship of all government information. At a time when Congress was beginning to move on legislation to address the growing tensions between branches over access to information, the Kennedy administration reaffirmed the Cold War Paradigm by asserting censorship authority during wartime as a justification for stemming the flow of information to the public and Congress. Despite the gains made through the Moss-Kennedy agreement regarding authority for executive privilege, Kennedy's assertion that Cold War activity constituted active wartime gave the administration another unilateral avenue with which to retain control. The move by Kennedy left Congress in a tenuous position politically in that any member of Congress would have to claim that Cold War activity, like Cuba, Vietnam, and Soviet containment, was not an active threat. Again, in this

---

[31] Letter from Edward A. McDermott to Samuel Archibald, March 19, 1963. Folder: Information Hearing [1963; Folder 1 of 2], Box M-16. Center for Legislative Archives, National Archives, Washington, DC.

situation as similar to Eisenhower, the president was able to take an action that expanded authority based on a learned response. This left Congress in the awkward position of either accepting this assertion or taking action to oppose the president, neither of which were politically popular.

However, Moss and Congress had a strong and vocal ally in this situation. Press organizations like ASNE began making the argument that such censorship policies during peacetime were unacceptable. This forced the administration to justify the necessity of wartime planning. Kennedy would state,

> This nation's foes have openly boasted of acquiring through our newspapers information they would otherwise hire agents to acquire through theft, bribery, or espionage. ... If the press is awaiting a declaration of war before it imposes the self-discipline of combat conditions, then I can only say that no war has posed a greater threat to our security.[32]

Once the press was able to sufficiently hammer Kennedy, Moss had the space to weigh in on the situation. Cautioning the White House in order to avoid an unnecessary shutdown of information based on political instead of security concerns, he stated,

> In almost every past instance the so-called security breach has turned out to be a careful controlled leak of information favorable to some government official, federal agency or military service. If such information leaks damage the national security, the perpetrators should be punished under the already adequate laws established for that purpose.

Moss would continue by asserting that his subcommittee:

> [h]as uncovered information withheld by officials who contend the disclosure would endanger national security whereas they were merely trying to protect their own political security. We must not use the excuse of the cold war dangers to weaken the critical self-appraisal which is a basic ingredient of our democratic government.[33]

---

[32] Draft of 1962 ASNE Freedom of Information Report. Folder: American Society of Newspaper Editors [1960–1962; Folder 1 of 2], Box M-24, Center for Legislative Archives, National Archives, Washington, DC.

[33] Ibid.

With considerable attacks coming from both the press and Congress, Kennedy backed away from his position, opting to provide voluntary guidelines for the media as opposed to mandating censorship under wartime authority.

When the 88th Congress (1963–5) convened in January 1963 these issues remained dominant on the agenda, as the Senate immediately introduced several bills seeking to curb executive secrecy through amending the APA.[34] Negotiations within Congress and with the press offer insight as discussions centered on portions of Senator Proxmire's bill, which was deemed to have "teeth" due to it being practical by defining public records, including exceptions, as well as a court enforcement mechanism.[35] While Moss continued to develop his own legislation, the consensus being reached between the Senate and House, along with press approval, was to develop a bill that would include a legal mechanism with clear definitions, along with certain exemptions for legitimate secrecy which could be acceptable enough to gain presidential approval. The learning process is demonstrated here, as Congress began to construct a new type of FOI bill that would not only address their concerns but provide a balance in order to gain presidential support. While this development continued through the remainder of the Kennedy administration, no other contentious issues arose, nor did any legislation pass to address these issues. Kennedy's assassination in November 1963 cut short his administration and would reshape the debate going forward.

Conclusion

The Kennedy administration in many ways was a transitional period in the development of FOIA and surrounding the issues of

[34] The first bill was S.1663, introduced by Senators Dirksen and Long; and the second, S.1666, was introduced by Senator Long with 21 co-sponsors. US Senate, Committee on the Judiciary, Subcommittee on Administrative Practice and Procedure, 1974. *Freedom of Information Act Sourcebook.* 93rd Congress, 2nd Session. Washington: US Government Printing Office.

[35] Draft of 1962 ASNE Freedom of Information Report. Folder: American Society of Newspaper Editors [1960–1962; Folder 1 of 2], Box M-24, Center for Legislative Archives, National Archives, Washington, DC.

secrecy and executive privilege. The change in partisan political and government control left the entrepreneurial activities of Moss stunted by his closeness with Kennedy, his own party loyalties, and in facing House leadership determined to keep his actions in check to avoid embarrassing the new president. Party politics influenced congressional Democrats by forcing them into a position where they needed to work with the administration on their policy agenda without being overtly adversarial. Congressional Republicans, however, found themselves in the easier position of playing defense, which afforded them the opportunity of attacking the administration by using the example set by Moss in his treatment of Eisenhower. Republican attacks landed hard, opening political opportunities for Moss to respond to administration actions without seeming too combative.

Kennedy had come into office with a record of support on public records and open access issues, claiming to have countered many of the policies that Eisenhower had put in place. He quickly found himself imperiled by the Cold War when faced with global issues in Cuba and Vietnam, along with continued Soviet interference and containment. Kennedy quickly learned that what worked well on Capitol Hill was no longer tenable in the White House. While both Kennedy and Johnson supported the Housekeeping Statute amendment in 1958, as well as other policy and oversight actions on executive secrecy, Kennedy's positions shifted by early 1961 when he reaffirmed the Cold War Paradigm mindset and began taking unilateral action to better control the flow of information through executive orders and privilege. Such executive power claims immediately opened up space for a congressional response. While the response was not in the form of legislation, Moss had learned to utilize his relationship with Kennedy and the position he held in the House to bargain directly with the administration in trying to gain some type of agreement that would be less publicly embarrassing than having to pass a bill. Moss achieved that goal in 1962 when Kennedy altered existing policy, countering Eisenhower's 1954 EO and letter, by asserting that executive privilege would only be used with explicit presidential authority. While this agreement would alter the way presidents would use executive privilege going forward, the effect was less than what Moss and Congress were hoping for. Kennedy was still able to maintain strict control over information and access and, as the wartime censorship example demonstrated, find new avenues from which to assert authority in doing so. Congress had learned that their response was proving to be as ineffective as the Housekeeping amendment, and in order to properly check executive power on this issue, stronger legislation was needed.

Within the CLDC, the Kennedy era offers several junctures and moments of clarity within the development period. The learning process unfolded in such a manner as to provide insight into how partisan control altered the politics within Congress, and between branches. While Republicans learned how salient the issue of executive secrecy was in attacking the administration, Democrats were left to learn how to check administration actions without causing political embarrassment, all while trying to fend off Republican accusations. Moss demonstrated the learning process through his subcommittee actions and in coalition building with other members of Congress, in both the House and Senate, to develop policy to address these issues. As the politics shifted, the actors had to learn new processes through which they could act in order to take advantage of the situation. Kennedy demonstrated how the president was able to be the central power player by making power claims that forced Congress to respond, providing examples of the action-reaction responses that dominate the development cycle. The president maintains the ability to make such claims, like executive privilege or declaring national security reasoning in refusing to make information available, which serve to alter the political power dynamics between branches. Congress is then forced to take defensive actions once they learn what the president has done, or take no action at all and face the political ramifications created by their action or inaction. The president then holds a clear advantage in the situation, where claims of executive power or authority stand unless checked by another branch. The political calculus also works in the president's favor within the CLDC, at least with Eisenhower and Kennedy, as the Cold War Paradigm had given support to claims of national security in the public interest. So at least within society, and with Congress, the politics required a deft touch to counter presidential claims of secrecy for security purposes. However, as we will see in the next chapter, even with these advantages, sometimes Congress can place the president into an untenable situation in order to check executive power.

5

LBJ and the politics of passing FOIA

What is Moss trying to do to me? I thought Moss was one of our boys, but the Justice Department tells me this goddamn bill will screw the Johnson Administration.
— Lyndon B. Johnson to House Democratic Leadership, April 1965

To no fanfare or ceremony, President Lyndon Johnson reluctantly signed the Freedom of Information Act on July 4, 1966. His advisor and press secretary, Bill Moyers, had been pushing the president to not only sign the bill but to hold a ceremony and invite prominent members of Congress and the press. Johnson could have pocket vetoed the bill, as Congress had adjourned for the July 4th break, which would have killed the bill outright. While there was heavy support in Congress, with such a busy legislative agenda and considering the work it took to get it to his desk, it was hard to imagine that, if pocket vetoed, FOIA would be back anytime soon. Through discussions with leadership and in looking at the House votes, LBJ was fairly certain that if he vetoed the bill, Congress would not have the two-thirds majorities in both houses to override. Yet he signed the bill and then followed Eisenhower's example, issuing a brief signing statement praising the bill and the importance of open government, but reiterating that the president has the authority to withhold any information from Congress or the public for national security concerns if it is in the public interest. In the end, LBJ was able to have it both ways—he could claim credit for FOIA being part of his "Great Society" agenda, while continuing to assert executive authority over information.

The Great Society period is an interesting moment in the history of government reform and policymaking. The politics of this period created an environment that would allow a policy like FOIA to not just pass through Congress, but garner an unwilling president's signature. Johnson seized the moment, built upon Kennedy's assassination, and with large congressional majorities in both houses pressed forward with a robust agenda. As a masterful politician and policymaker, Johnson placed himself in a position to bargain and work with Congress on policy. His insistence in seeking to influence legislation and love of the legislative process created a weakness that John Moss was able to exploit in imposing a bill on a president of his own party that limited executive power. In the midst of one of the most policy-productive periods in history, with so much social and political change, FOIA fit within the congressional agenda as an issue Johnson was forced to deal with. As alluded to by Bill Moyers, in the end, Johnson made a pragmatic political decision to sign FOIA and deal with it, rather than upset Moss and his coalition, whom he was relying on to help pass other bills and move his agenda forward.

The shifting political environment gave Congress an advantage over Johnson, in part due to the coalition building that had already taken place. Moss had strong allies in the Senate and the support of House leadership, although they remained reluctant early into the Johnson administration. Going forward, Moss gained support from several key players, including Republican Representative Donald Rumsfeld (IL), who requested to be on the Moss Subcommittee and then helped get Republican support for FOIA, including from House Minority Leader Gerald Ford. Another key political player who was not in Congress at all, but within the administration, was Bill Moyers. While he was reluctant to support FOIA at first, after compromises were made Moyers was able to help sell the legislation within the executive branch. In the end, he saw FOIA as a bill that Johnson could use politically. What makes this last period of development, prior to passage, interesting is how Congress was able to use the politics of the moment to continue to build support in order to foist a bill on one of the most politically astute presidents of the modern era. As we will see, the work that Moss had already done around the issue, including investigations and hearings, introducing bills that failed but kept the issue moving forward, and using his institutional power to develop admiration from other members of Congress, would all prove vital in the final months leading to passage of the bill.

This chapter provides a perspective focused on one single issue, demonstrating how policy evolves and develops in response to the politics of the moment, made possible by continued intransigence from the president over executive privilege. What cannot be ignored is that the Johnson administration was a period of massive change, and the additional factors playing out politically, socially, and institutionally around all of the other issues had an influence on FOIA. While the CLDC is developed to examine a single issue through multiple iterations, politics never happens in a vacuum, and in this instance, we are able to understand how moments for other policy issues can have an impact on different issues. While Johnson still operated under the Cold War Paradigm, the politics of this moment changed as domestic unrest with issues like Vietnam and Civil Rights grew. In a sense, as Kingdon would say, the 'window of opportunity' would open for FOIA in this moment, but the opening was only created by the masterful use of institutional power, which Moss proved deftly capable of using. The confluence of factors that contributed to the politics of passing FOIA were grounded in reform, where actors within Congress, the administration, and the press worked together in achieving a new law that would fit within the political and social reforms of that moment. While we can see how policy like FOIA brings about institutional reform, this chapter offers a look at the individuals who were able to successfully bring about that change.

Executive privilege, coalition building, and committee jurisdictions

The untimely death of Kennedy brought President Johnson into the White House and opened the door to a productive period of legislative reform, and thus an opportunity for Moss to take advantage. Moss did not have the personal connection to Johnson that he did with Kennedy, though he would use his

111

entrepreneurial skills to begin to build relationships. In the days following Kennedy's assassination, Moss sent LBJ a telegram on behalf of himself and the entire California congressional delegation expressing their grief and pledging their "unreserved support" for the president.[1] The Democratic National Committee (DNC) would send a response a few weeks later thanking Moss on behalf of the president and letting him know how appreciative LBJ was of his support.[2] The letter would continue by thanking Moss for his leadership and "prompt cooperation in what became an unprecedented demonstration of unity." In quickly moving to support LBJ and the party in the moments following Kennedy's death, Moss would continue to ensure access to the White House and keep congressional leadership on his side now that he was serving as House Deputy Whip. Moss would use this moment to take stock of the political terrain in order to develop a strategy going forward, and to see Johnson's position on executive privilege and freedom of information. As Senate Majority Leader, Johnson had supported efforts at curtailing government secrecy under Eisenhower and voted in favor of the Housekeeping Statute amendment, but now as president, Moss was doubtful he would be as supportive of those same efforts. However, partisan concerns remained the same, with the Democrats in unified control of government.

Prior to Kennedy's death the Senate introduced a public records bill, an early iteration of what would become FOIA, which sought to amend the APA in providing a congressional pathway to executive information. Moss had his own version of the bill in the House, and began to lobby colleagues for their support. One colleague he reached out to in particular was Judiciary Committee Chair Celler. If the Senate passed their version, because it amended the APA, the bill when introduced

---

[1] Telegram to President Lyndon B. Johnson from John Moss, November 26, 1963. Folder 3, Box 111, Series 3. John E. Moss Archive, California State University, Sacramento.

[2] Letter to John Moss from Democratic National Committee, December 6, 1963. Folder 3, Box 111, Series 3. John E. Moss Archive, California State University, Sacramento.

in the House would fall under the jurisdiction of the Judiciary Committee and not Government Operations, meaning that Moss would have no committee control over the bill. Moss sent a letter to Celler asking for his evaluation of feedback on his bill, which he states is better than the Senate version, and ends the letter by saying, "I would like to discuss this with you at your convenience."[3] Moss prepared to introduce his own bill, which would be nearly identical to the Senate version but would amend the Federal Register Act, which was the Housekeeping Statute, as opposed to the APA, just so Moss would have jurisdiction and control over the bill in the House. Archibald and Moss discussed the need to talk with Celler and Speaker McCormack about having the bill referred to the Moss Subcommittee instead of Judiciary if the Senate bill came to the House.[4] After so much time and work being put into the issue, Moss did not want to lose control and influence in shaping the final bill in the House.

Moss introduced his bill in the House, and while Long pushed his through the Senate, the issue of executive privilege under Johnson moved to the fore as well. By early 1964, with the Johnson administration strongly pushing their agenda, Moss and Archibald pursued their own agenda to get Johnson to take a public position on executive privilege. In a meeting with Press Secretary George Reedy, Archibald discussed and urged Johnson to follow Kennedy's example by providing a letter to Moss delineating the use of executive privilege.[5] Archibald told Reedy that Moss could send Johnson a letter to prompt his actions, and Reedy assured Archibald that he would speak about it with the president. Archibald followed his meeting with Reedy by reaching out to Pierre Salinger, noting concerns the subcommittee had

---

[3] Letter to Emanuel Celler from John Moss, July 1, 1963. Folder: Alphabetical Files—1963—"Archibald Memos" [Folder 1 of 2], Box M-42, Center for Legislative Archives, National Archives, Washington, DC.

[4] Letter to John Moss from Sam Archibald, September 14, 1964. Folder: Alphabetical Files—1964—"Archibald Memos" [Folder 2 of 2], Box M-43, Center for Legislative Archives, National Archives, Washington, DC.

[5] Memorandum to John Moss from Sam Archibald, February 13, 1964. Folder: Alphabetical Files—1964—"Archibald Memos" [Folder 1 of 2], Box M-43, Center for Legislative Archives, National Archives, Washington, DC.

received from multiple press associations about Johnson's position on executive privilege.[6] Archibald warned Salinger that the press groups would make the "executive privilege problem" a campaign issue, but Johnson could prevent that by taking a public position. Archibald said,

> You could wait for a public inquiry from one of the FOI professionals; you could take the initiative and issue a statement on President Johnson's position, or we could exchange letters as we did before. In case you want to follow the latter tactic, here's a draft of a letter John Moss could send.

The warning from Archibald was twofold. First, he noted how press groups were going to use the executive privilege issue against the administration, and that the subcommittee would be unable to prevent them. Second, this provided Archibald with ammunition to work out an agreement with the administration in pressing them to follow Kennedy's lead, and ending with a public clarification position on the issue. Moss and Archibald followed a private bargaining strategy with the administration to keep political tensions from becoming public and giving Republicans ammunition to use in the upcoming election.

The response to Archibald's letter inside the administration was not pleasant. White House Counsel Lee White sent a memo to Salinger in response, which stated,

> My reaction to the attached [Archibald letter] is that the President should re-affirm the position taken by President Kennedy on executive privilege simply because I do not think anyone in a position of responsibility now would undertake such action without personal knowledge on the part of the President. The prospect of cooperating with Sam Archibald gives me a headache and a stomach-ache. However, I guess we ought to do it anyway.[7]

---

[6] Letter to Pierre Salinger from Sam Archibald, March 5, 1964. Folder: Executive Folder—FE 4-1 Presidential Power, EX FE 3-2 Box 6, LBJ Presidential Library.

[7] Memo to Pierre Salinger from Lee White, March 16, 1964. Folder: Executive Folder—FE 4-1 Presidential Power, EX FE 3-2 Box 6, LBJ Presidential Library.

Salinger took White's comments to LBJ, with the president directing them to make arrangements with Moss on the matter.[8] By June, Reedy responded to Archibald, stating,

> I have given the matter some consideration and have discussed it generally with the president. He believes that President Kennedy's decision to make it perfectly clear that the claim of executive privilege be exercised only by the President is the only sensible policy. Obviously, if the question should come to him in written or oral form, that is the type of response he would give. Thus, if Congressman Moss were to write the President, this is the response that would be received.[9]

Reedy asked Archibald to keep him apprised of their intentions on this, but the administration and Johnson had already determined that reaffirming the Kennedy position would be in their best interest at this time. Archibald sent Reedy a draft letter to get White House feedback prior to Moss sending the public letter to Johnson. Moss again demonstrated a skillful touch in handling the administration through private communications in order to prevent the issue from becoming more political during an election year.

After receiving commentary on the draft letter from the White House, Moss sent Johnson a letter on August 19, 1964, discussing the problems surrounding executive privilege, establishing the creation of Eisenhower's 1954 memo and noting how Kennedy sought to change its use. Moss wrote,

> The use of the claim of "executive privilege" to withhold government information from the Congress and the public is an issue of importance to those who recognize the need for a fully informed electorate, and for a Congress operating as a co-equal branch of the Federal Government. . . . As a result of President Kennedy's clear statement, there was no longer a rash of "executive privilege" claims to withhold information from the Congress and the public. I am confident you share my views on the importance to our form of government of

---

[8] Memo to President Johnson from Pierre Salinger. Folder: Executive Folder— FE 4-1 Presidential Power, EX FE 3-2 Box 6, LBJ Presidential Library.

[9] Letter to Sam Archibald from George Reedy, June 8, 1964. Folder: Executive Folder—FE 4-1 Presidential Power, EX FE 3-2 Box 6, LBJ Presidential Library.

a free flow of information, and I hope you will reaffirm the principle that "executive privilege" can be invoked only by you alone and will not be used without your specific approval.

Through working with the administration, Moss sought to get Johnson on record to limit the use of executive privilege without the issue becoming too much of a political liability. By giving the White House the ability to have input on the situation, Moss was able to keep allies in the administration while still getting what he wanted.

It was not until spring 1965 that the White House would finally respond to Moss. A memo from White to Reedy through Larry O'Brien mentions that they had been all set to respond to the request, but it never got done. White mentions having no recollection as to why the request to Moss was never made, and in fact, he had thought it had already been done. It was brought back to their attention when Moss and Long issued statements about their new freedom of information bills, introduced in February 1965, that noted Johnson's silence on the executive privilege request.[10] On April 2, 1965, Johnson sent Moss a letter clarifying his position on executive privilege. LBJ stated,

> Since assuming the Presidency, I have followed the policy laid down by President Kennedy in his letter to you of March 7, 1962, dealing with this subject. Thus, the claim of "executive privilege" will continue to be made only by the President. This administration has attempted to cooperate completely with the Congress in making available to it all information possible, and that will continue to be our policy. I appreciate the time and energy that you and your subcommittee have devoted to this subject and welcome the opportunity to state formally my policy on this important subject.[11]

The letter from Johnson became a double-edged sword. Now that he had publicly affirmed the Kennedy position on EP, any

---

[10] Press Release from Moss and Long, February 17, 1965. Folder: Freedom of Information Miscellaneous [1965–1966], Box M-25, Center for Legislative Archives, National Archives, Washington, DC.

[11] Letter to John Moss from Lyndon Johnson, April 2, 1965. Folder: Office Files of Harry McPherson—Executive Privilege, Office Files of White House Aids Box 22, LBJ Presidential Library.

deviation from that position, or in fact any claim of executive privilege, would become a political rallying cry, in particular for Republicans and the press. However, by working with Moss and the Democrats he maintained support with his congressional majority and kept them happy as they worked on the Great Society agenda items.

The FOIA endgame: How Congress sought to check the President

While the Senate had passed Long's FOI bill in 1964, the House never moved forward on either the Senate bill or Moss's version, ending the 88th Congress with no legislative action on freedom of information. Another setback for Moss was that the Senate bill, when introduced in the House was sent to Celler and the Judiciary Committee, not his own. While it made no difference on policy, as the bill died in committee, the episode demonstrated to Moss that he needed to be better prepared if and when the Senate passed a new version. The 89th Congress (1965–7) in 1965 began with Moss and Long jointly introducing FOI bills, S.1160 and H.R.5012, that would "require every agency of the Federal Government to make all its records promptly available to any person."[12] A press release discussed the scope of the legislation and noted that eight categories of sensitive information would be made exempt, along with the fact that the legislation had more than twenty-five co-sponsors across the House and Senate. Long notes that the bill, based on the bill passed by the Senate the previous year, would be passed again during the current term. The introduction prompted the administration to move forward with the executive privilege position letter, but Moss and Long sent a clear message with the press release as well. The message put both the White House and congressional leadership on notice that they planned on moving forward.

Congressional Republicans became more vocal in opposing

---

[12] Press Release, 17 February 1965: Papers of Lyndon Baines Johnson, President 1963–1969, EX FE 3-2 Wreath Laying (11/22/63–9/18/65), Folder: FE 4-1 Presidential Powers, Box 6, LBJ Presidential Library.

administration secrecy policies, bringing Moss a new ally to help push his bill forward in a sophomore Republican from Illinois, Donald Rumsfeld. Rumsfeld held a deep respect for Moss and had requested a place on his subcommittee, as he sought to influence policy on public records issues.[13] As the politics had altered for House Republicans, Rumsfeld was able to gain support for the FOI bill within his caucus, including the support of House Minority Leader Gerald Ford. Republican support helped to bolster Moss with the House leadership as well as putting additional pressure on Johnson, especially looking toward the 1966 midterm election. Within the CLDC, the issue evolved again in response to the altered political environment, creating a new juncture. While Johnson sought movement on his Great Society agenda, it was clear that Congress was moving forward on FOI legislation, pressing their own agenda issues on the president. The politics began to change as congressional Republicans offered a learned response to the issue and strategy that had worked for Democrats, especially in seeing how Rumsfeld adopted the same initiative as Moss, placing the issue squarely on LBJ's shoulders.

As the CLD cycle continued through iterative development, the administration stood strong in opposition to the FOI legislation in Congress, providing a challenge for Moss in getting his legislation passed. It had become clear during the negotiations over the executive privilege memo that the administration had no patience for Moss or his subcommittee, viewing them as a distraction from their agenda at best, and at worst, seeking to undermine the power of the president. As Congress pressed forward, many agency heads and officials within the administration fervently made their opposition known by following the Justice Department's (DOJ) lead in citing the unconstitutionality of the legislation, and that the bill would prevent "their ability to discharge their responsibilities effectively."[14] By spring 1965, Phillip Hughes, assistant director for legislative reference at BOB, sent a memo to Lee White, special counsel to LBJ, discussing the

---

[13] Foerstel, *Freedom of Information*, 1999; Lemov, *People's Warrior*, 2011.
[14] Memo for the President from Wilfred Rommel, June 29, 1966. Folder: Executive Folder LE/FE 14-1, WHCF Box 44, LBJ Presidential Library.

upcoming hearings in the House scheduled on H.R.5012. In the memo, Hughes stated that BOB regarded the bill as "threatening a serious legislative encroachment on executive power."[15] Hughes continued by speculating that the Senate would wait for the House to act, but noted that if the House passed the bill, the Senate would move quickly to do the same. He ranted that freedom of information was too sensitive an issue, and would be difficult to handle at a hearing. Hughes then recommended that the issue warranted immediate attention and they needed to talk with House leadership to urge them to prevent the bill from coming to a floor vote.

At the same time, several administration officials including Moyers and McPherson reached out to the DOJ and requested they examine both S.1160 and H.R.5012, and then draft language for a bill that would be acceptable to the president. In doing so, the discussion detailed concerns within the administration that the proposed FOI bills would create an opening for complete public access without concern for the government's responsibility in the public interest. In other words, the bills went too far. The Office of Legal Counsel (OLC) told Moyers,

> The agencies' opposition to S.1160 is simply that—opposition to the particular proposed formula as a wholly inadequate effort to resolve this intricate problem. The bill seeks to eliminate any application of judgement to questions of disclosure or non-disclosure, substituting a simple, self-executing word-formula which would exempt a few enumerated kinds of information and otherwise open all government files, except Congressional files and whatever non-public files courts may maintain, to anyone who might wish to go through them, whatever his motive and irrespective of the consequences of disclosure. The Administration opposes this particular approach, not the principle or the purpose of freedom of information.[16]

In making their case, the OLC and the DOJ were walking a fine line in opposing the bills on substantive, rather than ideological,

---

[15] Memorandum for Mr. Lee White, March 19, 1965: Office Files of Harry McPherson, folder: Office Files of Harry McPherson Executive Privilege, Box 22, LBJ Presidential Library.

[16] Memo for Bill Moyers from Leon Ulman, March 16, 1966. Folder: Executive Folder LE/FE 14-1, WHCF Box 44, LBJ Presidential Library.

grounds. Within this current iteration, it was becoming clearer to the administration that Congress was moving forward and they needed to be prepared, which was why the DOJ was already involved in developing draft language for a bill. Demonstrating the learning process, the administration showed that now was the time to try to influence the final language of any FOI bill that might come from Congress, to make it more palatable, while standing firm in opposition as it gave them a stronger bargaining position.

The administration's position was publicly expressed during the Moss Subcommittee hearings on H.R.5012, which featured representatives from the DOJ who testified that the proposed legislation was unconstitutional, and that all executive agencies involved objected. That same day, Hughes sent a detailed letter to House Government Operations Committee Chair William Dawson outlining BOB's position on the bill. In the letter, Hughes ripped apart the legislation, noting that it did not adequately protect the public interest and ending by stating that BOB strongly opposed enactment.[17] The issue had evolved into a final position, where Congress was holding public hearings on a bill and seeking administration feedback, while the administration was attempting to press their opposition privately with congressional leadership to stop the bill, or at least change the language and scope. Reflecting the politics of this moment, LBJ needed his congressional majority to pass his agenda, but was fighting tooth and nail against this bill that Congress was foisting on him.

A few weeks later, in April 1965, House Democratic leaders were holding their weekly meeting with President Johnson, who requested that Speaker McCormack, Majority Leader Carl Albert, and Majority Whip Hale Boggs explain why Moss was holding hearings and moving forward on his government secrecy bill. Johnson remarked that the legislation was terrible, asking, "What is Moss trying to do to me?" He continued, "I thought

---

[17] Letter to William L. Dawson, March 30, 1965: Office Files of Harry McPherson, folder: Office Files of Harry McPherson Executive Privilege, Box 22, LBJ Presidential Library.

Moss was one of our boys, but the Justice Department tells me this goddamn bill will screw the Johnson Administration."[18] Johnson then recommended to House leadership that Moss be "brought in line." Within an hour of this meeting, Moss was called out of his own hearing and summoned to the Speaker's office. McCormack expressed the president's outrage over the bill, and while the Speaker did not specifically direct Moss to kill it, the message was implied. After more than a decade of hearings and investigations into issues of government secrecy and access to public records, Moss was not deterred by Johnson's irritation. With support from his colleagues in the Senate, and with congressional Republicans ramping up their "credibility gap" campaign against Johnson for the midterm elections, Moss knew he could get this done without causing political damage to the president or his party. [19]

By August, regardless of the president's opposition, Moss was moving forward, but cautiously keeping channels open with the White House. Archibald sent Lee White an updated version of H.R.5012, noting that any comments White could offer would be helpful.[20] This letter prompted an internal exchange within the Johnson administration, with White forwarding the letter and bill to Hughes at BOB with a memo attached that merely said, "HELP!"[21] Hughes responded noting that although some changes had been made to the language of the bill, it remained

[18] Lemov, *People's Warrior*, 2011, p. 53.
[19] The Ford Presidential Library archive contains documents on the Republican efforts to run a discrediting campaign against LBJ and congressional Democrats during the 1966 midterm elections. With Rep. Donald Rumsfeld on the Moss Subcommittee pushing from the inside, House Minority Leader Ford was able to get a large group of Republican House members on board to support FOIA, which could be used as a partisan attack on LBJ. This was referred to as the "Credibility Gap" campaign for the 1966 midterms.
[20] Letter to Mr. Lee White, August 2, 1965: Office Files of Harry McPherson, folder: Office Files of Harry McPherson Executive Privilege, Box 22, LBJ Presidential Library.
[21] Letter to Mr. Sam Hughes, August 4, 1965, Office Files of Harry McPherson, folder: Office Files of Harry McPherson Executive Privilege, Box 22, LBJ Presidential Library.

objectionable, and he recommended continued opposition.[22] The next day, White sent the correspondence to Moyers, who commented that he agreed with BOB's objections and they should continue to oppose the bill.[23] Two weeks later, White sent a letter back to Archibald noting that after having some of their legislative specialists look over the bill, the lawyers still agreed that the legislation was unconstitutional and would provide an undue burden on the agencies. White ended by saying that he hoped Archibald and Moss would continue to work with the administration on developing a bill that overcame their objections.[24] Prior to White responding back to Archibald, he sent a memo to Moyers stating, "I have not been bothered by Sam Archibald about this, but it seems to me we ought to at least make it clear that our silence does not mean agreement. Additionally, I did not think it desirable to just say "no," but wanted to kind of preserve our "harmonious" working relationship by sticking poor old Norb [Schlei] with the duty of working with Sam."[25]

As the administration continued to privately bargain over the focus of the legislation, they were getting frustrated and beginning to show concern among themselves about the possibility that a FOI bill could actually pass. Within the White House, legal counsels and the DOJ continued to assert to Congress that the proposed legislation was unconstitutional by attempting to alter power solely provided to the president. A main area of contention between the sides was over the provision that would allow requestors of information a legal process for appealing

---

[22] Memorandum for Mr. Lee White, August 12, 1965: Office Files of Harry McPherson, folder: Office Files of Harry McPherson Executive Privilege, Box 22, LBJ Presidential Library.

[23] Memo to Bill Moyers, August 13, 1965: Office Files of Harry McPherson, folder: Office Files of Harry McPherson Executive Privilege, Box 22, LBJ Presidential Library.

[24] Letter to Sam Archibald, August 27, 1965: Office Files of Harry McPherson, folder: Office Files of Harry McPherson Executive Privilege, Box 22, LBJ Presidential Library.

[25] Memo to Bill Moyers, August 27, 1965: Office Files of Harry McPherson, folder: Office Files of Harry McPherson Executive Privilege, Box 22, LBJ Presidential Library.

denials through the courts. This legal mechanism did not sit well amongst many in the White House. A memo on the DOJ review of H.R.5012 firmly opposed court intervention in executive branch activities, stating,

> Mr. Schlei pointed out that it was his opinion that the president would never approve a bill with the court review provision. Not only does the Executive not like the watchful eye of the court peering over its shoulder, but also the Judges are "not equipped to handle the informational problems which occur within the Executive."[26]

For Moss and Congress, the legal mechanism that offered judicial oversight upon denial of information was an integral part of the legislation, without which it had no teeth or enforcement mechanism. After so many years of investigations, Moss had learned the importance of needing teeth in the bill, and the legal mechanism was the best option.

The Senate passed S.1160 by unanimous voice-vote on October 1, 1965. Long issued a press release stating, "This action will bring us much nearer realization of a strong Freedom of Information bill, as the Senate unanimously adopted a bill very similar to the present one last session. The public has a right to know what its Government is doing."[27] With the Senate moving first in placing increased pressure on the White House, Moss now had momentum, but he was faced with the same problem from the previous congressional session, where the Senate bill would not be referred to his subcommittee.

With S.1160 coming to the House with jurisdiction falling to the Judiciary Committee, Moss needed to get control through his subcommittee. He decided his best chance was to go directly to Celler. After the Senate passed their bill in the previous Congress, Moss was prepared for this contingency. At that time, he had

---

[26] Memorandum for the Record, "Justice Department Views on Current Draft of HR 5012," Folder: Alphabetical Files—1965—"Kass Memos," Box M-45, National Archives, Washington, DC.

[27] Press release from the Subcommittee on Administrative Practice and Procedure, October 1, 1965. Folder: Executive Folder LE/FE 14-1, WHCF Box 44, LBJ Presidential Library.

met with Celler and discussed a plan to get the bill through.[28] Once the Senate had passed S.1160, Moss wasted no time in reaching out to Celler again. Moss and Celler then met for a brief conversation. Following the meeting, Celler informed Moss that he would waive jurisdiction of S.1160, leaving it to the Speaker to determine assignment of the bill. Celler had noted previous instances when Moss had assisted him and his committee with obtaining information from executive agencies, and since Moss had been so doggedly determined in his pursuit of the issue, Celler believed Moss deserved to have control of the bill for the final push.[29] Speaker McCormack then assigned the bill to the Government Operations Committee, thereby giving it over to the Moss Subcommittee. This incident demonstrated the power and influence Moss had accrued during his time as subcommittee chair. To have the Judiciary Committee Chair waive jurisdiction and gain the support of the Speaker to hand over the bill was entrepreneurial prowess at its zenith. Moss was now in a position to get the bill through the House, with the continued resistance from the administration being the only remaining obstacle.

The private bargaining between the administration and the Moss Subcommittee continued into December, with Archibald sending Moyers a letter in the aftermath of the Senate passing S.1160. Archibald asserted that the subcommittee was planning to pass H.R.5012 in January and that things were going to get "hot," so he wanted to prepare Moyers for what to expect.[30] Archibald discussed that the Subcommittee would take up S.1160, which did not include any of the language he had worked out with Norb Schlei and members of the Justice Department that

---

[28] Letter to Emanuel Celler from John Moss, July 1, 1963. Folder: Freedom of Information Act—Legislative Background—Legislative Proposals 1962–1963 [Folder 2 of 2], Box M-187, National Archives, Washington, DC.

[29] Memorandum to Moss Subcommittee from Sam Archibald, October 14, 1965. Folder: Freedom of Information Act—Legislative Background—S.1160, Analysis S.1160 & H.R. 5012 [Folder 2 of 2], Box M-189, National Archives, Washington, DC.

[30] Letter to Mr. Bill Moyers, December 13, 1965: White House Central File, Subject File, folder: Executive Folder LE/FE 14-1, Box 44, LBJ Presidential Library.

was included in the House version, which had made the bill more acceptable to some administration officials. Archibald states, "But even those changes would not make the bill acceptable to those agency witnesses. In fact, I doubt whether any improvements in the present law would be acceptable to the Executive Branch holdovers." Archibald continued by mentioning the press organizations who would begin to push for House approval, adding that Gene Patterson from the *Atlanta Constitution* and other editors would argue, "that it would be politically damaging for the President to oppose freedom of information."[31] Regardless of the relationship between Moss and Rumsfeld, Archibald was less concerned over congressional Republicans. However, he did warn Moyers by stating,

> Although the Republicans generally have been on the wrong side of the freedom of information issue, I think they are going to take partisan advantage of any further delays of the proposed Federal Public Records Law. The Republican Congressional Campaign Committee has issued one press release—sort of weak—and they have been trying to get background information from us—without success.

Archibald ended by saying that he would keep Moyers informed about what the press and Republicans would do on the issue. This warning shows the continued communication between the Moss Subcommittee and the White House, with Archibald sending Moyers a clear signal of determination to get the bill passed, along with his concerns for the potential political damage if the administration continued to oppose the bill.

The forward momentum from Congress prompted Moyers to send the correspondence from Archibald to White seeking his advice, noting, "This could be a potential time bomb."[32] White's response to Moyers recommended that any "Congressional liaison types" in the White House be prepared to talk with House leadership, including Moss, in order to get the subcommittee to

---

[31] Ibid.
[32] Memorandum for Lee White, December 15, 1965: White House Central File, Subject File, folder: Executive Folder LE/FE 14-1, Box 44, LBJ Presidential Library.

change the bill to something more acceptable.[33] By January 1966 White sent a memo to Schlei and Hughes with Archibald's letter, warning them of the potential upcoming problems as outlined in the letter. His memo asked them to look over S.1160 and get back to him on what the administration would be willing to accept. He then noted that they should, without delay, sit down with Moss and come to an accord on amending the bill in a way that would be acceptable to them, so that they "would not be in the awkward position of opposing freedom of information."[34] It had become clear to the administration that the bill was moving forward despite their objections, so they were pursuing an alternative strategy of bargaining in an attempt to change the language of the bill to make it more acceptable.

After several months of negotiations, a deal was made with Moss and House leadership, working with the DOJ, Moyers, White, Schlei, Hughes and others within the Johnson administration to come to an agreement that would allow S.1160 to come to a vote in the House. The agreement was necessary if Moss wanted to gain White House support, which would allow House leadership to bring the bill to a floor vote. Numerous agencies had followed the DOJ position, making claims that the legislation was unconstitutional and would place a heavy administrative burden which would interfere with the public interest. Moss had refused to consider adding provisions to the legislation written by the DOJ, and would not remove the legal mechanism contained in the bill. While the administration agreed with the nine exemptions to public record disclosures contained in the bill, the agreement was to allow the DOJ to help write the House conference report that would accompany the final bill.[35]

---

[33] Memorandum for Bill Moyers, December 17, 1965: White House Central File, Subject File, folder: Executive Folder LE/FE 14-1, Box 44, LBJ Presidential Library.

[34] Memorandum for Mr. Norbert Schlei and Mr. Phillip Hughes, January 15, 1966: White House Central File, Subject File, folder: Executive Folder LE/FE 14-1, Box 44, LBJ Presidential Library.

[35] Letter to Charles Schultze from Ramsey Clark, June 28, 1966. Folder: P.L. 89-487, 7/4/66, S.1160. Enrolled Legislation Box 36, LBJ Presidential Library.

The report provided clarification and directions on implementation for the agencies and the courts, and the DOJ was satisfied that their input on implementation would overcome many of their constitutional concerns with the bill. In this moment, the pressure was mounting for Johnson politically as increased attacks from Republicans continued, while he stayed focused on the Great Society agenda. Moss was under pressure from House leadership to compromise with the administration that would get his legislation passed without forcing a political showdown between LBJ and his own party in Congress, which would be politically embarrassing heading into a midterm election. The private bargaining strategy between the president and Congress paid off, in creating the space for compromise on all sides that would bring the bill to a floor vote in the House. The possibility did exist for LBJ to remain publicly quiet and veto any bill that came to him, which was a concern for Moss, as Johnson could back out of the agreement in the end. Even with the support of allies in both the House and Senate that Moss had gained, he was worried there were not enough votes to override LBJ's veto.[36]

The agreement reached was that Moss would drop his own bill, H.R.5012, and move forward with the Senate version, S.1160, as it had already passed in the Senate and would allow the House to move quickly. Moss and the House leaders agreed to press forward with S.1160 unamended, so that when passed it would skip the need for a conference committee and go right to LBJ for his signature. The bill moved forward under a closed rule so that no amendments could be offered, giving Moss the political cushion to get the bill passed with White House agreement.[37] Concessions were given from both ends of Pennsylvania Avenue, but even with administration officials now agreeing to support the legislation, no one in the White House knew for sure if LBJ would actually sign the bill or issue a veto.

---

[36] Interview with Bill Moyers, conducted via email between March 17, 2015 and May 5, 2015.

[37] Memorandum to John Moss from Sam Archibald, January 7, 1966. Folder: Alphabetical Files—1966—"Archibald Memos," Box M-46, National Archives, Washington, DC.

On March 30, 1966, a press release went out noting that the Moss Subcommittee had favorably reported S.1160 out of committee and it would be taken up by the full Government Operations Committee.[38] The next day, Milton Semer, counsel to LBJ, sent a letter to Johnson's administrative assistant, Henry Wilson, informing him that he and Moss had spoken about the bill coming out of his subcommittee and going before the full committee. Semer notes that Moss agreed that the bill should go to DOJ officials for comment, showing that the deal was being implemented, and asserts that he believes Moss and the administration can work things out. Semer also notes that both Moss and Moyers will be in Vietnam at the same time, and he suggests to both that they get together and talk then.[39] While Moyers never went to Vietnam with Moss, they did talk several times to discuss the legislation and the issue. Moyers stated that

> Moss was so persistent, so dogged and determined, that one had to take him seriously. He was like Hubert Humphrey on civil rights, although less publicly exuberant. The man understood what it took to pass such a crucial game-changing bill, just as HHH did. He was one of those students of Congress who knew that no victory was solo.[40]

During this time, Moss was able to convince and gain an ally in the White House—Bill Moyers. Moyers commented that when he became Press Secretary in 1965, after turning LBJ down several times in the past, he began meeting regularly with various press officials, including strong FOI advocates like Russ Wiggins from the *Washington Post*. In discussing the issue and reading some of ASNE's reports, Moyers began to understand that the constitutional problems expressed by DOJ were open to interpretation,

---

[38] News Release from the Foreign Operations and Government Information Subcommittee, March 30, 1966: White House Central File, Subject File, folder: Executive Folder LE/FE 14-1, Box 44, LBJ Presidential Library.

[39] Memo to Henry Wilson, March 31, 1966: GEN FE 14 Records—Archives (11/22/63–5/25/65), folder: FE 14-1 (4/6/65–5/10/67), Box 25, LBJ Presidential Library.

[40] Interview with Bill Moyers, conducted via email between March 17, 2015 and May 5, 2015.

which provided him flexibility in pushing other administration officials toward working with Moss to influence the construction of the legislation instead of just outright opposition. Moyers had respect for Moss and understood that he was willing to work with the administration on solving the access and secrecy problem, not just in scoring political points. Where the issue stood within the CLDC at this time, having already passed the Senate, Moyers preferred to work with Moss in crafting the final bill, where the White House could have input, rather than continue to push it off.

By the end of April, the full House Government Operations Committee reported S.1160 out of committee, paving the way for the bill to be voted on by the full House. A press release marks the occasion, and another juncture in the CLDC, by quoting Moss, who predicted House approval and LBJ's signature. Moss stated,

> This legislation, which strengthens the right of access to government information, reflects many years of study in the Congress and in the Executive branch of problems created by restrictions to Federal records. Legislation in this complicated field was most difficult to draft, and I want to express my appreciation for the cooperative attitude of administration officials. I also want to express my appreciation to Congressman Rumsfeld, who has rendered able assistance in drafting the legislation.[41]

The public rhetoric clearly glossed over much of the internal tension between congressional Democrats and the administration. The praise Moss gave to Rumsfeld helped to keep congressional Republicans supportive by offering them credit for the process. The House Republican Policy Committee would respond with their own press release, praising the progress of the bill and condemning the Johnson administration for delaying progress and creating a "screen of secrecy" in barring reporters, members of Congress, and the public from being able to access vital information important to their welfare.[42] The constant Republican

[41] Press Release, House Committee on Government Operation, April 27, 1966. Folder: Freedom of Information Miscellaneous [1965–1966], Box M-25, Center for Legislative Archives, National Archives, Washington, DC.

[42] Press Release, House Republican Policy Committee, May 18, 1966: folder:

attacks, coupled with concerns over the 1966 midterm elections, were placing pressure on the administration to finalize a deal on FOIA and get the bill passed.[43] At the end of May, Moyers sent Cabinet secretary and special assistant to the president Robert Kintner a memo, with an attached booklet written by then Vice President Elect Johnson in 1960 detailing how the Kennedy administration would be an open government, overcoming the access to information and government secrecy problems that had been rampant in the Eisenhower administration. Moyers notes to Kintner that he kept this information on hand for LBJ to use in a signing ceremony or statement on FOIA.[44] With the House on the verge of passing the bill, Moyers pushed administration officials and those close to the president to think through potential outcomes and how passage of FOIA could be used to their advantage. In gaining an ally in the White House like Moyers, Moss had acquired the advantage of having someone within the administration pressing for passage and trying to convince LBJ to sign, instead of veto the bill.

By mid-June, with passage of FOIA looming in the House, Semer sent a memo to Moyers offering suggestions on how to handle the freedom of information bill. Semer suggested that Moyers help LBJ frame the issue as one between the transient president and the power of the permanent bureaucracy.[45] Semer ended by recommending that Johnson sign the bill at the Governor's Conference on July 4. The shift within the administration at this point shows that many officials who had been

Credibility Gap 1966–1967, Press Secretary and Speech File 1947–1973, Press Releases, Agriculture 1966 to Press Releases, Crime 1973, Box D6, Gerald R. Ford Presidential Library.

[43] It was not just the 1966 midterms that had LBJ politically worried; at that time, LBJ was planning to run for reelection in 1968 as well, so rationally, he would have been concerned about the political impacts the issue would have on his reelection campaign, which would offer additional pressure that would impact the situation and play into a potential veto consideration.

[44] Memo to Robert Kintner, May 28, 1966, White House Central File, Subject File, folder: Executive Folder LE/FE 14-1, Box 44, LBJ Presidential Library.

[45] Memorandum for Bill Moyers, June 15, 1966: GEN FE 14 Records— Archives (11/22/63–5/25/65), folder: FE 14-1 (4/6/65–5/10/67), Box 25, LBJ Presidential Library.

consistent in opposing the bill with LBJ were now discussing the inevitable outcome of how to handle the bill passing, including how the president could position himself. While Johnson was publicly silent about whether he would sign the bill, White House officials like Moyers were planning for passage. The stringent opposition to FOIA from numerous agency officials began to weaken once it became known that the DOJ had clarified the implementation practices in the final report.[46] However, Johnson continued to face increased pressure to veto the bill from Hoover at the FBI, who staunchly opposed any public records law.[47] The tide had turned in Congress's favor, yet no one in the Capitol quite knew how this would end. Moyers was being heavily lobbied by members of the press and Congress to hold a signing ceremony, which he in turn lobbied LBJ to do, although the president was reluctant.

FOIA came up for a floor vote and passed on June 20 with a unanimous vote of 306 to 0, with 126 members not voting. The final vote tally showed 207 Democrats and 99 Republicans voting yea.[48] As the tally demonstrated, Moss had plenty of support, but he lacked a veto-proof majority.[49] Moss remained hopeful that the deal made with the DOJ would be enough to push the bill into law. Now that the House had passed the bill and it was making its way to the president, no one in the White House was certain what LBJ's response would be. To complicate matters more, Congress adjourned a week later for the 4th of July recess. The adjournment added an additional worry for

[46] There are numerous letters from cabinet secretaries to the Bureau of the Budget discussing their final position on FOIA. Folder: P.L. 89-487, 7/4/66 S.1160. Enrolled Legislation, Box 36. LBJ Presidential Library.

[47] Interview with Bill Moyers, conducted via email between March 17, 2015 and May 5, 2015.

[48] The roll call vote count is available online through GovTrack.us, and can be accessed at <http://www.govtrack.us/congress/votes/89-1966/h277> (last accessed November 10, 2018).

[49] I must acknowledge the vote tally in the House on FOIA. In all of the archives and documents I have examined on this bill, there is nothing to account for why 126 members abstained from voting. Rather than speculate at this moment, I will leave it for future research.

Moss: with Congress now out of session for several weeks, LBJ was given the ability to pocket veto. The pocket veto would kill the bill outright, not giving Congress a chance to override. With legislative priorities focused on other Great Society agenda items, and with the increased attention given to Vietnam, Moss was uncertain that he would be able to get another iteration of FOIA through Congress if Johnson vetoed this bill.

The day FOIA passed the House, Archibald sent a letter to Semer that offered suggestions on what Johnson should do to promote the legislation. Archibald recommended Johnson hold a "full-dress signing ceremony" that included prominent members of the press and Congress who had been supporting the bill.[50] Archibald also noted that General Eisenhower had had a similar opportunity in 1958, but he "muffed it" and issued a "weasel-worded statement" that drew the wrath of his detractors, who received more favorable press coverage. Archibald emphasized that LBJ should not make that same mistake. Considering that Johnson had been Senate Majority Leader in 1958, behind the efforts in the Senate to pass an open records bill at that time, and one of the detractors who took advantage of Eisenhower's weasel-worded response, this message from Archibald made a clear and poignant statement. The next day, Senator Long, who had shepherded FOIA through the Senate, sent a letter to Mike Manatos, administrative assistant to Johnson, offering similar suggestions about a signing ceremony. Manatos sent a letter back to Long the following day noting that no decisions had been made about a signing ceremony, and giving no indication as to whether LBJ would even sign the bill.[51]

Several days later, Kintner sent a memo to LBJ outlining a phone call he had had earlier in the day with Moss, who continued to urge the president to sign the bill and to host a signing ceremony in order to take full advantage and claim credit.[52]

[50] Letter to Milton P. Semer, June 20, 1966: GEN FE 14 Records—Archives (11/22/63–5/25/65), folder: FE 14-1, Access to Records, Box 25, LBJ Presidential Library.

[51] Letter to Senator Edward V. Long, June 22, 1966: GEN FE 14 Records—Archives (11/22/63–5/25/65), folder: FE 14-1, Access to Records, Box 25, LBJ Presidential Library.

[52] Confidential Memorandum for the President, June 24, 1966: Handwriting

Kintner relayed Moss's theory that the president could use the signing ceremony, accompanied by a statement that would counteract the accusations Republicans had been leveling at him, to overcome the credibility gap. Across the bottom of the memo in large letters, LBJ wrote "No Ceremony." This is the first indication that Johnson had decided he would sign the bill, but at this point, no one other than he and Kintner knew that a decision had been made, and records indicate that no official statement or position by the president was indicated to anyone in the White House or administration.

With the deadline and possibility of a pocket veto mounting, supporters of FOIA in Congress and a multitude of press organizations inundated the White House, urging LBJ to sign the bill. Congressional Republicans kept up the pressure by issuing press releases blasting Johnson for his refusal to sign. On June 29, Hughes sent a report to Johnson that contained responses from all federal agencies impacted by FOIA, all of whom, except the Department of Health, Education and Welfare, approved of FOIA or at least no longer objected. Hughes explained the impact of the legislation in detail and recommended that, even though they still disagreed with some of the language, LBJ should not withhold his signature, provided he issued a signing statement outlining his position and ability to still keep information secret in the interest of national security.[53] Moyers notes that by the end of June, the president had "entered into a séance" with himself over whether he should sign the bill. Moyers spent this time urging several of his close journalist friends to contact the president personally to make the case for his signature, in order to show a favorable press response to the bill.

On July 1, Semer sent a memo to Johnson discussing the options and impacts of FOIA. In it, he offered suggestions on a signing statement and noted the BOB report Hughes sent a few

File Lyndon B. Johnson, folder: Handwriting–President Johnson June, 1966 (notes, instructions, doodles), Box 15, LBJ Presidential Library.

[53] Memorandum for the President, June 29, 1966: White House Central File, Subject File, folder: Executive Folder LE/FE 14-1, Box 44, LBJ Presidential Library.

days earlier, which removed most of the agency and bureaucratic objections to the legislation, and he recommended LBJ sign the bill. Semer mentioned that the agencies believed a strong signing statement, coupled with the House report, would be sufficient to overcome most objections. He recommended that if Johnson did not want to sign the bill, he could use the pocket veto. Semer did ask if LBJ wanted him to have the Attorney General begin working with the agencies on developing rules for implementing FOIA—to which Johnson checked YES at the bottom.[54] It was now clear that Johnson had decided to sign FOIA, as he would have the Justice Department begin preparations for implementation. Within the CLDC, this demarcates the final iteration prior to passage, as it now appeared LBJ would no longer veto the legislation. While the president was successful in shifting the language and having control over implementation, he was not successful in keeping FOIA from getting through Congress. The constant attacks from Republicans, electoral concerns, Moss, and a strong coalition within his own party pressing the issue left him with the inability to publicly veto; there was no political support for it. Johnson was left with little choice but to sign the bill and issue a statement asserting a continued measure of executive power.

On the morning of July 4, LBJ, albeit reluctantly and with no ceremony or fanfare, signed the Freedom of Information Act at his ranch in Texas. Moyers would later recount the incident:

> LBJ had to be dragged, kicking and screaming, to the signing. . . . He hated the very idea of open government, hated the thought of journalists rummaging in government closets, hated them challenging the official view of reality. He dug in his heels and even threatened to pocket veto the bill after it reached the White House. Only the tenacity of a congressman named John Moss got the bill passed at all, and that was after a 12-year battle against his elders in Congress. . . . He [Johnson] signed "the f-ing thing" as he called it and then set out to claim credit for it.[55]

---

[54] Memorandum for the President, July 1, 1966: GEN FE 14 Records— Archives (11/22/63–5/25/65), folder: FE 14-1, Access to Records, Box 25, LBJ Presidential Library.

[55] Moyers 2005, pp. 157–8.

Moyers asserted that regardless of Johnson's opposition to the legislation, he was a pragmatic politician, which is exactly what led him to sign the bill. In the end, Moyers said that LBJ understood the politics surrounding the larger policy agenda of the Great Society and knew he would need the support of those individuals in Congress, like Moss, to help him on future legislation. Therefore, it was in his best pragmatic and rational interest to sign FOIA and deal with it rather than upset a large coalition in the House and Senate, from which he wanted and needed continued support. Moyers said that LBJ was more concerned about the process rather than the substance of policy, and wanted to be on the right side in the end, which played into Johnson's strategy of keeping positions secret and everyone guessing until he made a final decision.[56]

The White House issued a signing statement that paid lip service to the importance of the legislation and of government transparency in a democracy. Much like Eisenhower's, and despite Moss warning him against it, Johnson's weasel-worded statement reiterated the president's authority to withhold information for national security reasons in the public interest. When it comes to public access to government information, the statement asserts,

> [T]he welfare of the nation or the rights of individuals may require that some documents not be made available. As long as threats to peace exist, for example, there must be military secrets. . . . Moreover, this bill in no way impairs the President's power under our Constitution to provide for confidentiality when the national interest so requires.[57]

Johnson's signature ended the legislative development period of the CLDC, and illustrated how Congress can successfully use

[56] Interview with Bill Moyers, conducted via email between March 17, 2015 and May 5, 2015. Moyers also mentioned that part of LBJ's hesitation toward FOIA may have come from pressure from J. Edgar Hoover. LBJ had needed Hoover's continued support over civil rights, and Hoover adamantly opposed FOIA, and according to Moyers, Hoover hated Moss, due to Moss's persistence in making public police records from the South. So one aspect of LBJ's reluctance was based on attempting to keep Hoover appeased.

[57] Statement by the President upon signing S.1160, July 4, 1966: Reports on Enrolled Legislation, P.L. 89-465 to P.L. 89-491, 6/22/66 to 7/4/66, folder: P.L. 89-487 S.1160, Box 36, LBJ Presidential Library.

policy as a check on presidential power. Over a dozen years, Moss had proved himself a successful power entrepreneur who utilized his position and institutional power by learning and responding to executive actions and the politics of the moment. However, even with the passage of FOIA, it was clear in Johnson's signing statement that he believed the president still maintained the authority to deny any information to Congress or the public, provided doing so was in the public interest.

Per the agreement made by Moss and Johnson, FOIA would be implemented one year later, on 4 July 1967, in order to give the administration enough time to build the bureaucratic infrastructure to manage the new process of requests, appeals, and potential legal action. Implementation was guided by the final committee report, developed in conjunction with the Justice Department, which detailed how agencies should handle the procedures and processes created by the new law. However, there were shortfalls in the language of the law, which continue to prove problematic to the present day. One major fault of FOIA was that the legislation did not establish a uniform procedure for all agencies to follow regarding requests, appeals, and lawsuits. The lack of a clear and consistent process allowed each agency and department to create its own unique procedures and processes, resulting in a very uneven practice subject to variation and driven by internal bureaucratic politics. Included with this issue, the agreement created nine exemptions that can be applied to any FOIA request that will serve as grounds for denial of that request. The ambiguous language of these exemptions, and the flexibility each agency now held over the procedures, gave department lawyers and managers the ability to continue to control information, following previous institutionalized secrecy policies out of continued concerns within the Cold War Paradigm. While Congress, and especially Moss, would provide continued oversight on implementation, shortfalls within the language of the law coupled with ongoing assertions of executive power served to keep FOIA restrained and public information private. As we will see in the next chapter, Nixon's resurgence in use of executive privilege demonstrated that presidential power remained dominant when it came to control over information, with FOIA only having minimal impact during these early implementation years.

Conclusion

The Johnson administration saw the end of the legislative development of FOIA with the passage of the bill. This marks a transition point within the CLDC from development to implementation, evaluation, oversight, and amendment. While the bill passed, the issue by no means went away, nor did concerns for public access to government information. As we will see in the following chapter, the issue of executive privilege came back with a vengeance under Nixon, even though it rarely concerned LBJ. On executive privilege specifically, LBJ helped set a precedent by agreeing to uphold the same position Kennedy had, and doing so provided Moss with a tool with which to attempt to constrain presidential power for future administrations. However, at this point, inter-branch power had swung further to the president on executive privilege. Once Eisenhower established the position of inherent constitutional power, it became more difficult for Congress to push back against these claims, which continued and will continue to influence inter-branch interactions showing how the Cold War Paradigm persisted. Moss had learned that with Johnson it was best to take a direct approach, asking Johnson to reaffirm Kennedy's position, as it would at least put the president on record. The president learned that even committing to such a position did not prevent or remove the ability to invoke executive privilege when needed, as Congress held very little recourse in those instances.

The politics of the moment was favorable to both Moss and Johnson, as unified Democratic control of government opened the opportunity for Congress to work with the administration on the issue, regardless of Johnson's objections. The Johnson administration provided Moss with the opportunity to develop allies in Congress and the White House in a moment that allowed him to leverage his institutional power to get the bill passed. While the administration opposed the bill from the beginning, due to Johnson's need to maintain a favorable coalition with congressional Democrats, Moss was able to press forward with FOIA by seeking private channels to bargain with administration officials. Even though his subcommittee and their Senate counterparts continued with hearings and investigations, it became clear from this chapter how engaged in bargaining Moss and administration officials were behind the scenes. Neither were interested in allowing party infighting over FOIA to tarnish the Great Society agenda, and with constant Republican attacks, the politics of the moment provided them with the space to work together. Moss was assisted by unlikely allies like Donald Rumsfeld, who had learned how politically viable the issue was as an attack point for congressional Republicans to use against Johnson. Additionally, as Bill Moyers learned about the legislation through the Moss Subcommittee, he determined that the DOJ and agency objections were largely overblown, giving him the ability to try to convince agency officials and Johnson that it would be in their interest to work with Moss to influence the legislation. Moyers gave Moss a White House ally to help bolster negotiations, which proved successful in the end. Once Moyers and administration officials realized FOIA was moving forward, they scrambled to make a deal on the final bill, as a veto would not be politically viable for Johnson at that time. Moss was able to capitalize on the moment after years of building expertise on the issue and winning over allies like Celler, which ultimately paid off.

Johnson proved to be a pragmatic policy negotiator, willing to work with Congress and unafraid to voice his positions to try to influence policy. FOIA was not on his agenda, but Congress was able to place it firmly in front of him regardless of what he wanted. Faced with a Congress controlled by his own party, Johnson was in a much better position to negotiate and work with Congress than Eisenhower had been, and he utilized a private strategy to keep the intra-party fighting from becoming public fodder. The politics of the moment thrust Moss and LBJ together on the issue, demanding they work together on getting bills passed, as they needed each other to meet their own political and policy goals. In the end, the deal that was made was satisfactory to all. Within the Cold War Paradigm, Johnson issued a statement that made clear the president still maintained control over information, regardless of FOIA. As we will see in the next chapter, Nixon faced a much different situation with an opposition Congress under divided government. Unlike Johnson, Nixon was far less willing to engage in the policymaking process with a Democratic Congress. He opted instead to follow the lead of Eisenhower, whom he had served under as vice president for eight years. The CLDC moves into the next iteration, where the policy is implemented and Nixon brings about a resurgence of executive privilege.

6

Nixon and the resurgence of executive privilege

I know that most people think that executive privilege was just a cloak that I drew around me to protect myself from the disclosure of my wrongdoing. But the fact that I wanted to protect myself did not alter the fact that I believed deeply and strongly in the principle and was convinced then—as I am now—that it stands at the very heart of a strong presidency. Even though the application of the principle to this case was flawed by the nature and extent of my personal interest and involvement, I did not want to be the first President in history who acquiesced in a diminution of the principle.

—Richard M. Nixon, *RN: The Memoirs of Richard M. Nixon*, 1978

Unlike his predecessor, Nixon faced an opposition Congress under divided government. However, it was not just partisan politics that would influence Nixon's behavior and his relations with Congress. The altered political landscape of the Vietnam War, civil unrest at home, and the ever-present threat of the Cold War continued as the dominant mindset within the executive branch. What Nixon brought to the White House that set him apart within the Cold War Paradigm was his previous government experience. As a member of Congress, Nixon served on HUAC, where he pursued a fervent anti-communist agenda with McCarthyesque enthusiasm, helping to institutionalize the Cold War Paradigm and driving Congress to overreach on anti-communist policies, leading to Truman's rejection. Truman's veto of the Internal Security Act of 1950 helped create a rift between branches that led Truman to become more cautious over information flows to Congress. But it was not just Nixon's congressional experience that would influence his policies and positions on secrecy and executive privilege as president; it was also his White House experience as Eisenhower's vice president.

The chapter on Eisenhower details the strong positions taken on public records and control of information by the administration, including the first full-throated constitutional defense of executive privilege in its contemporary form. By serving under Eisenhower, Nixon's perceptions of the need for a strong president, in particular when it came to Cold War politics with Congress, were reaffirmed and fortified by Eisenhower's position and policies. As we will see, Nixon positioned himself and justified his actions based on the precedent set by previous presidents, in particular Eisenhower and Truman. The mindset and positioning taken by Nixon during his formative political years would now provide guidance to his presidency.

Nixon also became the first president to take office with FOIA being fully implemented. Within the CLDC, we have moved from development to implementation and oversight, which creates an altered set of politics. Now that FOIA had become institutionalized within the executive branch, Congress had jurisdiction and oversight capabilities in a manner they lacked before. The Moss Subcommittee continued its work, but now shared responsibility across Congress as different committees within the House and Senate held jurisdiction on FOIA processes and oversight across all executive agencies and departments. The move from development to oversight established a new inter-branch power dimension that would influence the action-reaction learning process between Congress and the president. As Nixon began to reassert authority under executive privilege and control information to Congress, Congress could respond through increased oversight capabilities, as well as through the amendment process to strengthen FOIA as a response to presidential actions. The cycle moved forward as Nixon brought about a resurgence in executive authority and control, regardless of FOIA or congressional assertions. However, the law being in place now provided Congress with new tools for targeting Nixon's policies as a means of checking executive power. The previous chapters provided insight into the legislative development of FOIA, but the CLDC continues by providing insight into the politics of public information as tied to the unilateral power of executive privilege.

The Johnson administration had taken less unilateral action

on executive privilege than his predecessors, perhaps due to his being far more politically engaged with Congress in the legislative process, incentivized by having a Democratic-controlled Congress willing to work with him. Where LBJ relished the politics with Congress, his successor had a much different perspective. Nixon came into office pushing an agenda of reform and claimed a desire to work with Congress, but quickly revived the Eisenhower approach of total shutdown when it came to providing information to Congress. Ten days into his presidency, Nixon sent a special message to Congress requesting authority to reorganize the executive branch, as "New times call for new ideas and fresh approaches."[1] A memo just a few weeks later from Nixon's assistant H. R. Haldeman to the White House staff notified all offices of the need to establish "internal procedures to assure that classified and sensitive documents and related materials are protected at all times."[2] Beyond the desire to reorganize and establish security procedures, Haldeman's memo noted how White House Police would carry out security inspections of each staff office on a nightly basis. Nixon was making it clear from the beginning that control over information was vital and would be heavily monitored.

Nixon was not just a reflection of Eisenhower, but moved far beyond him as part of the inevitable outgrowth of presidential politics of public records and information control. While Nixon attempted to assure cooperation with the Democratic Congress, he immediately began to institute policies grounded in the Cold War Paradigm of executive authority to ensure strict control over information and personnel within the executive branch. His utilization of White House Police to monitor and inspect staff made Truman's loyalty oaths seem quaint by comparison, but nonetheless had the desired impact of promoting security and

---

[1] Richard Nixon: "Special Message to the Congress Requesting New Authority To Reorganize the Executive Branch," January 30, 1969. Available online at *The American Presidency Project*, <https://www.presidency.ucsb.edu/docu ments/special-message-the-congress-requesting-new-authority-reorganize-the-executive-branch> (last accessed November 10, 2018).

[2] Memorandum for the White House Staff from H. R. Haldeman, February 24, 1969. Folder: National Security—Defense (ND), Box 98, Richard M. Nixon Presidential Library.

recentralizing control through the Oval Office. Nixon sought complete control over information, and was not intimidated by Congress. He relied on the past precedent of constitutional authority to support his position, countering congressional claims of overreach. The politics within the country had shifted under Johnson's presidency through civil rights and the Great Society programs, which led to party reforms that Nixon utilized through his "silent majority" to push back on Congress. Less concerned over social reform than Johnson had been, Nixon was focused on institutional reform of the presidency, central to which was a reestablishment of authority that relied on control of information. On the issue of executive privilege, Nixon demarcates several junctures within the CLDC, including his resurgent use of executive authority, and in the congressional and judicial response, the latter of which changed the use of executive privilege for all future administrations.

Nixon, Moss, and the renewed politics of executive privilege

As a shrewd politician in observing the development of FOIA and how the Democratic Congress engaged with Kennedy and Johnson on executive privilege, Nixon knew exactly what was coming and was able to prepare. While Moss reached out to the administration early on, Nixon never directly engaged Moss or the executive privilege issue until he was ready to do so. Two months into his presidency, in March 1969, Nixon sent a signed memo to all executive departments and agencies detailing procedures to govern compliance with congressional demands for information. It was focused specifically upon the appropriate use of executive privilege.[3] Nixon asserted:

> The policy of this Administration is to comply to the fullest extent possible with Congressional requests for information. While the

[3] Memorandum for the Heads of Executive Departments and Agencies from President Nixon, March 24, 1969. Folder: Executive Privilege—Congressional Invocation #3—L. H. Fountain, Folder 8. WHCF Box 13, Richard M. Nixon Presidential Library.

Executive branch has the responsibility of withholding certain information the disclosure of which would be incompatible with the public interest, this Administration will invoke this authority only in the most compelling circumstances and after a rigorous inquiry into the actual need for its exercise. For those reasons Executive privilege will not be used without specific Presidential approval.

The memo provided Nixon with a footing on executive privilege use, grounding his position as inherent authority to withhold information in the public interest, just as his predecessors had done. Nixon's learned response was that national security concerns demanded control over information, which was not just situational to his presidency, but also demonstrated what he had learned as Eisenhower's vice president, and supported the Cold War Paradigm mindset. Throughout his administration, Nixon continued to utilize past precedent to justify executive privilege claims, generally invoking executive orders, memos, and directives from Eisenhower. In the weeks prior to the memo, an ongoing discussion between Attorney General John Mitchell, John Ehrlichman, and Nixon delved deeply into previous uses of executive privilege, with an emphasis on Eisenhower. The conversation demonstrated how Eisenhower's claims of an inherent constitutional right of executive privilege had become institutionalized and then impacted future political debates and policies. While the memos signed by Kennedy and LBJ were discussed, the conclusions reached were to provide flexibility for Nixon to claim privilege as needed once departments had cleared all congressional informational requests with the Attorney General and the Office of Legal Counsel.[4]

These actions taken in the early months of the Nixon administration were influenced by Congress. Eight days into the Nixon presidency, Moss sent a letter detailing concerns over claims of executive privilege to withhold information by "those of us who support the principle that the survival of a representative government depends on an electorate and a Congress that are well

[4] Memorandum for the President, from John Mitchell to Richard Nixon, March 17, 1969. Folder: [EX] FE 4-1 Presidential Powers [1969–70], WHCF Box 6, Richard M. Nixon Presidential Library.

144

informed."[5] Moss discussed how past administrations had justified such claims, and how Kennedy and Johnson had pledged to
limit the use of executive privilege. He ended the letter by stating,
"In view of the urgent need to safeguard and maintain a free
flow of information to the Congress, I hope you will favorably
consider a reaffirmation of the policy which provides, in essence,
that the claim of 'executive privilege' will be invoked only by the
president."[6] Nixon sent Moss his response in April 1969, using
his March memo as evidence to Moss and Congress of how
his administration would limit executive privilege.[7] In the April
letter Nixon asserted that, like his predecessors, he believed the
scope of executive privilege must be "narrowly construed" and
exercised with discretion. He continued by stating,

> I want to take this opportunity to assure you and your committee that
> this Administration is dedicated to insuring a free flow of information
> to the Congress and the news media-and, thus, to the citizens. . . . I
> want open government to be a reality in every way possible. This
> Administration has already given a positive emphasis to freedom
> of information. I am committed to insuring that both the letter and
> spirit of the Public Records Law will be implemented throughout the
> Executive Branch of the government.

In reaffirming the position of Kennedy and Johnson, Nixon took a
public stance with Congress in limiting executive privilege claims
and ensuring implementation of FOIA to keep an open flow of
information from the White House to Congress. The position
gave Nixon some latitude with Moss in the short term, as Moss
sent Nixon a letter thanking him for supporting the principle of
freedom of information. Moss continued by saying, "Your spirit
of cooperation and attention to this important issue of mutual
concern is most welcome and helpful."[8]

---

[5] Letter to Richard M. Nixon from John E. Moss, January 28, 1969. Folder:
[EX] FE 4-1 Presidential Powers [1969–70], WHCF Box 6, Richard M.
Nixon Presidential Library.

[6] Ibid.

[7] Letter to John E. Moss from Richard M. Nixon, April 7, 1969. Folder: [EX]
FE 4-1 Presidential Powers [1969–70], WHCF Box 6, Richard M. Nixon
Presidential Library.

[8] Letter to Richard Nixon from John Moss, April 25, 1969. Folder: [EX]

The issue was taken seriously by administration officials. The following month, Ehrlichman sent a memo to numerous advisors and counsels in the White House detailing how to use executive privilege when handling formal congressional requests for testimony. In the memo, Ehrlichman stated that executive privilege should only be an issue when it came to official hearings before committees where records would be made, noting less of a concern for off-the-record or informal briefings.[9] The focus on formal committee hearings demonstrated the political concerns within the administration over allowing officials to testify before Congress on the record, or potentially under oath; however, Ehrlichman noted that executive privilege should not be regularly invoked. He stated,

> We feel, however, that Executive privilege should only be used as a last resort. Congressional invasion of the President's official staff family is often more a matter of impropriety and poor form than of breaching separation of powers doctrine.

The direction given by Ehrlichman was for staff to work through Bryce Harlow, counselor to Nixon, on any congressional requests or questions. Ehrlichman was optimistic in the early days of Nixon's tenure that the administration and Congress could work together on staff testimony, and would be able to come to an agreement; although Ehrlichman's position confirmed that the administration was getting prepared to deal with the inevitable breakdown of inter-branch politics. When faced with requests and demands for information from Congress, the administration's position of cooperation would wilt. For all the public rhetoric about open access, discretion, and limited use, the Nixon administration quickly began to use executive privilege in more creative ways to counter congressional inquiries.

By the spring of 1970, Representative L. H. Fountain, Chair,

FE 4-1 Presidential Powers [1969–70], WHCF Box 6, Richard M. Nixon Presidential Library.

[9] Memo titled, "Congressional Committee Requests for Testimony from White House Staff," from John Ehrlichman, May 22, 1969. Folder: [EX] FE 4-1 Presidential Powers [1969–70], WHCF Box 6, Richard M. Nixon Presidential Library.

House Intergovernmental Relations Subcommittee, was conducting an investigation focused on evaluations of scientists to serve on advisory boards for the Department of Health, Education, and Welfare (HEW). Fountain requested investigative reports prepared by the FBI that had been provided to HEW in this matter. Attorney General Mitchell responded to Fountain claiming executive privilege with Nixon's authority in denying the FBI reports to Congress. In his letter, Mitchell cited an opinion from Attorney General Jackson from April 30, 1941, claiming that investigative reports from the FBI are confidential in nature and that "congressional or public access to them would not be in the public interest."[10] The conversation inside the administration focused on justifying executive privilege and handling the congressional response. A memo from Egil "Bud" Krogh to Ehrlichman discussing the situation included a lengthy opinion from Assistant Attorney General in the Office of Legal Counsel (OLC) William Rehnquist, providing justification for, and strongly recommending, the invocation of executive privilege in this matter as grounded in past precedent.[11] Krogh and Ehrlichman discussed that any information provided to a congressional committee would ultimately result in public disclosure, thereby making executive privilege necessary. Krogh stated, "The Attorney General and Rehnquist both feel that this is a necessary precedent to set now, and they see no real public relations problem."[12] Fountain and his subcommittee pushed back, requesting that Nixon reconsider his position. This back and forth continued into the fall, when Ehrlichman responded to Fountain, reaffirming the president's original position. In his letter, Ehrlichman states,

---

[10] Letter to L. H. Fountain from John Mitchell, June 29, 1970. Folder: Executive Privilege—Congressional Invocation #1—L. H. Fountain, Folder 7. WHCF Box 13, Richard M. Nixon Presidential Library.

[11] Memorandum for the Honorable Egil Krogh, June 18, 1970. Folder: Executive Privilege—Congressional Invocation #1—L. H. Fountain, Folder 7. WHCF Box 13, Richard M. Nixon Presidential Library.

[12] Memorandum for John Ehrlichman from Bud Krogh, June 23, 1970. Folder: Executive Privilege—Congressional Invocation #1—L. H. Fountain, Folder 7. WHCF Box 13, Richard M. Nixon Presidential Library.

To our knowledge, no president has ever authorized the release of such reports except in connection with proceedings involving the confirmation or the impeachment of officers of the United States. . . . Since neither of those categories is applicable here, the President has decided to adhere to his earlier decision approving the invocation of privilege in this case.[13]

The exchange demonstrated the power held by the president in using executive privilege, and how past precedent gave cover for Nixon to not only invoke privilege, but to expand its use based on new interpretations. Congress was left powerless to respond as FOIA, or any other oversight measure, would not overcome the claim, leaving members in the position of needing to learn new strategies.

Very quickly and publicly the Nixon administration began to spin out of control on executive privilege. First, growing tensions between Congress and the administration over continued refusal to provide information, access, or testimony from officials, especially on war issues, began to mount. Back in May 1969, Senator Fulbright (D-AR) requested that the DOD provide access to the "Five Year Plan for the Military Assistance Program," which would later become part of the document known as the Pentagon Papers.[14] In his request, Fulbright specifically wanted National Security Advisor Henry Kissinger to testify before Congress on this matter. Defense Secretary Melvin Laird responded a month later that the Plan was a staff planning document and therefore would not be made available, as it was protected by executive privilege. Into the next year, Fulbright continued to press the administration, writing to Laird demanding access as required under the Legislative Reorganization Act of 1970 so that Congress could determine long-term cost estimates for military aid. By spring 1971, after continued delays and inaction from Laird, Fulbright

---

[13] Letter to L. H. Fountain from John Ehrlichman, November 21, 1970. Folder: [EX] FE 4-1 Presidential Powers [1969–1970]. WHCF FE Box 6, Richard M. Nixon Presidential Library.

[14] Memo to Henry Kissinger from John Dean, August 20, 1971. Folder: [EX] FE 4-1 Presidential Powers, Succession and Term of Office 1/1/71 [12/31/72, 1 of 2], WHCF Box 6, Richard M. Nixon Presidential Library.

delivered an ultimatum—that the requested documents be made available, or the president specifically invoke executive privilege as authority for withholding the information—otherwise, Congress would suspend all funding for military aid. Internal deliberations within the administration demonstrated concern over the ability of Congress to compel White House staff to testify. While Rehnquist's opinion and continued legal memos gave cover to use executive privilege, John Dean and others determined to use it only on a case-by-case basis.[15]

Faced with continued stubbornness from the administration, Congress decided a public investigative approach could work to check the president. Inquiries from the Senate Subcommittee on Separation of Powers, chaired by Senator Sam Ervin (D-NC), grew in fervency as Congress began to target the legal foundations of Nixon's assertions on executive privilege as an attempt to challenge claims of inherent constitutional authority. Early in March 1971, Fulbright introduced legislation to amend FOIA to include language that would force executive branch employees to appear before Congress, even if they planned to invoke executive privilege.[16] Dean noted how Fulbright's actions were "conveniently timed to coincide with Senator Ervin's inquiry into the entire questions of Executive Privilege," and that the hearings on Fulbright's bill would "require the President to personally and formally invoke any exercise of Executive Privilege."[17] The congressional strategy now directly targeted the constitutional justifications of executive privilege, as past precedent had relied on Congress accepting the legal arguments as valid. The problem now was the mounting political ramifications Congress faced from continued White House intransigence. Administration officials began to seek help to overcome congressional attacks.

---

[15] Memo for Clark MacGregor and Bill Timmons from John Dean, February 10, 1971. Folder: Executive Privilege—Congressional, Folder 5. WCHF Box 14, Richard M. Nixon Presidential Library.

[16] The bill, S.1125, was introduced by Senators Fulbright and Cranston on February 17, 1971.

[17] Memo to Henry Kissinger from John Dean, August 20, 1971. Folder: [EX] FE 4-1 Presidential Powers, Succession and Term of Office 1/1/71 [12/31/72, 1 of 2], WHCF Box 6, Richard M. Nixon Presidential Library.

Charles Colson and John Dean sought assistance from constitutional scholars and the American Enterprise Institute (AEI) to produce studies that would support the administration's position.[18] Dean prepared to defend the president's position on the issue, focusing staff resources to respond quickly to Congress. In a memo to Fielding, Dean stated that he was certain Congress was hoping to "stick it to us" on the executive privilege issue, but believed they could withstand such attacks and bolster their position with AEI's help.[19] The White House strategized on how to veto bargain against the Fulbright bill, and refused to work with Fulbright or any of the committee members to offer language that would make it palatable to the administration. Dean commented, "It is my strong feeling that at this juncture we should offer no suggestions for the improvement of the proposed bill or in any way indicate the Administration acquiescence in it."[20] While the bill would make it through committee, the administration knew it lacked the votes to pass the Senate and would ultimately die in Congress; however, this was only the first attempt to amend FOIA.

At the same time, pressure from multiple committees in the House, centered on spending in Southeast Asia through the US Agency for International Development (USAID), had Nixon making continued claims of executive privilege to Congress.[21] In response to numerous requests for information and testimony,

[18] Memo for John Dean from Charles Colson, June 1, 1971. Folder: Executive Privilege—AID/September 1973, Folder 1. WHCF Box 13, Richard M. Nixon Presidential Library.

[19] Memo for Fred Fielding from John Dean, July 22, 1971. Folder: Executive Privilege—AID/September 1973, Folder 1. WHCF Box 13, Richard M. Nixon Presidential Library.

  In digging through the archives, it would appear that AEI never actually produced a report to constitutionally justify executive privilege by request of the White House at this time.

[20] Memo to Wilfred Rommel from John Dean, November 19, 1971. Folder: Executive Privilege—Congressional Folder 5, Staff Member Office Files, Buzhardt, Box 14, Richard M. Nixon Presidential Library.

[21] Memo for Alexander Haig et al. from Leonard Garment, September 4, 1973. Folder: Executive Privilege—AID/September 1973, Folder 1. WHCF Box 13, Richard M. Nixon Presidential Library.

Nixon issued a directive to the Secretaries of State and Defense detailing his position on executive privilege for congressional inquiries on anything related to "military assistance."[22] In the memo, Nixon states,

> The precedents on separation of powers established by my predecessors from the first to last clearly demonstrate, however, that the President has the responsibility not to make available any information and material which would impair the orderly function of the Executive Branch of the Government, since to do so would not be in the public interest. As indicated in my memorandum of March 24, 1969, this Administration will invoke Executive Privilege to withhold information only in the most compelling circumstances and only after a rigorous inquiry into the actual need for its exercise. I have accordingly conducted such an inquiry with regard to the Congressional requests brought to my attention in this instance.

Nixon asserted that providing Congress with any information on military assistance programs would not be in the public interest, and he directed the Secretaries of State and Defense not to disclose any related documents to Congress under executive privilege.

By this time, and facing ever increasing pressure from Congress on a host of issues, Nixon had learned that executive privilege was the only option he had to completely shut down Congress, and he began to use it more frequently. The 1971 directive demonstrates how the use evolved with Nixon: he not only grounds his claims in past precedent, but also states that information that would impair the functions of the executive branch is not in the public interest and is therefore subject to executive privilege authority. The evolving issue also included new interpretations to provide cover to the White House as well. Rehnquist testified before Ervin's subcommittee, vigorously defending the president's authority to withhold information from Congress. The administration now began to redefine the term "agency," arguing that certain agencies and their staff did not fit the congressional definition and would therefore be exempt from FOIA and protected

---

[22] Memo for the Secretary of State and Secretary of Defense from Richard Nixon, August 30, 1971. Folder: Executive Privilege—AID/September 1973, Folder 1. WHCF Box 13, Richard M. Nixon Presidential Library.

under executive privilege claims.[23] The argument of ambiguous legal language and broad assertions of what constituted the public interest would allow Nixon to increase the frequency and scope of executive privilege. In responding to a request for Vice President Agnew to appear before the Senate, Nixon would tell Agnew, "I feel very strongly that as Vice President you should never appear before a Committee of Congress."[24] A related political outcome from Nixon's strategy was that his constant reinterpretation of executive power created a stonewalling effect with Congress. Politically, then, every time Congress would request information, Nixon would deny based on his interpretation, which continued to evolve and continued to keep Congress from information that could be used against the administration. This strategy, however, would only be successful for a short period of time.

One other important factor playing into the political and power struggles between Congress and the administration, one that held Fulbright's attention, was the Pentagon Papers and the subsequent lawsuit from the *New York Times* and *Washington Post*, resulting in *New York Times Co. v. United States*. The relevant part of the Pentagon Papers case was not the legal decision by the Supreme Court, which found that the government had failed to provide adequate justification for national security to overcome the First Amendment rights of press freedom, but rather the political ramifications of the public spectacle of what the papers revealed coupled with the fight the administration made in asserting authority to prevent the publication. Nixon deployed the same justifications and arguments he used in claiming executive privilege: that "[a]dvisors must be able to rely on the confidentiality of their advice for a free flow of ideas," in the White House.[25]

---

[23] Memo to Eugene Cowen from Wallace Johnson, November 9, 1971. Folder: [EX] FE 4-1 Presidential Powers, Succession and Term of Office 1/1/71 [12/31/72, 2 of 2], WHCF Box 6, Richard M. Nixon Presidential Library.

[24] Memo to Spiro Agnew from Richard Nixon, November 9, 1971. Folder: [EX] FE 4-1 Presidential Powers, Succession and Term of Office 1/1/71 [12/31/72, 1 of 2], WHCF Box 6, Richard M. Nixon Presidential Library.

[25] Memo to Richard Nixon from John Ehrlichman, June 17, 1971. Folder: EX ND 13-3 Classified Information, National Security—Defense (ND) Box 98, the Richard M. Nixon Library.

The assertions of authority to block publication of the Pentagon Papers was grounded in the same arguments he and his predecessors used to deny information to Congress, except in this case the Courts ruled that such authority, which exists in part, was not proven to overcome the First Amendment arguments made by the newspapers. While not a direct legal check on executive privilege, the court decision chipped at the foundational claims for which the White House continued to operate, with some of those claims going back to Eisenhower. The other major political impact the Pentagon Papers case had on congressional-presidential relations was to weaken public trust in the administration. The public legal battle ending with Nixon losing in the Supreme Court served to provide Congress with a boost in public support to target secrecy issues with the president.

Revisions, recreations, and resurgence of privilege while amending FOIA

Early in 1972, Nixon responded to the Court decision in the Pentagon Papers case and the ongoing demands from Congress by issuing Executive Order 11652, "Classification and Declassification of National Security Information and Material."[26] This lengthy order would amend previous orders, such as Eisenhower's EO 10501 and Kennedy's EO 10964, to reestablish authority for classification and denial within the departments and agencies. Nixon was reasserting power that had decreased under Kennedy and Johnson, but moving even further than Eisenhower when it came to information control. Over the previous few months, the administration had been working on ways to overcome and address the fallout from the Pentagon Papers case in a manner that would allow Nixon the

---

[26] Richard Nixon: "Executive Order 11652—Classification and Declassification of National Security Information and Material," March 8, 1972. Available online at *The American Presidency Project*, <https://www.presidency.ucsb.edu/documents/executive-order-11652-classification-and-declassification-national-security-information > (last accessed November 10, 2018).

ability to reassert executive authority.[27] The decision to pursue a new Executive Order on the classification issue was targeted to gain positive public relations. The administration hoped the new order would counter credibility attacks and change the narrative to show Nixon as a champion who eliminated abuses of government secrecy. Just days after Nixon issued EO 11652, a memo to Ehrlichman from Young established a game plan to reinvent Nixon as credible on overcoming secrecy, an issue that was vital to the upcoming election. In the memo, Young stated, "if we can identify the President in the eyes of the electorate as the man that eliminated the abuses of government secrecy—thereby clearly indicating that he has nothing to fear from having his record made public as soon as it is possible—then we can picture him as a man to be trusted and believed."[28] Young's opinion was that the new order provided for the public release of administration information within six, eight, or ten years after Nixon left office, which created credibility and would influence Nixon's actions knowing how soon his decisions would be open to public scrutiny. Young stated,

> The point is simply that this President, unlike any other President in the past, has personally stripped himself of the protection which secrecy can provide for hiding his mistakes in the future. Why? Because he has nothing to hide and he is confident that in 6, 8, or 10 years the record will show he had nothing to hide. By knowing that the public will have access in a relatively short period to such information as he alone now has access to, the President completely undercuts the criticism that he can't be trusted now.

After describing a ten-point plan to achieve credibility and reelection, Young ends his memo by asserting,

> The common thread in the above moves is to constantly identify the President with the flow of information from government to the

---

[27] Memo to John Ehrlichman from David Young, January 18, 1972. Folder: Classification/Declassification and Unauthorized Disclosure Legislation. WHCF David R. Young, Box 3, Richard M. Nixon Presidential Library.

[28] Memo to John Ehrlichman from David Young, March 10, 1972. Folder: Credibility and the Election. WHCF David R. Young, Box 3, Richard M. Nixon Presidential Library.

people. And, as a man that is not afraid to have his record public, he can be trusted.

While Young was energetic in conveying the possibilities of his proposal, others within the administration, like Dean, Ehrlichman, and Edward Morgan, seemed less enthusiastic. Morgan acknowledged the premise and importance of building Nixon's credibility for his reelection, but though Young's plan was "much ado about nothing" when it came to campaign impact.[29] He felt Young's plan should be implemented, but would have a more historical than immediate impact; yet the decision to remake the president's image as an anti-secrecy champion would be positive for the campaign. At the same time, the administration noted its strained relations with Congress and sought to take an aggressive approach to conducting personal outreach to members, in particular Republican members, to help push Nixon's agenda forward.[30] Politically, the new executive order provided an additional layer of justification that the administration began to use in continued denial of information to Congress. Demonstrating a learned response to the public outcry over the Pentagon Papers and an onslaught of requests from Congress that challenged foundational assertions of executive authority, Nixon's EO reestablished justification to help position the White House to counter requests. Additionally, Nixon offered a learned response by seeking to sway public opinion through rebranding efforts as a means not just of reelection, but to help move his agenda forward in Congress.

Responding to these actions from Nixon, the House Subcommittee on Foreign Operations and Government Information (FOGI), formerly the Moss Subcommittee, continued to apply pressure.[31] Congress began considering multiple

---

[29] Memo to John Ehrlichman from Edward Morgan, April 11, 1972. Folder: Credibility and the Election. WHCF David R. Young, Box 3, Richard M. Nixon Presidential Library.

[30] Memo for Richard Nixon from William Timmons, January 21, 1972. Folder: EX LE Legislation. (LE) Legislation, Box 5, Richard M. Nixon Presidential Library.

[31] The House Special Committee on Government Information became a

approaches to targeting the new EO and identified problems with FOIA implementation. An exchange between Dean and press official Margita White highlighted the concerns building within the administration. White discussed having lunch with Archibald, who informed her that Rep. William Moorhead (D-PA) had planned to introduce a declassification bill that targeted Nixon's order and changed parts which Congress found disagreeable.[32] White also discussed that the subcommittee was continuing with hearings and oversight on problems arising from FOIA, including the subcommittee feeling that decisions to withhold information under the exemptions were coming from bureaucrats "at too low a level . . . who are not trained to handle FOI requests."[33] White noted Archibald's complaints that the administration had not done enough to centralize control over FOIA implementation, and that potential legislation to amend might be forthcoming. Another issue White raised with Dean was that the subcommittee planned to continue hearings on executive privilege; White asked that she be kept in the loop on those decisions, as she often had to justify such uses to the press. With the Watergate scandal appearing on the horizon, Congress continued to push back on Nixon through investigations, hearings, and legislation coming from both the House and Senate, which served to increase pressure on the administration throughout the rest of Nixon's tenure. Nixon's hopes of having a positive working relationship with Congress before the election quickly became dashed.

The heated politics of the 1972 campaign kept the administration in a tenuous position with Congress. The fallout of the I.T.T. scandal, surrounding the company pledging money to the Republican Convention and Nixon's intervention in an antitrust suit against the company through the Justice Department,

permanent subcommittee under the House Government Operations Committee in 1964 with Moss as Chair. However, the name and scope was changed to Foreign Operations and Government Information. By this time, Rep. William Moorhead (D-PA) had taken over as Chair, although Moss remained on the subcommittee and active.

[32] Memo to John Dean from Margita White, April 19, 1972. Folder: FOIA #2. WHCF: Buzhardt, Box 15, Richard M. Nixon Presidential Library.

[33] Ibid.

raised concerns within Congress, leading to investigations and hearings.[34] Senator Ervin requested that White House aide Peter Flanigan testify before his subcommittee on the issue, to which Dean responded with a refusal, invoking executive privilege. In his response to Ervin, Dean stated,

> Under the doctrine of separation of powers and long established historical precedents the principle that members of the President's immediate staff not appear and testify before Congressional committees with respect to the performance of their duties is firmly established.[35]

While this response had become routine for Dean, Ervin was not pleased and began to push strongly against the arguments being made as justification. Ervin's frustration was palpable in his response to Nixon. In a letter to the president, Ervin asked for clarification to Dean's reference of "long established historical precedents" that were used as justification. He asked Nixon to provide him with every specific instance in which, "White House staff was requested or subpoenaed to testify before a congressional committee and declined to appear by formally claiming 'executive privilege,' or as in the instant example, informally asserting the privilege."[36] Ervin was by no means done. He continued,

> In addition, please include information on all instances when a White House employee has testified before a congressional committee, regardless of the capacity in which he may have appeared. I realize that individual members of the White House staff sometimes function in different capacities, therefore, in each example cited, it would be most helpful if you would specify the capacity in which the individual appeared, as well as identifying the committee he appeared before,

---

[34] For an overview of the I.T.T. scandal, see Ciara Torres-Spelliscy, "The I.T.T. Affair and Why Public Financing Matters for Political Conventions," March 19, 2014, from The Brennen Center for Justice, available at https://www.brennancenter.org/blog/itt-affair-why-public-financing-matters-political-conventions (last accessed November 10, 2018).

[35] Letter to Richard Nixon from Sam Ervin, April 21, 1972. Folder: Executive Privilege—Congressional Folder 5. WHCF: Buzhardt, Box 14, Richard M. Nixon Presidential Library.

[36] Ibid.

the date, and the subject of his testimony. I would appreciate your giving me this information for all the instances from the administration of Franklin Roosevelt to the present.

Evident through the exchange, Ervin exemplified where Congress was on the issue of executive privilege and government secrecy with Nixon. Ervin was trying to get the administration on the record to specifically justify their claims of past precedent, placing a check on executive power while giving Congress insight into potential avenues of policy to overcome such claims. Ervin and Congress had learned to no longer accept assertions of past precedent from the White House. In trying to force clarification from the White House, Congress sought to shift the politics in their favor, while attempting to create space to counter the constitutional claims that underpinned executive privilege.

Dean notified Clark MacGregor, White House congressional liaison, about the Ervin letter, noting that he was waiting for the controversy with I.T.T. to cool down or Ervin to make additional inquiries before responding.[37] However, by late June they decided it was time to respond, sending Ervin a four-page letter that included three examples where White House staff had declined to testify under presidential instructions, and three examples where staff did testify. Dean stated in his letter,

> As I am certain you realize, the White House maintains no records in this regard as to past administrations. The Department of Justice, however, through its records and other research, has knowledge of six incidents involving Presidential Assistants which occurred prior to Mr. Flanigan's recent testimony. In additional to those six, I understand that there have been numerous occasions in past administrations as well as this Administration when Presidential Assistants have declined congressional invitations to appear and testify on an informal basis.[38]

---

[37] Memo to Clark MacGregor from John Dean, June 28, 1972. Folder: Executive Privilege—Congressional Folder 5. WHCF: Buzhardt, Box 14, Richard M. Nixon Presidential Library.

[38] Letter to Sam Ervin from John Dean. Folder: Executive Privilege—Congressional Folder 5. WHCF: Buzhardt, Box 14, Richard M. Nixon Presidential Library.

The exchange demonstrated the growing frustration of Congress as they sought to overcome continued denials, while scandals, controversies, and electoral politics were increasing tensions. Nixon's reliance on past precedent was becoming more precarious, as Congress pursued various means to overcome continued secrecy and claims of executive privilege.

Watergate, the Supreme Court, and amending FOIA

The learning process surrounding the ongoing issues continued through this phase of the CLDC, as the Nixon administration had become dependent on past precedent of executive actions, even as the context changed. While Nixon adhered to the same mindset of the Cold War Paradigm, Congress learned that the situation with Nixon required additional action. FOIA was one avenue that Congress pursued for oversight purposes, but the law did not have the moderating or restraining effect on Nixon that Moss and others believed it would. The Watergate scandal broke just prior to Nixon's reelection, yet no one at that time knew the extent to which the president was involved. Congress began Nixon's second term seeking new means of checking continued White House secrecy using whatever tools available. The Watergate scandal and the last two years of the Nixon administration provide a fascinating examination of presidential power gone awry, and how Congress responded. Scholars, researchers, and authors have devoted so much attention and work to the scandal that it serves no use to recall it here. My purpose is to offer a much narrower perspective on how Nixon's use of executive privilege during this episode brought about congressional responses in several ways, and ultimately led to the Supreme Court decision that would check executive privilege, though not alter it greatly. By continuing to focus on the CLDC and the unfolding learning process, I will show the internal White House discourse on secrecy and its response to Congress developing legislation to target these issues, including the first amendments to FOIA. My focus is on the unfolding political situation that intertwines government secrecy with open records as it pertains to power struggles between the legislative and executive branches.

159

The 93rd Congress (1973–5) began in January 1973 right where the previous Congress ended. Nixon attended a bipartisan leadership breakfast where the subject of executive privilege was a top concern.[39] Nixon directed members of Congress to raise their concerns with Ehrlichman, and behind the scenes ordered Dean to support Ehrlichman in these efforts. Congress responded aggressively when Senate Majority Leader Mike Mansfield (D-MT) helped pass a resolution from the Majority Conference of the Senate detailing their concerns over cabinet and other officials' refusal to testify before the Senate.[40] The resolution invoked Article II of the Constitution, which requires the advice and consent of the Senate, and asserted the Senate has the power to summon witnesses to appear and testify. Mansfield reminded Nixon that presidential appointees and officials have a commitment to appear before Senate committees, and the committees require testimony and cooperation for evaluation purposes. Nearly two weeks later, Dean responded to Mansfield thanking him for forwarding the resolution and noted that it did not conflict with current administration policy.[41] Dean mentioned that many of the problems were administrative in nature, commenting that it was merely scheduling conflicts that prevented witnesses and officials from appearing. He complained that with more than 300 congressional committees and subcommittees demanding testimony, it was difficult to arrange for White House officials.

Beyond the organizational complications, Dean launched into telling Mansfield about "the recurring problem of 'leaks' of classified information given in closed, executive sessions of Senate committees."[42] He discussed how these leaks had prevented the

[39] Memo to John Dean from Todd Hullin, January 13, 1973. Folder: [EX] FE 4-1 Presidential Powers, Succession, and Term of Office 1/1/73–4/30/73. WHCF: Subject Files FE, Box 6, Richard M. Nixon Presidential Library.

[40] Memo to Richard Nixon from Mike Mansfield, January 11, 1973. Folder: Executive Privilege—Congressional Folder 5. WHCF: Buzhardt, Box 14, Richard M. Nixon Presidential Library.

[41] Letter to Mike Mansfield from John Dean, January 25, 1973. Folder: Executive Privilege—Congressional Folder 5. WHCF: Buzhardt, Box 14, Richard M. Nixon Presidential Library.

[42] Ibid.

administration from fully sharing information with the Senate, "especially in areas of national security and foreign policy." Dean continued by reiterating the White House position on executive privilege, which he maintained adhered to the policies established early in Nixon's first term, and said that these policies would continue to guide their actions into the second term. He stated, "The President directed that Executive Privilege would be used only with specific Presidential approval after a rigorous inquiry into actual need for its exercise."

In between Mansfield sending Nixon the Senate Conference resolution and Dean's response, the Senate Democratic Policy Committee chaired by Mansfield passed a different resolution specifically targeting executive privilege.[43] The resolution conferred how the failure of administration officials to appear and testify before the Senate prevented Congress from exercising its constitutional responsibilities. The resolution specifically targeted Nixon's reasoning in this matter by stating, "The Executive Branch has asserted that the refusal to testify before Senate Committees is based upon the notion of privileged communications between the President and officials requested to testify."[44] The resolution served notice to the White House that the Democratic Senate was no longer willing to accept Nixon's rationale and past precedent as justification when refusing to allow officials to appear before Congress. The resolution stated,

> RESOLVED, That all such witnesses appear; that all questions propounded by Senate Committees be answered unless the President expressly pleads in writing that he has requested the witness to refuse to answer specific questions dealing with a specific matter because the President desires to invoke executive privilege, in which event it shall then be a question of fact for the committee to decide as to whether or not the plea of executive privilege will be taken. If not well taken, the witness shall be ordered to answer the question or questions; and Be It Further

[43] Resolution of Senate Democratic Policy Committee, RE: Executive Privilege, January 18, 1973. Folder: Executive Privilege—Congressional Folder 5. WHCF: Buzhardt, Box 14, Richard M. Nixon Presidential Library.
[44] Ibid.

RESOLVED, That when any Committee upholds or denies the invocation of executive privilege, it shall within ten days file with the Senate a resolution together with a report and record of its proceedings bearing on such claim of executive privilege, and the Senate shall take such action as it deems proper on disposition of said resolution.

The resolution, while only passed by the Democratic majority of the Senate, provided a rationale and strategy that required clear invocations of executive privilege from Nixon, and then provided for the Senate to override such invocations and compel testimony from White House officials. While the legal implications of this congressional action may have been questionable, the political implications were clear. Congressional Democrats took a page from the president's playbook, demonstrating a learning process, by simply declaring that Congress had the power to not only force witnesses to testify, but to override a presidential invocation of executive privilege. In many ways, this was similar to the strategy that Eisenhower took when first asserting the inherent constitutional power of privilege, a strategy that Nixon had expanded upon. Senate Democrats now asserted an inherent congressional privilege that would counter the continued claims coming from the administration.

Nixon's Deputy Assistant, Tom Korologos, sent Ehrlichman a hand-written note with a copy of the resolution and a floor speech given by Mansfield explaining his support. The note from Korologos simply stated,

> You'll be happy know Democrat Conference (all of them) passed this thing this morning. (note reference to you in Mansfield's speech) Nobody seems to know what the resolution means.[45]

The timing of the resolution offers additional context to understanding Dean's response to Mansfield a week later, and his seeking to reassure the Senate that administration policy had remained consistent. The resolutions from congressional Democrats put the White House on notice as they would have

---

[45] Memo to John Ehrlichman from Tom Korologos, January 18, 1973. Folder: Executive Privilege—Congressional Folder 5. WHCF: Buzhardt, Box 14, Richard M. Nixon Presidential Library.

to develop new strategies and justifications for further actions around claims of secrecy and executive privilege. Congress was again using the issue of executive privilege as a political tool of opposition to the president, in a manner similar to their actions when Nixon was vice president.

Faced with a resurgent opposition Congress, White House deliberations on the Senate resolutions proved troubling. In a memo to Ehrlichman from administration attorney Jonathan Rose lamented the notion that Congress could compel testimony from officials, and that witnesses would be forced to invoke executive privilege in person before the committee.[46] Rose observed the political situation to Ehrlichman,

> Obviously the whole subject of testimony by the White House staff is governed largely by the election returns. Instead of Republican chairmen, we are confronted with a hostile opposition Congress out to embarrass the President in any way possible. A number of the current Assistants have been accused of incidents with good smear potential in the hands of a skillful committee. In this unfortunate setting arises the necessity to define the applicability and scope of executive privilege for Presidential assistants.

Adding to his frustrations with the current political climate, Rose continued by noting how Dean had been able to deflect Congress thus far:

> In the past, John Dean has sent artfully drafted letters declining all invitations to Presidential assistants to appear before Congressional committees. The letters allude to, but do not claim, executive privilege.

The point made by Rose to Ehrlichman is stark: Dean had been able to deny Congress testimony and access without having to actually use executive privilege. By alluding to it, but not actually invoking it, additional power surrounding executive privilege had been created. If Congress believed that privilege had been asserted when the president had not specifically done so, but the effect still remained the same, then Dean had been successful in

[46] Memo to John Ehrlichman from Jonathan Rose, January 26, 1973. Folder: Executive Privilege—Congressional Folder 5. WHCF: Buzhardt, Box 14, Richard M. Nixon Presidential Library.

duping Congress and getting away with it. Simultaneously, this tactic had provided Nixon with additional cover in being able to assert that his administration had only used executive privilege in a small handful of cases. Rose concluded by noting that there was no clear or easy way out this situation, especially politically. With Congress reasserting authority in challenging these White House practices, Rose told Ehrlichman to prepare, and that while he believed Congress's authority to compel testimony was weak, they must be ready and more discerning when preventing officials from appearing before Congress in the future.

Just a few days after Rose sent his comments to Ehrlichman, Nixon was confronted directly with his administration's use of executive privilege during a press conference by Clark Mollenhoff from the *Des Moines Register and Tribune*. Mollenhoff questioned whether Nixon had approved the use of executive privilege by Air Force Secretary Seamans during a congressional hearing the previous day, when it was invoked. Mollenhoff reminded Nixon that he had previously stated that executive privilege would only be used with his approval, and then proceeded to ask if the administration now allowed others to use it on their own.[47] Nixon astutely danced around the question by reaffirming that his position on executive privilege had not changed, but he stated,

> In this case, as I understand it—and I did not approve this directly, but it was approved at my direction by those who have the responsibility within the White House—in this case it was a proper area in which the executive privilege should have been used. On the other hand, I can assure you that all of these cases will be handled on a case-by-case basis, and we are not going to be in a position where an individual, when he gets under heat from a Congressional committee, can say, "Look, I am going to assert executive privilege." He will call down here, and Mr. Dean, the White House Counsel, will then advise him as to whether or not we approve it.

[47] Richard Nixon: "The President's News Conference," January 31, 1973. Available online at *The American Presidency Project*, <https://www.presid ency.ucsb.edu/documents/the-presidents-news-conference-86> (last accessed November 10, 2018).

Mollenhoff pressed Nixon with a follow-up question, asserting that as a Member of Congress in 1948 he was critical of executive privilege, yet it seemed now that under his administration the White House had expanded its use from only covering conversations with the president, to now covering anyone in the executive branch. Mollenhoff asked Nixon to cite any law or court decision that supported this position as justification.

Mollenhoff's questioning caught Nixon off guard, leaving the president in a position to do the only thing he could at that moment, which was to divert by offering to prepare a more precise statement on executive privilege, which he would personally approve so there would be no question as to his position on the issue. Nixon continued,

> But I would rather, at this point, not like to have just my off-the-top-of-my-head press conference statement delineate what executive privilege will be. I will simply say the general attitude I have is to be as liberal as possible in terms of making people available to testify before the Congress, as we are not going to use executive privilege as a shield for conversations that might be just embarrassing to us, but that really don't deserve executive privilege.

With this statement, Nixon now placed a heavy burden on himself and Dean to clearly justify the intent and use of executive privilege. While past precedent created a foundation, it was clear that the press and Congress were no longer willing to accept the justification that executive privilege was warranted, valid, and useful merely because previous presidents had claimed it was. The societal shift was also present, underlying Mollenhoff's questions. The perception among the public and the press was that the administration had expanded the use of executive privilege, which was evident by the actions congressional Democrats were taking in the face of continued repudiation from the White House. As the Watergate scandal continued to unfold, the political pressure was mounting and Nixon needed to respond. It was at this point that Nixon had to develop a position and justification beyond those of his predecessors in order to maintain power and control over information in the face of congressional actions to constrain his own.

Following the press conference, the White House immediately sprang into action. One particular action was John Dean reaching out to the Office of Legal Counsel (OLC) in the Justice Department, asking for a policy statement on the procedures for invoking executive privilege in judicial proceedings.[48] Dean noted that, as opposed to dealing with Congress, he wanted legal footing and the creation of a committee within the Justice Department to advise on any and all situations where the White House would have to invoke executive privilege during a judicial proceeding. While the political pressure from Congress mounted, Dean took the additional step of instructing OLC to provide justification for court cases and legal action that would shield administration officials and prevent testimony before a judge. Within a few days, Assistant Attorney General and head of OLC Roger Cramton responded to Dean with a memo detailing the uses, justifications, and reasoning of executive privilege as carried out under Eisenhower, Kennedy, and Johnson.[49] The memo included copies of Eisenhower's May 17, 1954 memo, and the letters sent to Moss from Kennedy and Johnson. In providing the historical documentation, Nixon was preparing to solidify his position in keeping to past precedent, thereby providing justification of his usage as merely an outgrowth of normal politics.

By the end of February, the House Committee on Government Operations readied to move forward with new legislation, introducing H.R.4938, which would amend FOIA to require executive information be provided to Congress. The bill stipulated that any congressional request for White House information needed to be fulfilled within 30 days unless the president submitted to Congress a statement invoking executive privilege. It also required any administration official to appear before Congress and supply all information requested unless the president had

---

[48] Memo to Roger Cramton from John Dean, February 5, 1973. Folder: Presidential Statement on Executive Privilege—1973, Folder 4. WHCF: Buzhardt, Box 14, Richard M. Nixon Presidential Library.

[49] Memo to John Dean from Roger Cramton, February 7, 1973. Folder: Executive Privilege—Congressional Reference 2. WHCF: Buzhardt, Box 15, Richard M. Nixon Presidential Library.

specifically invoked executive privilege. The bill contained this clarification:

> Executive Privilege shall be invoked only by the President and only in those instances in which the requested information or testimony contains policy recommendations made to the President or agency head and the President determines that disclosure of such information will seriously jeopardize the national interest and his ability or that of the agency head to obtain forthright advice.[50]

In conjunction with the Mansfield Senate resolutions, the House bill was a more assertive maneuver from Congress to check executive power. Nixon had yet to issue his official statement on executive privilege as promised during the press conference, but Congress was no longer willing to take direction on the issue from the White House. With the institutional infrastructure FOIA created already in place within Congress, it was much easier for committees to assert power through oversight and investigation. As a policy, FOIA provided the structure for a congressional check on executive power.

As pressure from Congress began to reach a fever pitch, Nixon finally released his statement on executive privilege in mid-March. The statement reiterated what Nixon had said in the press conference and cited his March 1969 memo establishing the use of executive privilege only at times when disclosure would harm the public interest.[51] He cited the historic precedent back to Washington, and the inherent constitutional authority granted to the president. The reasoning provided in the early portion of the statement was consistent with the past precedent arguments Nixon had been making since coming into office. Regarding the denials of permission for officials to testify and appear before

---

[50] H.R.4938, "To amend the Freedom of Information Act to require that all information be made available to Congress except where Executive privilege is invoked," February 28, 1973. Folder: Executive Privilege—Congressional Declinations, Folder 5. WHCF: Buzhardt, Box 13, Richard M. Nixon Presidential Library.

[51] Statement by the President, March 12, 1973. Folder: Presidential Statement on Executive Privilege—1973, Folder 4. WHCF: Buzhardt, Box 14, Richard M. Nixon Presidential Library.

Congress, Nixon noted concerns about allowing his personal staff to testify, asserting that he was merely following the same tradition as past administrations in routinely denying such congressional requests. He stated:

> Under the doctrine of separation of powers, the manner in which the President personally exercises his assigned executive powers is not subject to questioning by another branch of Government. If the President is not subject to such questioning, it is equally appropriate that members of his staff not be so questioned, for their roles are in effect an extension of the Presidency.
>
> This tradition rests on more than constitutional doctrine: It is also a practical necessity. To insure the effective discharge of the executive responsibility, a President must be able to place absolute confidence in the advice and assistance offered by the members of his staff. And in the performance of their duties for the President, those staff members must not be inhibited by the possibility that their advice and assistance will ever become a matter of public debate, either during their tenure in Government or at a later date. Otherwise, the candor with which advice is rendered and the quality of such assistance will inevitably be compromised and weakened. What is at stake, therefore, is not simply a question of confidentiality but the integrity of the decision making process at the very highest levels of our Government.

Nixon thoroughly made his case in justifying his actions on the subject before providing guidelines on how the White House would deal with congressional requests and staff appearances. He reaffirmed that he would be diligent about invoking executive privilege only in extreme matters, on a case-by-case basis. Substantively, while the memo served to position the administration on the matter, it did little to break any new ground, especially politically. The arguments used to justify executive privilege and denials of congressional requests were the same ones Eisenhower had used, and that Nixon had already reiterated in his 1969 memo. Politically, the statement served as a warning to Congress that the administration remained persistent in its belief on the issue and would not cower nor give in to congressional demands, especially ones of inherent congressional constitutional powers. This left Congress little recourse but to continue to take action through hearings and targeted legislative development.

Within days of Nixon's statement going public, multiple congressional committees requested John Dean to testify on the matter. The Chair and Ranking Member of the House FOGI Subcommittee wrote directly to Nixon requesting Dean to appear, stating that "many Members of Congress of both political parties are concerned over your March 12 statement."[52] The letter from FOGI notes upcoming hearings on their new bill, H.R. 4938, to amend FOIA, and asks Dean to appear during these hearings so the subcommittee can, "obtain the depth of understanding of current Executive branch views on this subject." The request states,

> This subcommittee held extensive investigative hearings on this subject in the last Congress and its oversight activity involving claims of "Executive privilege" date back to the mid 1950's, spanning four administrations. Subcommittee members have varying opinions over the extent to which "Executive privilege" actually exists from a legal standpoint, and, if it does, what limitations can or should be placed upon it. Moreover, there is substantial concern about what role the courts should have in this question which involves delicate Executive-Legislative relationships and the Constitutional prerogatives of both branches.

Any clarification and potential comity Nixon had hoped to achieve from the memo were clearly dispelled in this single request. The pushback from Congress at this point was fierce. No longer were members willing to accept even the shaky legal foundations of executive privilege, especially at a time when the White House was shielding information more than ever. Just as Dean had shown concerns over whether they could invoke a judicial executive privilege, Congress now too was raising concerns over what impacts judicial decisions might have on this inter-branch power struggle. The political ramifications were quickly mounting on the administration as Congress had already introduced legislation to amend FOIA specifically to counter claims of executive privilege. Dean responded to the FOGI request by declining the

[52] Letter to Richard Nixon from William Moorhead and John Erlenborn, March 23, 1973. Folder: Executive Privilege—Congressional Declinations, Folder 5. WHCF: Buzhardt, Box 13, Richard M. Nixon Presidential Library.

invitation to appear. He claimed his refusal was consistent with Nixon's March 12 statement and administration position in preventing personal staff to appear before Congress.

By summer, the administration was fending off several more bills from Congress. The first was a House bill, H.R.7645, which reauthorized the Department of State-United States Information Agency (State-USIA), which had passed out of committee at this point. Congress utilized a strategy here to stop all funding for the agency if it failed to comply with congressional requests for information, a position the White House found unconstitutional.[53] The internal White House and OLC discussion found the bill to violate the separation of powers doctrine of the Constitution by removing the president's ability to prevent harmful information from going to Congress that would damage the public interest. The discussion between Special Consultant and Counsel to the President Leonard Garment, OLC Head Leon Ulman, Assistant Attorney General Mike McKivett, Dr. Henry Kissinger and his assistant Bud McFarlane, and Nixon's legislative affairs assistant Bill Timmons all agreed a veto strategy on the bill was necessary, which also received Nixon's approval.[54] The strategy from Congress to withhold funding created an uproar within the White House and placed Nixon on a veto strategy, but demonstrated that Congress had learned to utilize funding as a tool to check the president.

The other bill that created similar outrage came from Senators Ervin and Fulbright that would amend FOIA in a similar manner to its House counterpart.[55] The bill, S.858, received the same

---

[53] Memo to Leonard Garment from Leon Ulman, July 16, 1973. Folder: Executive Privilege—General, Folder 11. WHCF: Buzhardt, Box 13, Richard M. Nixon Presidential Library.

[54] Memo to Leonard Garment from Bud McFarlane, July 16, 1973. Folder: Executive Privilege—General, Folder 11. WHCF: Buzhardt, Box 13, Richard M. Nixon Presidential Library; Memo to Leonard Garment from Mike McKivett, July 16, 1973. Folder: Executive Privilege—General, Folder 11. WHCF: Buzhardt, Box 13, Richard M. Nixon Presidential Library.

[55] Memo to Fred Fielding from Bill Timmons, July 16, 1973. Folder: Executive Privilege—General, Folder 11. WHCF: Buzhardt, Box 13, Richard M. Nixon Presidential Library.

outrage as the State-USIA funding bill. Ervin, as chair of the Senate subcommittee with oversight on FOIA, requested the Justice Department to offer comment on the bill, and what he received was an eight-page memo from McKivitt citing precedent and reasoning all the way back to "the St. Clair incident of 1792" as to why the bill was unconstitutional.[56] In targeting the politics of the moment and a particular section of the bill that would compel testimony over invocations of executive privilege, McKivitt told Ervin,

> The statements made by Senator Fulbright in introducing the bill, however, suggest that the clause is designed to assert for Congress the power of ultimate determination of the propriety of invoking executive privilege, and thus substitute the judgement of the committee for that of the President. If this is the correct interpretation, this subsection would be a trespass on the constitutional power of the Executive.

While Nixon also approved the position to veto this bill, it demonstrated how the power politics between Congress and the president had disintegrated during this period. Congress was attempting an end-run around executive privilege by passing a law that provided for a congressional privilege that would compel information and testimony regardless of the president's position. The example serves to show a learned response from Congress to the overuse of executive privilege as defined by Nixon. In this case, Congress followed Eisenhower's example by now making the constitutional claims of privilege where none had existed before and forcing the White House to defend itself. Politically, Congress knew Nixon would veto this legislation, and it would be difficult to override, but it served to place the administration in the position of having to veto a bill on government secrecy at a time when the administration was under increased scrutiny.

Over the course of the next year, Congress continued in the same manner of introducing new bills to amend FOIA, holding hearings and investigations on the lack of access to executive

---

[56] Memo to Sam Ervin from Mike McKivitt, July 10, 1973. Folder: Executive Privilege—General, Folder 11. WHCF: Buzhardt, Box 13, Richard M. Nixon Presidential Library.

branch information and staff, while the Nixon administration continued to stonewall and threaten to use the veto, adhering the same position as previously established—which was that any action to remove executive privilege, including amending FOIA to strengthen the law, was considered an unconstitutional violation of executive power. Two incidents challenged and altered the stalemate of this period, and served to mark a new juncture in the CLDC. The first was Congress finally passing legislation to amend FOIA, and the second was the Supreme Court decision in *US v. Nixon* that impacted executive privilege. In March 1974 the House passed a cooperative bill, H.R.12471, which amended FOIA by increasing disclosure policies and enforcement procedures. The bill had come from the FOGI Subcommittee and was being pushed by Moss and Moorhead as the product of combining several previous bills and taking concerns from the administration into account. The administration objected to the House bill, calling it "unacceptable" and noted that a less objectionable version should be coming from the Senate Judiciary Committee.[57]

The administration made efforts to bargain with the Senate to secure a more favorable bill, but the problem became that Nixon and many within the administration could not compromise on any FOIA amendment bill that they saw as diminishing presidential authority. The administration was unwilling to bend on any notion of strengthening the nine exemptions in the law, or in giving Congress or the courts the ability to override any presidential decision. The negotiations between the White House and the Senate evaporated quickly, and the Senate passed their version on May 30, 1974, which included much stronger provisions than the House version, including some Nixon did not want.[58] The two FOIA amendment bills now moved to a conference com-

---

[57] Memo to Jerry Jones from Powell Moore, May 20, 1974. Folder: EX LE Legislation [39 of 39, February–July 1974]. WHCF: (LE) Legislation, Box 7, Richard M. Nixon Presidential Library.

[58] Memo to Richard Nixon from Roy Ash, June 27, 1974. Folder: [EX] FE 14-1 5/1/74–8/9/74. WHCF: FE (Federal Government) Box 22, Richard M. Nixon Presidential Library.

mittee to hash out their differences. Within the White House officials were determined to see the bill fail and pressed Nixon to engage in a veto bargaining strategy of outright opposition, arguing that the bill was too objectionable to win over enough senators to sustain a veto.[59] The internal discussion noted that the conference committee was not in favor of working with the administration, thereby leaving Nixon little chance of changing the bill, especially given the quick timeline; the committee wanted to finish by mid-July. Nixon decided to take a more open veto bargaining strategy than his advisors counseled, by recommending they advise the conference committee of their specific objections and threaten to veto only if the bill is not rewritten.[60] Much as Johnson had tried to stop FOIA from becoming law, Nixon had tried to prevent Congress from passing any legislation, then attempted to influence the bills, before succumbing to a veto bargaining strategy of seeking to get the final version altered before the final vote in Congress.

The main problem Nixon faced in attempting to veto bargain with the conference committee over the FOIA amendment bill was the Watergate scandal, and the subsequent Supreme Court decision in *US v. Nixon* handed down on July 24, 1974. The decision weighed in on executive privilege and served as the final blow leading to Nixon's resignation on August 9, 1974, after the House filed Articles of Impeachment on July 27, 1974. Without retelling the story of Watergate, I am going to focus here on the power dynamics between Congress and the president that unfolded simultaneously as Congress passed the first amendments to FOIA in response to both Watergate and Nixon's assertions of presidential authority to deny staff testimony or information to Congress. The significance is in how the White House continued to expand assertions of executive privilege over the Watergate

---

[59] Memo to Richard Nixon from Ken Cole, July 2, 1973. Folder: [EX] FE 14-1 5/1/74–8/9/74. WHCF: FE (Federal Government) Box 22, Richard M. Nixon Presidential Library.

[60] Memo to Richard Nixon from Roy Ash, June 27, 1974. Folder: [EX] FE 14-1 5/1/74–8/9/74. WHCF: FE (Federal Government) Box 22, Richard M. Nixon Presidential Library.

tapes, claiming inherent executive control over all internal communications and documents at the discretion of the president. Nixon's position was an outgrowth from Eisenhower's, but where his predecessors had kept their reasoning and justification of executive privilege within the realm of national security issues centered on the public interest, Nixon expanded further by claiming the privilege power was inherent to the executive, and that it covered any employees and information within the entirety of the executive branch.

The Watergate scandal unfolded through 1973 and into 1974. Aside from the struggles with the Justice Department over the Saturday Night Massacre and the ongoing investigation from the special prosecutor, Congress was conducting its own investigations. Senator Ervin and his subcommittee hotly pursued information from Nixon on a host of issues related to the campaign and beyond. Ervin demonstrated his entrepreneurial prowess, much as Moss had a decade earlier, in doggedly pressuring the administration on testimony and documentation. As Nixon continued to obstruct, based on his 1973 memo, Ervin began to subpoena for specific information. Nixon strongly and publicly responded to Ervin, refusing to turn over any information to his subcommittee, including the infamous tapes on which the Supreme Court would weigh in.[61] Nixon recounted the vast amount of information being requested by Ervin, and responded,

> As I stated in my letter to you of July 6, 1973, "Formulation of sound public policy requires that the President and his personal staff be able to communicate among themselves in complete candor, and that their tentative judgements, their exploration of alternatives, and their frank comments on issues and personalities at home and abroad remain confidential." I anticipated that even quite limited, selected disclosures of Presidential recordings and documents "would inevitably result in the attrition, and the eventual destruction of the indispensable principle of confidentiality of Presidential papers."

[61] Text of a Letter from the President to Senator Sam Ervin, Jr., January 4, 1974. Folder: [EX] FE 4-1 12/1/73–8/9/74. WHCF: FE (Federal Government) Box 7, Richard M. Nixon Presidential Library.

Nixon's argument echoed the same position he had taken since coming into office and used the same reasoning expressed in his statement on executive privilege from March 1973. However, he continued to Ervin,

> To produce the materials you now seek would unquestioningly destroy any vestige of confidentiality of Presidential communications, thereby irreparably impairing the constitutional functions of the Office of the Presidency. Neither the Judiciary nor the Congress could survive a similar power asserted by the Executive Branch to rummage through their files and confidential processes. Under the circumstances, I can only view your subpoena as an overt attempt to intrude into the Executive to a degree that constitutes an unconstitutional usurpation of power.

Nixon's assertion of presidential authority in this manner was absolute and could not be abridged by either Congress or the Courts. It was this very notion that the Supreme Court examined once the case made its way to them in July 1974, just as the FOIA amendment bills made their way through conference committee.

The special prosecutor filed a subpoena for specific tape recordings and documents related to White House conversations about the Watergate break-in and the political fallout. Nixon at first complied by releasing some of the records, though partially edited or redacted, but then filed a motion to quash the subpoena based on executive privilege.[62] Nixon asserted the absolute right of privilege, meaning that the courts were not qualified or capable of having access to the tapes or papers, as it violated the separation of powers doctrine in the constitution. The case went before the Supreme Court on July 9, 1974, and two weeks later, the court delivered an 8-0 decision, with Justice Rehnquist having recused himself due to his work on these issues while at OLC under Nixon. The Burger majority decision focused on executive privilege, arguing that in circumstances of alleged criminality the president's authority did not extend to the courts, and therefore the courts had a right to the information under consideration. The

---

[62] A summary of the case can be found on the Justia, US Supreme Court website, <https://supreme.justia.com/cases/federal/us/418/683/#annotation> (last accessed November 10, 2018).

decision gave the court the ability to counter the constitutional arguments of violation of the separation of powers doctrine, confirming that presidential confidentiality in communication did not override due process of law in cases of suspected criminality. The court did however acknowledge an executive privilege, in particular in areas of diplomatic affairs or national security, thus having the judicial branch officially recognize the legitimacy of at least some privilege claims.

The political impact of the Supreme Court decision had ramifications beyond leading directly to Nixon's resignation. The first was that the court provided a clear barrier demonstrating a limit to executive privilege claims. In contrast to the assertions from the administration, the court held that the president did not have unlimited authority to withhold information at his sole discretion. Cases of potential criminality in the matter of due process and justice superseded the president's need for confidentiality. From this aspect, the court was able to check executive power by delineating between a qualified privilege that a president would need while in office and an abuse of authority. The second political impact of the decision was the legitimization of executive privilege as a constitutional presidential power by the Supreme Court. While Congress had previously spent decades offering a measure of legitimacy to such claims, the court involvement helped to institutionalize the power as a valid and acceptable tool of the presidency. While limited in certain circumstances, the court was able to provide an increase in the power of executive privilege as it largely withstood legal scrutiny. A third political impact was that the Court's decision and Nixon's resignation halted much of the legislative development Congress had been working on. As we will see in the next chapter, the FOIA amendment bill proceeded in the conference committee, but legislation focused on limiting executive privilege and asserting a congressional privilege ceased.

The final political impact of the decision built upon the previous ones. The president now had a legitimate constitutional claim to utilize this power at will, unless countered by the courts or Congress. Going forward from Nixon, the politics surrounding executive privilege have changed little, and therefore the impact

176

has been more muted than originally thought. While the political fallout of the decision in the wake of impeachment and resignation for Nixon was huge, for future presidents, claims of executive privilege for national security purposes in the public interest would continue largely unabated. While Nixon's staff had been fearful of the courts intervening in executive-legislative power debates, the final outcome left the courts largely hesitant to intervene in politics, keeping the focus on the specific situation and the potential criminality. This left the larger political grey area of executive privilege in place, whereby the president and Congress would continue their arguing over access to information and government secrecy into the contemporary period. More recent examples have provided evidence that presidents will continue to use executive privilege at times that suit their needs, leaving Congress in the same difficult situation of attempting to overcome those claims. Congress will continue to utilize tools like FOIA, hearings, and oversight to pressure administrations on public information, but the politics surrounding the issue since Nixon have hardly changed.

Conclusion

The Nixon administration brought about the next iteration within the CLDC that began the oversight and amendment period of FOIA, along with the resurgence of executive privilege that had been largely absent under the unified Democratic governments of Kennedy and Johnson. It was not just the politics of divided government that made Nixon unique within the context of this research; otherwise he would not have pushed much further than his former boss, Eisenhower. The evolving context of the issues surrounding government secrecy and FOIA implementation gave Nixon footing to expand the use and scope of executive privilege beyond his predecessors. The Cold War Paradigm still simmered below the surface, influencing decision making within the White House on foreign and domestic policy. However, Nixon's own personal proclivities led him to take actions both illegal and unethical. In the fallout over such actions he turned to executive privilege as a shield, finally forcing the Supreme Court to intervene, and thus leading to his resignation from office.

From early on in his administration, Nixon took a strong position on issues of government secrecy, demonstrating how much he had learned as vice president in the Eisenhower administration and as a keen observer during the eight years of Kennedy-Johnson. Nixon immediately sought to position himself with Moss and Congress on issues of access and executive privilege, a position that only hardened throughout this tenure. Within the constant feedback loops of the CLDC, the learning process became clear as Congress sought to overcome the continued denials of access from the White House. Through oversight and investigations, hearings, the introduction of legislation, to Democratic majority resolutions, as well as asserting a congressional privilege that superseded the president's authority, Congress pursued a multi-faceted strategy to counter Nixon's positions. The action-reaction model of the learning process unfolded in numerous ways during the Nixon administration, leaving Congress in a position to learn and continuously alter strategy to overcome Nixon's expansion of authority. Fortunately for Congress, the Watergate scandal helped to turn the politics of the moment in their favor. In the end, Congress was able to pass amendments to strengthen FOIA, which Nixon threatened to veto, and as we will see in the next chapter, President Ford was left to veto bargain. By late summer 1974, Congress finally responded to Nixon with the one tool left unused and the final course of action: impeachment. Nixon resigned before being officially impeached and was pardoned by Ford for any wrongdoing while he was president.

7

Ford and veto bargaining over amending FOIA

With all due respect, I do not believe many Federal judges are experts in the complex weighing of defense and intelligence needs for security or secrecy. I also think that the transfer of this judgment from the executive to the judicial branch of Government may be unconstitutional.

—Gerald R. Ford, Remarks at the Annual Convention
of the Society of Professional Journalists, Phoenix, AZ,
November 14, 1974

On 8 September 1974, President Ford addressed the nation on live television after signing a full and complete pardon of Nixon. Ford claimed that to have done so was in the best interest of the country. He argued that the continued pursuit of the investigation and indictments of Nixon would be damaging to the nation, stating, "The prospects of such a trial will cause prolonged and divisive debate over the propriety of exposing to further punishment and degradation a man who has already paid the unprecedented penalty of relinquishing the highest elective office of the United States."[1] While Ford asserted the pardon was the right thing to do to bring the country back together in repairing the damage caused by Watergate and Nixon's resignation, the political fallout haunted Ford for the remainder of his presidency. His pardon served to complicate political matters with Congress, in particular over unfinished legislation like the FOIA amendments that were still sitting in conference committee when Nixon resigned. The early months of the Ford administration

[1] Gerald R. Ford: "Proclamation 4311—Granting Pardon to Richard Nixon," September 8, 1974. Available online at *The American Presidency Project*, <https://www.presidency.ucsb.edu/documents/proclamation-4311-granting-pardon-richard-nixon> (last accessed November 10, 2018).

were politically fraught and marked by contentious legislative battles and veto bargaining.

A month after issuing the pardon, Ford sat before a hearing of the House Judiciary Committee to answer questions about his pardon. During his opening statement, Ford discussed the need for any branch of government to have confidence in its internal communications, and therefore the need for certain communications to remain secret. He cited the Supreme Court decision in *United States v. Nixon* as recognizing a sphere of confidentiality within the executive branch.[2] He provided his view on executive privilege, stating:

> As I have stated before, my own view is that the right of executive privilege is to be exercised with caution and restraint. When I was a Member of Congress, I did not hesitate to question the right of the executive branch to claim a privilege against supplying information to the Congress if I thought the claim of privilege was being abused. Yet, I did then, and I do now, respect the right of executive privilege when it protects advice given to a President in the expectation that it will not be disclosed. Otherwise, no President could any longer count on receiving free and frank views from people designated to help him reach his official decisions.

While Ford was not in a position to utilize privilege in the same manner as his predecessors due to the tenuous politics of that period, he does provide a reasoned assertion that aligns with past use and creates the space to use it going forward. While the abuses of Nixon were still fresh, Ford was not willing to walk back nearly thirty years of power by giving up on executive privilege—in particular since the Supreme Court upheld an appropriate use of it within specific circumstances, thereby justifying the power as constitutional. Ford was willing to appear before Congress and justify his actions in the pardon, but at the

---

[2] Gerald R. Ford: "Statement and Responses to Questions From Members of the House Judiciary Committee Concerning the Pardon of Richard Nixon," October 17, 1974. Available online at *The American Presidency Project*, <https://www.presidency.ucsb.edu/documents/and-responses-questions-from-members-the-house-judiciary-committee-concerning-the-pardon> (last accessed November 10, 2018).

same time, he established a position that was consistent with past use.

This brief chapter will be slightly different than the previous ones, as I am only examining the political fallout as it relates to Ford's fight with Congress over the FOIA amendments. This chapter will examine the situation Ford found himself in during the first week of his presidency, and how he sought to influence the final bill with the conference committee, followed by his decision to veto, and Congress's subsequent override. In many ways, the examination of Ford here functions as a continuation of the examination of the Nixon administration; but it cannot be ignored, as it marks the final battle over the first amendments to FOIA, which offers insight into the continuing politics of issue evolution during the oversight and amendment process within the CLDC. For me, Ford marks the end of this early period defined through the Cold War Paradigm that tied freedom of information and executive privilege together through the politics of policymaking. The politics of this moment demanded that Ford attempt to reconcile the perceived abuses of the Nixon administration while trying to establish his own agenda—and also tackling Congress's ongoing legislative agenda, which included the FOIA amendments and issues surrounding executive privilege.

Previous scholarship has focused on Nixon as the turning point on executive privilege as it relates to the contemporary period. However, as we have already seen, Congress reacted by learning from presidential actions, often using policy as a check on power, as with the original passage of FOIA in 1966. As the issue of executive privilege remained and expanded under Nixon, after implementation the CLDC adjusts to focus on the debates leading to amendment. The issue has evolved, but as the inter-branch power struggles over access to information remain, we can continue to examine how the politics have changed surrounding the same issue that led to eventual policy outcomes. Ready or not, Ford found himself mired in a legislative battle with Congress from day one over amending FOIA. Muddying the politics with Congress was the fact that Ford had supported the bill's passage when he was House Minority Leader, and he appointed Don Rumsfeld, who had been a fierce FOIA advocate when LBJ was president, as his Chief of Staff. The politics of this moment would lead Ford and his staff to push back against Congress over the FOIA amendments by asserting the bill was unconstitutional under the separation of powers doctrine. Continuing to utilize past precedent, Ford would attempt to veto bargain as a means of altering the legislation to his liking, but his efforts would eventually fail, leading him to make good on his veto threats.

Veto bargaining and congressional blowback

As the previous chapter demonstrated, Congress had already been working on several different bills to target both amending FOIA and executive privilege. Nixon opposed all of the bills, and took a strong veto position.[3] However, even in the depths of the Watergate scandal and facing a potential Supreme Court rebuke, Nixon indicated that he was willing to work with the conference committee on changing the language of the FOIA amendments to something more acceptable.[4] Senator Ted Kennedy (D-MA) was leading the conference committee, which included other members like John Moss and William Moorhead, showing the committee was comprised of members with a strong record of advocacy on this particular issue. Negotiating with the conference committee would have been difficult for Nixon, and Ford's position was no better. Even in facing an opposition Congress of Democrats determined to push reforms in the Watergate fallout, Ford began his presidency with one advantage—he was not Nixon. Congress was willing to give him some latitude in attempts at bringing a sense of calm and normalcy back to politics. Ford took advantage of the Democrats' attitude in order to gain leverage for bargaining on the FOIA amendments.

---

[3] Memorandum for Richard Nixon from Roy Ash, 28 June 1974. Folder: Freedom of Information 6/1–17/74, Congressional Relations, O'Donnell and Jenckes Files (1971) 74–76, Box 5. Gerald R. Ford Presidential Library.

[4] Memorandum to Jerry Jones from Kenneth Cole, 11 July 1974. Folder: Freedom of Information, 6/18–8/16/74, Congressional Relations, O'Donnell and Jenckes Files (1971) 74–76, Box 5. Gerald R. Ford Presidential Library.

The administration's opposition to the FOIA amendments began while Nixon was president, but is relevant to revisit here as it influences the position Ford will take, in part due to many of Nixon's staff staying on to work under Ford. Once the House passed the FOIA amendments in March 1974, internal White House discussion focused on the need to stop the bill in the Senate. William Timmons was seeking input on a viable strategy, noting, "This bill is absolutely terrible and must be stopped in the Senate."[5] Timmons was seeking a "game plan" on how to halt the bill and discussed three specific provisions that were particularly objectionable. In conversations with Assistant for National Security Affairs Brent Scowcroft, Timmons deliberated on the need to prevent the legislation from moving forward. Regarding the House bill, Scowcroft noted,

> This bill is only one of several being contemplated that have the aim of opening up public access to Executive documents and Congressional oversight of the process. These moves have far reaching implications for the Executive Branch and deserve careful, coordinated attention. Justice is fighting H.R.12471 but will need all the help it can get, if the bill is to be blocked in the Senate.[6]

As we know, the administration was unsuccessful in preventing the Senate from passing amendments to FOIA, but the Senate did not pass the same bill as the House, setting up a position for negotiating with the conference committee. The position taken by staff under Nixon influenced Ford in setting the terms of debate and bargaining with Congress over specific objectionable provisions. Within the CLDC, while a junction is marked with Ford becoming president, the legislative development process is ongoing and continuous with Ford being an extension of Nixon.

The first week of the Ford administration was rife with action on two fronts, the first being executive privilege. Moss sent

[5] Memo to Tom Korologos from William Timmons, April 18, 1974. Folder: Freedom of Information 6/1–17/74 (2). Congressional Relations, O'Donnell and Jenkes Files (1971) 74–76, Box 5. Gerald R. Ford Presidential Library.

[6] Memo to Bill Timmons from Brent Scowcroft, April 15, 1974. Folder: Freedom of Information 6/1–17/74 (2). Congressional Relations, O'Donnell and Jenkes Files (1971) 74–76, Box 5, Gerald R. Ford Presidential Library.

Ford a letter a week into his presidency noting his concerns over executive privilege and the positions taken by Kennedy, Johnson, and Nixon, and asked Ford to reaffirm the same position that executive privilege would only be invoked by the president.[7] At the same time, Chair of the FOGI Subcommittee Moorhead and Ranking Minority Member John Erlenborn sent Ford a letter detailing the positions taken by his three previous predecessors on executive privilege, noting the track record of Moss and the subcommittee's investigations spanning two decades. The letter discussed newly introduced legislation targeting executive privilege in the fallout of Watergate and the Supreme Court decision. Moorhead and Erlenborn wanted Ford to provide input and feedback on the bill. They pressed Ford on his past position and how the issue had evolved. The letter stated,

> As you were a long-time Member of the House, it is not necessary to spell out to you details about the steady erosion in the flow of information from the Executive to the Congress which has taken place over the past generation. You are well aware of such problems and of the disastrous effect which the wholesale withholding of information from the Congress under "Executive Privilege" has had on the credibility of our government and its leaders. Last Friday's *New York Times* quoted remarks you made on this subject more than a decade ago: "Congress cannot help but conclude that executive privilege is most often used in opposition to the public interest."[8]

While this particular bill would not pass, the political ramifications of Nixon's actions had already set the terms of debate for Ford, with Congress taking aggressive action from the beginning on these issues. Ford found himself in the tenuous position of having to justify his administration's position in Nixon's shadow, while Congress levied political attacks using his past positions on the issues against him.

---

[7] Letter to Gerald Ford from John Moss, August 15, 1974. Folder: FE 14-1 Access to Records 8/9/74–9/30/74. WHCF Subject File Box 5. Gerald R. Ford Presidency Library.

[8] Letter to Gerald Ford from William Moorhead and John Erlenborn, August 13, 1974. Folder: Freedom of Information Act Veto (1), William E. Timmons Files Box 4 Gerald R. Ford Presidential Library.

The second front was on the FOIA amendment legislation sitting in conference committee. A few days after being sworn in, Ford received a letter from Roy Ash, Director of the Office of Management and Budget (OMB), discussing that the conference committee on FOIA was meeting that week to vote on a final bill.[9] Ash advised Ford to request the committee give him time to offer a response and position on the bill. Ash noted that most agencies and advisors in the administration, including the Justice Department, felt that the bill could not be fixed to overcome what the administration viewed as usurpation of executive authority, and therefore recommended that Ford veto. Although he believed the committee would be unwilling to amend the pending legislation, Ash thought Kennedy and Moss would be agreeable to giving Ford more time to provide comment. Ash recommended that Ford use the opportunity to at least try and amend the bill, as working with Congress would be a preferable strategy to a veto threat. At the same time, Domestic Advisor Ken Cole and outgoing Chief of Staff Al Haig (quickly replaced by Don Rumsfeld) discussed Ford meeting with Attorney General William Saxbe to confer on several pending bills that needed attention. Cole noted that Nixon wanted to try to bargain with Congress on the FOIA amendments rather than veto, but that option no longer existed due to the timeframe as the conference committee was prepared to pass the final version.[10] Cole hoped that Saxbe could buy some additional time so Ford was not forced to take a position until he had put his new staff together.

The following day, Timmons sent Haig a memo discussing his morning meeting with Ford where they attempted to plan a best solution strategy for "that obnoxious" FOIA bill, and decided to ask the conference committee for more time in order to bargain on changing the language.[11] The memo noted the ranking

[9] Memorandum for Gerald Ford from Roy L. Ash, August 12, 1974. Folder: Legislative Issues Pending (1), William E. Timmons Files Box 4. Gerald R. Ford Presidential Library.

[10] Memo to Al Haig from Ken Cole, August 12, 1974. Folder: Department of Justice 8/9/74–9/30/74. WHCF Subject File Box 86. Gerald R. Ford Presidential Library.

[11] Memorandum for Gen. Alexander Haig, August 13, 1974. Folder: Legislative

Republican on the conference committee, Senator Roman Hruska (NE), was asking for a signal from the administration on what they wanted so that he could act within the committee to support Ford. That same day, White House Counsel Philip Buchen sent a memo to Ford letting him know the conference committee had scheduled a vote for that afternoon, placing increased pressure on the administration. Buchen stated,

> Although President Nixon had been advised to veto it, it would be contrary to your policy of furthering openness and candor in government to oppose this legislation. Efforts are being undertaken by Deputy Attorney General Silberman to seek a week's delay so that you can be more fully apprised of the issues proposed by the bill, and to permit negotiations on some of the language which has troubled the Executive branch. If, however, delay and accommodations cannot be effected, you should sign this bill accompanied by comments strongly commending the Congress for action which tips the scales further in favor of the public's right to know about the processes of government.[12]

There was mixed positioning within the administration on what action Ford should take with the amendments. It was clear that nearly all the staff and officials wanted more time before having to weigh in on the bill, but the Nixon holdovers remained adamantly opposed and pressed Ford to veto, while others believed negotiation would be a more politically viable strategy that could potentially yield results from Congress. The strategy of seeking more time paid off, as Kennedy and the committee were willing to give Ford a week to offer his comments on the bill before the committee would reconvene for a final vote on August 20.[13] The

Issues Pending (1), William E. Timmons Files, Freedom of Information Act Veto to Meetings with Congressional Leaders September 1974, Box 4, Gerald R. Ford Presidential Library.

[12] Memo to the President from Philip Buchen, August 13, 1974. Folder: FG 17 Department of Justice 8/9/74–9/30/74, WHCF Subject File Box 86. Gerald R. Ford Presidential Library.

[13] Memo for William Timmons from Patrick O'Donnell, August 14, 1974. Folder: Freedom of Information, 6/18–8/16/74, Congressional Relations, O'Donnell and Jenckes Files (1971) 74–76, Box 5. Gerald R. Ford Presidential Library.

administration moved quickly to get feedback from as many agencies and departments as possible on the final version of the bill. Ford wanted to gauge just how unpalatable the FOIA amendments were to his Cabinet officials, and where in the language of the bill they should press for change.

Negotiations and deliberations between the White House and the conferees took place over the following week "on the troublesome bill," as Timmons called it.[14] Timmons reached out to Ford the day before the final conference meeting on August 20 to inform him of the progress made and to ask for his direct involvement, as it would be the only way to get an acceptable bill. Timmons had drafted a letter for Ford to send to Kennedy and Moorhead, the heads of conference committee, detailing the administration's position on the bill and which provisions they would specifically like to change. Timmons recommended that Ford immediately sign and send the letters before the committee moved on a final vote. Taking the recommendation, Ford sent the letter to the committee the following day. In the letter, he thanked the committee for providing additional time and allowing him input. Ford noted the success of FOIA and the need to make improvements, but he also warned Congress of looming problems, stating,

> There are, however, more significant costs to government that would be extracted by this bill—not in dollar terms, but relating more fundamentally to the way Government, and the Executive branch in particular, has and must function. In evaluating the costs, I must take care to avoid seriously impairing the Government we all seek to make more open. I am concerned with some of the provisions which are before you as well as some which I understand you may not have considered. I want to share my concerns with you so that we may accommodate our reservations in achieving a common objective.[15]

Ford continued by detailing three specific provisions he found unacceptable and unconstitutional, which were the same

---

[14] Memo for Gerald Ford from William Timmons, August 19, 1974. Folder: Freedom of Information, 6/18–8/16/74, Congressional Relations, O'Donnell and Jenckes Files (1971) 74–76, Box 5. Gerald R. Ford Presidential Library.

[15] Letter to William Moorhead and Edward Kennedy from Gerald Ford, August 20, 1974. Folder: Legislative Issues Pending (1), William E. Timmons Files, Box 4. Gerald R. Ford Presidential Library.

provisions Nixon had objected to. While he never overtly threatened to veto the bill, Ford made that intention clear while concealing it in the language of cooperation in wanting to work with Congress on resolving their differences to achieve the same desired goal. Ford ended the letter by asking for more time, telling Moorhead and Kennedy,

> I have stated publicly and I reiterate here that I intend to go more than halfway to accommodate Congressional concerns. I have followed that commitment in this letter, and I have attempted where I cannot agree with certain provisions to explain my reasons and to offer a constructive alternative. Your acceptance of my suggestions will enable us to move forward with this progressive effort to make Government still more responsive to the People.

It was clear that Ford had learned from Nixon's mistakes and sought to bargain with Congress to change the final bill instead of just offering strong opposition. Ford took a more friendly approach with Congress, offering a public position of seeking cooperation and compromise, while clearly stating his objections. Congress had set the terms of this debate, and now Ford had been able to offer input, thus moving the CLDC into a veto bargaining position.

Ford's strategy paid off, at least in part, as the committee postponed a final vote in order to consider the president's position and recommendations. A month later, Kennedy and Moorhead responded to Ford with a very detailed letter discussing the points of disagreement the president had raised.[16] The letter opened by thanking Ford for his personal interest in the issue and the bill. Kennedy and Moorhead state,

> And we appreciate your recognition of the fundamental purposes of this milestone law and the importance you attach to these amendments. They of course would provide support for your own policy of "open government" which is so desperately needed to restore the public's confidence in our national government.

---

[16] Letter to Gerald Ford from Edward Kennedy and William Moorhead, September 23, 1974: folder: Legislative Issues Pending (1), William E. Timmons Files, Box 4. Gerald R. Ford Presidential Library.

They continued by noting how the committee had taken time to study and deliberate on the issues raised, giving them time to investigate and talk with administration officials. The letter stated that the committee had now held their final session, which addressed and was responsive to the major issues raised by Ford. The letter then detailed the specific policy issues and how the committee had compromised by changing the some of the language within the final bill to accommodate the president. Kennedy and Moorhead provided a detailed discussion of their internal deliberations and reasoning for the final bill, where they believed to have met and addressed many of the president's concerns by altering the language enough to have a compromise that would be acceptable to all concerned, while still achieving the goal of open government and public confidence.

By the following day, the Kennedy-Moorhead letter had reverberated around the White House. General Counsel Douglas Metz sent a letter to Presidential Counsel Stanley Ebner in which he stated that the president should approve the final version of the FOIA bill. Metz continued by noting the original version of the bill had passed through Congress by overwhelming majorities, and that the conference committee was diligent enough in addressing administration concerns. He goes on to state:

> There is no convincing evidence that a better bill could be obtained in a new Congress; nor is it likely that the Conferees could be persuaded to reopen their deliberations. Many in the Congress and the general public will regard the President's response to the action of the Conferees as a test of his sincere and strongly professed commitment to greater openness in government and to conciliation and compromise with the Congress.[17]

Metz continued by discussing that agencies should be happy with the new version as it clarified many of the issues they disliked about the original bill. He ended the memo with discussion of the timing and deep public distrust, meaning that Ford should sign and avoid the politically fraught debate that would arise if he vetoed

[17] Memo to Stanley Ebner from Douglas Metz, August 24, 1974. Folder: Freedom of Information, 8/19–9/30/74, Congressional Relations, O'Donnell and Jenckes Files (1971) 74–76, Box 5. Gerald R. Ford Presidential Library.

the bill. That same day, associate counsel Ken Lazarus sent a memo to Buchen, discussing the final conference report. Lazarus noted that three House and three Senate members, the Republicans on the committee, had not yet signed the report and were waiting to hear from the president on whether he accepted the proposed legislation.[18] He continued by asserting that their opposition to the conference report would be essential to sustain a veto, should that course be pursued. Lazarus was far more critical of the changes the committee made in addressing Ford's concerns, and while a veto would have political repercussions, he asserted that it would be best to make efforts at keeping the Republican Conferees from signing the report to preserve their support of a possible veto.

By the next day it was clear the Lazarus strategy had failed, with Senator Hruska being the only conferee not to sign the final report. Cole briefed Ford on the action taken by the committee and noted that Hruska's support in the Senate would be essential to sustain a veto.[19] While progress had been made, Cole noted two provisions in the final bill still remained objectionable, and he expected "State, Justice, Defense and the CIA to recommend a veto."[20] However, he noted that the Civil Service Commission and Privacy Committee staff would recommend that Ford sign. He continued,

> There is little question that the legislation is bad on the merits, the real question is whether opposing it is important enough to face the political consequences. Obviously, there is a significant political disadvantage to vetoing a Freedom of Information bill, especially before an election, when your Administration's theme is one of openness and candor.
>
> There is no likelihood of the Conferees altering their report to accommodate your objections to these two issues. Your response, if negative, will set the stage for a major veto.

[18] Memo to Philip Buchen from Ken Lazarus, September 24, 1974. Folder: Freedom of Information—Legislation (1), Philip Buchen Files 1974–77, Box 17. Gerald R. Ford Presidential Library.

[19] Memo to Gerald Ford from Kenneth Cole, September 25, 1974. Folder: Legislative Issues Pending (2), William E. Timmons Files, Box 4. Gerald R. Ford Presidential Library.

[20] Ibid.

Cole concluded by telling Ford that Timmons was pretty certain a veto would not be sustained in the House, but that there was potential to sustain a veto in the Senate. Ford was now in the position of deciding what to do—sign or veto, and then deal with the political ramifications of either. The similarity between Ford and LBJ must be noted here, in that LBJ also objected to the bill and had the option of using his veto pen. As we know, Johnson chose to sign the bill and issue a statement that continued to assert privilege in keeping information secret for national security reasons in the public interest. At this moment, it seemed the Ford administration was not interested in following the same strategy as its predecessors.

The Senate responded first by passing the final bill by voice vote on October 1. Knowing the House vote was coming and that the FOIA amendment bill would pass, OLC Head Antonin Scalia sent a memo to Domestic Council Assistant Director Geoffrey Shepard that included a draft memo of a veto message that Ford could use, which Scalia believed made a strong case and would be understood by the public.[21] Scalia believed that Ford could veto the bill and save face publicly by offering a veto message that included specific compromises on the objectionable language. A few days later, on October 7, the House passed the bill by an overwhelming majority, and then Congress adjourned for a month-long break due to the upcoming midterm elections in November. The congressional recess provided Ford with a potential third option, which was a pocket veto that would remove the ability for Congress to try to override. The similarity to LBJ grew more stark.

Cole huddled with Ford following the passage in Congress and strategized on what to do. Cole made the case that Ford had only two options.[22] Option one was to sign the bill, hold a

---

[21] Memo to Geoffrey Shepard from Antonin Scalia, October 3, 1974. Folder: Freedom of Information Act Amendments H.R. 12471 (1), Frederick Lynn May, Box 27. Gerald R. Ford Presidential Library.

[22] Memo to Gerald Ford from Ken Cole, October 9, 1974. Folder: Freedom of Information Act Amendments H.R. 12471 (2), Frederick Lynn May, Box 27. Gerald R. Ford Presidential Library.

signing ceremony and issue a statement, much as Eisenhower and Johnson had done before him. Cole noted that only Buchen and the Civil Service Commission were in the favor of this option, as they noted the political ramifications of the veto could be severe. Option two was to veto the bill and simultaneously submit to Congress identical legislation that included Ford's proposed changes, then call on Congress to work with the president to fix the legislation instead of overriding his veto. Cole also noted that the legal staff was looking into the propriety of using the pocket veto, but since Ford might be set to veto multiple bills, Cole argued that all vetoes should be uniform, which limited his options. Cole mentioned that every other agency and official supported the second option.

After several days, Ford sent a copy of the memo back to Cole with a check mark next to option two. Unlike his predecessors, Ford was in a weakened position in comparison to a resurgent Congress. The fallout from Nixon and his subsequent pardon had left Ford in a politically tenuous position as Congress pursued an aggressive reform strategy. In essence, Ford failed to learn from Nixon in this situation, and while attempting to find a workaround, he allowed his staff to pressure him to use the veto on one of the very issues he had made central to his administration. Additionally, Ford quickly dismissed following the past precedent of Eisenhower and Johnson in just signing the bill while reasserting executive authority over information. Beyond that, Ford was pushed by his staff to ignore the more powerful tool he had at hand—the pocket veto. Ford could have removed a political showdown with Congress, and a potential veto override, by using the pocket veto, which Congress could not override. While the chance existed that Congress would take up the FOIA amendment bill again, the pocket veto would have provided more time for Ford to convince Congress to change the language he objected to.

On October 17, Ford issued a veto message to the House, providing his justification for not signing the FOIA amendment bill.[23] He began the message by noting the correspondence with

[23] Message to the House of Representatives from Gerald Ford, October 17 1974.

192

the conference committee and their early efforts to change the language, making it more agreeable, but that the final bill still contained objectionable language. Ford detailed his reasoning on the sections he wanted changed and told Congress he would be submitting to them language that would overcome his concerns. He ended the statement by saying,

> It is only my conviction that the bill as enrolled is unconstitutional and unworkable that would cause me to return the bill without my approval. I sincerely hope that this legislation, which has come so far toward realizing its laudable goals, will be reenacted with the changes I propose and returned to me for signature during this session of Congress.

Cole's option two strategy was on full display in the veto message, as Ford attempted to overcome the negative politics surrounding his veto by appealing to Congress to continue negotiations on language. Ford was hopeful his public appeal was reasonable enough that he could win over public support to help pressure Congress to compromise and rewrite the bill rather than override his veto. Shortly after his veto was issued, and with Congress still in recess, Ford sent letters to congressional leadership, including both Kennedy and Moorhead, which included his proposals to change the bill.[24] Ford implored them to work with him, stating,

> While I realize we have had our differences on this bill, I think they are few compared to the many compromises and the substantial agreements which have been worked out over the past several months. I ask your further help and cooperation so that we may accomplish our common goal of producing viable freedom of information legislation before the close of the 93rd Congress.

Knowing the weakened position he was in, Ford was desperately trying to convince Congress to work with him instead of pursuing an override his veto. The strategy from Ford was sound,

Folder: Freedom of Information Act Amendments, Robert T. Hartmann Files, Box 12, Gerald R. Ford Presidential Library.

[24] Letters to Carl Albert, James O. Eastland, Edward M. Kennedy, William S. Moorhead, October 25, 1974. Folder: Freedom of Information Act Amendments, Robert T. Hartmann Files, Box 12. Gerald R. Ford Presidential Library.

but the politics surrounding the issue had placed Congress in a power position to push back against decades of executive power expansions, and Congress was not in a bargaining mood.

While Ford publicly sought a compromise with Congress, privately administration officials began outreach to individual Republican members of Congress seeking support to sustain the veto. They reached out to Hruska's office asking him to introduce Ford's version of the bill prior to an override vote being held, so that Senate Republicans could argue to move forward on that version with the new language.[25] The main problem with Ford's strategy was that Congress was still recessed for several more weeks, coming back into session on November 18, and no one within the administration knew how quickly Congress would move on override votes once back. While White House officials tried to negotiate time with the Democratic leadership in the hope of brokering a deal in the Senate, they continued their attempts to win over enough Republican senators to sustain the veto.[26] The near insurmountable difficulty of this strategy was driven home in a memo from Lazarus to Timmons explaining that discussions with Kennedy's staff had been unsuccessful and they showed no willingness to compromise on Ford's language.[27] The main political problem Ford faced in his alternative veto override strategy was that it required Democratic support, which was sorely lacking. In fact, congressional leadership was eager to move forward with holding a vote to override, leaving a targeted Senate outreach strategy as the only remaining option for the administration.[28]

[25] Memo to Doug Marvin and J.C. Argetsinger from Patrick O'Donnell, October 29, 1974. Folder: Freedom of Information 10–12/74, Congressional Relations, O'Donnell and Jenckes Files (1971) Box 5. Gerald R. Ford Presidential Library.

[26] Memo to William Timmons, Tom Korologos, and Max Friedersdorf, November 4, 1974. Folder: Freedom of Information 10–12/74, Congressional Relations, O'Donnell and Jenckes Files (1971) Box 5. Gerald R. Ford Presidential Library.

[27] Memo to Phil Areeda and William Timmons, November 11, 1974. Folder: Freedom of Information 10–12/74, Congressional Relations, O'Donnell and Jenckes Files (1971) Box 5. Gerald R. Ford Presidential Library.

[28] Memo to William Timmons from Tom Korologos, November 13, 1974. Folder: Freedom of Information 10–12/74, Congressional Relations,

As Congress neared return, Ford began outreach directly to Senate Republicans and Democrats asking for their help to sustain the veto and pursue a new bill that included the language Ford wanted.[29] While continuing his public appeals, Ford also appealed privately to several members to uphold his veto. On November 19, just after Congress returned from break, Ford was able to persuade a bipartisan group of seven prominent senators, including Hruska and Eastland, to send out a "Dear Colleague" letter to all members of the Senate imploring them to vote to sustain the veto, and to then vote on a new FOIA amendment bill that included the president's language.[30] The letter was a last-minute plea to offer the president a deal. It stated,

> In enlisting your support, we wish to make it clear that a vote in support of the President's veto does not, in any way, reflect a rejection of a commitment to the ideals of the Freedom of Information Act. Indeed, it is our conviction that the citizen should be granted the fullest access to the records of the Federal agencies that the right of privacy and effective government will permit.

The problem was not just in the timing of this effort, but in the language used. While a small bipartisan group of Senators may have been a good start, the reasonable plea they attempted to make sounded similar to the explanations Nixon had offered for his use of executive privilege. The ideas of national security, right of privacy, and effective governance are all ideals, but in this context their language resonated too close to Nixon's at a time when Congress was seeking specifically to keep such Nixonian abuses of power from happening again. The politics of Ford's pardon of Nixon were also a factor for many members of

O'Donnell and Jenckes Files (1971) Box 5. Gerald R. Ford Presidential Library.

[29] Letter to Congressman John J. Rhodes, November 10, 1974. Folder: Freedom of Information Act (1), William E. Timmons Files, Box 4. Gerald R. Ford Presidential Library.

[30] Dear Colleague Letter, November 19, 1974. Folder: Freedom of Information 10–12/74, Congressional Relations, O'Donnell and Jenckes Files (1971) Box 5. Gerald R. Ford Presidential Library. The signatories of the letter were Senators James Eastland, Roman Hruska, John McClellan, Robert Griffin, John Stennis, Bill Brock, and Robert Taft, Jr.

Congress in wanting to send a message to the White House. All of Ford's efforts were to no avail, as on November 20 the House voted 371 to 31 to override Ford's veto, and the Senate followed suit the next day voting 65 to 27. Ford had been defeated; the amendments to FOIA were now law.

Conclusion

The situation that encompassed the Ford administration was much different from the situations of the previous presidents examined here. The issue of executive privilege evolved through a continuous learning process driven by the Cold War Paradigm mindset established under Truman and expanded with Eisenhower. Each president from Truman through Nixon grew and expanded the use of executive privilege and government secrecy, forcing Congress to learn and respond in numerous ways, including by developing policy to target these actions, like FOIA. Due to the excesses of Nixon, the Watergate scandal, and his subsequent resignation, Ford could not take a bold stand on any of these issues, especially at a time when public trust was so shaken and a Democratic Congress was aggressively focused on reform. The past precedent in which Nixon had grounded his assertions and actions was no longer feasible for the president, at least at this moment. Ford sought to offer some type of reasoned balance to debates, but as many of the pieces and people involved in amending FOIA had already been put into place prior to his becoming president, the best he could manage was buying time and trying to veto bargain. Neither strategy proved successful for Ford in the end, as the politics of the moment demanded a response he was not willing to give. At this time, the politics of open government and oversight demanded that Ford move away from strong executive power assertions, but he still chose to veto numerous bills coming from Congress. Ford failed to grasp the changed public demands and the inter-branch power struggle, as exemplified in his foregoing either the pocket veto strategy on FOIA or the strategy of just signing the bill and issuing a statement as his predecessors had done. Either of those strategies would have proved more fruitful than the one he chose, which led to a veto override and a more weakened executive position.

I must note here that FOIA was again amended in September 1976 as part of the Government in Sunshine Act. The amendment was minor, just slightly altering the language of Exemption 3 in order to help prevent agency denials. Unlike the previous amendment as described in this chapter, Ford happily signed the bill and took credit. While minor in scope, the 1976 amendment demonstrates the continuation of the issue within the CLDC as it moves into the contemporary period. Ford was trapped by the politics of reform, which focused heavily on preventing future executive abuses of power. While he did pardon Nixon and fight back against Congress by vetoing sixty-six bills during his brief administration, Ford was forced to acquiesce to Congress and the public on the issues of executive privilege and government secrecy, especially after facing the veto override on the 1974 amendment.[31] The continuous feedback within the CLDC led Ford to downplay presidential power in the name of bringing the country back together following scandal, which influenced his decision making as noted above. Within the confines of this model there was little room to make claims of privilege or power as his predecessors had done. While the Supreme Court validated executive privilege in some circumstances, this period was marked by a reduction in presidential authority vis-à-vis the Congress. The Ford chapter here is more of an epilogue to the story, demarcating a juncture within the CLDC leading to a weakening of executive power that would continue through Carter.

---

[31] "Vetoes by President Gerald R. Ford," from the United States Senate. Available online at <https://www.senate.gov/reference/Legislation/Vetoes/FordG.htm> (last accessed November 10, 2018.)

8

Conclusion: The future of FOIA and executive privilege

The scope and purpose here is to take a deep dive into the legislative development of FOIA in order to understand how a political issue evolves, and how Congress can utilize policy to check executive power. Without the president seeking to keep information private, invoking executive privilege in order to prevent testimony or information from going to Congress, FOIA would never have been passed. Without the Cold War and all the threats that stemmed from it—wars in Korea and Vietnam, the Red Scare and McCarthyism, the Cuban Missile Crisis, and more, the need to control information flows would not have evolved to be so significant to the president. There has always been a need for government secrecy in specific areas, making claims of national security in the public interest a valid assertion for the president. Only when faced with new conditions, new information, and new threats did the policies of the executive branch shift to seek dominance and control over such information flows. This led to the creation of new politics, built around the Cold War, which created an action-reaction institutional power struggle between the president and Congress.

The model developed here provides analysis for how an issue evolves and the continuous political feedback loops that nurture change, based on the introduction of new information, and how that information is then processed and used. A social learning perspective underpins the analysis. Hall provides the ability to understand the learning process as overcoming outdated thinking and past policy failures, leading to new policy shifts that can be measured. Dodd takes us a step further to provide an understanding of how failed political regimes are based on outdated thinking, policy failures combined with changed societal demands that have been left unaddressed for too long, bringing about the ability to learn in creating a new political regime. Building upon this past scholarship, I have sought to push the model further. Social learning is a process built upon past failures, but as it moves forward it builds new systems, which invariably one day also fail and require the establishment of more new systems; thus the cycle moves on. The inability of past policies and politics to address the current needs and situations drives the learning process forward. Using Hall's terminology, the end of World War II and the beginning of the Cold War led to a paradigm shift in thinking, or a Third Order shift. When faced with the new information of threats at home and abroad that the Cold War brought, the president was forced to learn, but past policies and politics were impotent in dealing with the current situation. It was not just the policies that were inept, but the politics and institutional structures as well. The shift in foreign and domestic policy, coupled with the altered societal demands, created a Cold War Paradigm.

However, it is not only past failures that mark the learning process. Going forward, the Cold War Paradigm demonstrates how new thinking and new mindsets are built and put into place. The Cold War Paradigm created a new order of politics that was grounded in the control of information. Truman quickly learned that to face the threats posed by communism and the Soviet Union, actions needed to be taken, such as the Truman Doctrine of containment in foreign policy and loyalty oaths at home. Congress worked with and contributed to the institutionalization of the Cold War Paradigm under Truman, as the politics provided motivation for action against these new threats. In examining the newspaper data from Chapter 1, the public outcry reinforced and supported political action from both the legislative and executive branches. Figure 1.2 illustrates the massive dominance of Cold War issues in the press, driving public attention and thus influencing politics. The new information presented by the Soviet and communist threats fed into the feedback loops within society and politics that drove the rapid and profound change in the political order. The newspaper data provides evidence of changing public interest in the issue of government secrecy and executive privilege, as it grew from little attention in the late 1940s to massive attention during the Nixon administration. The rise in press attention provides support for public attention, as Figure 1.1 illustrates; attention to the issue rose and fell around the political actions being taken by Congress in response to presidential action. These feedback loops reinforced each other, creating the Cold War Paradigm mindset that would dominate the political order for the next forty-five years.

Within this new mindset we can see how individual actors, power entrepreneurs, are able to utilize institutional power to drive the issues forward. Just as the Truman Doctrine ushered in the Cold War Paradigm mindset, FOIA would not exist without the efforts of John Moss, who continued in his quest to push back on executive privilege and develop FOIA. Issue evolution and the politics at any given moment are made and progressed by individual actors like Moss, Ervin, and Moorhead, as well as by the president, the singular figure at the head of government. Without the entrepreneurial efforts of individuals who fight for specific issues, there would be no policy development. Many of these individuals within government set the tone and create the politics of the moment in which they find themselves. They utilize their position, such as a committee or subcommittee chair, and the institutional levers of power that come with it to move policy forward and push back against executive actions. Moss's ability to gain a subcommittee chair with jurisdiction on information gave him the platform from which to launch investigations, hold hearings, and develop policy. Through the entrepreneurial efforts of individual members, issues evolve and policy is made to address the demands of the moment. Entrepreneurs capitalize on partisan controls and institutional power to benefit their goals. These individuals are attuned to politics and demonstrate learned responses to actions, making their responses more effective.

The social learning process is demonstrated by the functionality of the interconnected double feedback loop of information flows between society and politics, as demonstrated throughout the book. Learning is based on the introduction, processing, and usage of new information. When Truman established a new doctrine of Soviet containment to actively fight communism, it demonstrated how the learning process led him to make those decisions. At the same time, it placed Congress into a position to learn from the actions taken by Truman in order to respond, which demonstrates how social learning functions within an action-reaction framework over time. Throughout this book, presidents learned to use executive privilege as justification for denying Congress information or testimony. Eisenhower helped to create the precedent that his successors would utilize, but even he grounded his argument for executive privilege in historical terms going all the way back to the Washington administration. Presidents have now learned to rely on executive privilege as a legitimate justification, especially post-Nixon, as the Supreme Court created the institutional space for its legitimacy. Eisenhower learned to depend on that strategy as it suited his needs, but in so doing, Congress learned to respond to his actions. Congress learned that the best approach was in the creation of the Moss Subcommittee, providing jurisdiction and investigative power over the administration on the issue. This subcommittee was created to respond to executive authority, institutionalizing the issue of government secrecy, executive privilege, and freedom of information within Congress. The institutionalization of the issue created a power struggle between the legislative and executive branches that continues to this day. Therefore the politics surrounding policy development and power issues becomes relevant context to understanding contemporary debates.

The learning process and continuous feedback loops providing information as a tool to seek influence function within an ongoing legislative process that I call the Continuing Legislative Development Cycle (CLDC). Many policy or political issues of the day can rise and fall off the agenda, but there is a continuous political agenda. Presidents normally serve four- to eight-year terms and come into office seeking to implement the agendas on which they campaigned. However, they also find themselves facing a continuing agenda from Congress on a host of issues. Situations can arise that foist an issue to the fore or open one of Kingdon's windows of opportunity, providing the space for an issue whose time has come. The CLDC is an analytical framework to view a single issue as it evolves over time, seeking to understand the junctures that alter the politics surrounding development. FOIA was an issue twenty years before being signed by Johnson and was institutionalized in Congress nearly twelve years prior to its final passage. Across four administrations and many alterations the policy developed into what finally passed, but that is not the end of the story. Policy is then implemented and the CLDC moves into a new phase characterized by oversight, evaluation, and the politics of amendment, which for all intents and purposes is back to the same policymaking politics but within a new and different context. Nixon fought against amending FOIA, but was open to dealing with Congress if they were willing to back away from what he saw as congressional usurpations of executive power. Ford followed suit, directly veto bargaining with Congress, but the politics of that moment left him unpopular and struggling against the weight Nixon left behind, leading Congress to override his veto, establishing the first amendments to FOIA. The CLDC provides a framework to talk about and understand the politics of learning and the interconnected double feedback loop that influence policy development and the politics that surround the policymaking process.

FOIA going forward and contemporary questions

Some issues come and go, while some seem to stay, merely with ebb and flow—meaning there are times that issues become resurgent and times when they wane, but are continuously lurking in the background. Freedom of information has been a part of US politics since the colonial period, when the Constitutional Framers began writing about the need of an informed citizenry for any type of self-government or democracy to work. However, it was not until the post-World War II era that the issue became institutionalized, rising to become a driving agenda issue underlying an inter-branch power struggle over access to information. The issue evolved as presidents made claims of inherent constitutional privilege to keep information from Congress, spurring action to counter denials and access. I have walked you through the history and politics of this period, from Truman through Ford, but FOIA and the dual issues of freedom of information and executive privilege have remained a constant issue ever since.

Using the CLDC model developed here, we can examine the five other times that FOIA has been amended since Ford was in office. Amendments were passed in 1986 under President Reagan as part of the Anti-Drug Abuse Act. It was amended again in 1996 under President Clinton, focusing on electronic and digital records. In 2002, following the attacks on 9/11, FOIA was amended again under President George W. Bush to limit the ability of foreign agents to request information from intelligence agencies. Again under Bush in 2007, FOIA was amended with the OPEN Government Act, seeking to address the administrative difficulties of the FOIA system. As mentioned earlier, in 2016 President Obama signed the last FOIA amendments thus far, seeking to strengthen government responsiveness and digital access to records. The CLDC continues on this issue, and it is clear from the amendment periods that the law was altered when faced with circumstances that demanded attention. It becomes possible now to examine each of these periods to better understand the politics leading to amendment, and that for fifty years, FOIA has been a part of the political agenda. It is not always at the forefront, but FOIA altered the political power balance, offering Congress, the press, and the public the ability to request information and documents. This process has helped establish citizen oversight, and with the legal mechanism, FOIA has given individuals the ability to hold executive branch agencies accountable when it comes to public information. Arguably this perhaps unintended outcome helps promote a healthy democracy, much in the way Ben Franklin envisioned.

Since Nixon, the use of executive privilege by any administration has largely remained routine, or at least holding to the precedent of past use and within the context of the Supreme Court decision. This book began by offering insight into the current Trump administration and the ongoing investigation into Russian interference in the 2016 election and the potential for Nixonian claims of executive power. Special Investigator Mueller has issued multiple indictments of former Trump campaign officials, including a past campaign manager, providing a reasonable argument for potential collusion or criminal intent. At the time of writing, much of this has yet to unfold, but so far, much of the administration and in particular Trump's response to the ongoing investigation and indictments is quite similar to Nixon's response to the Watergate break-in and subsequent cover-up. I am merely speculating at this moment by trying to place current events into an historical perspective whereby Nixon is the closest modern president to Trump, providing some insight as to the potential ramifications for Trump's firing of former FBI Director James Comey and his threatening to fire the special investigator. In the context of my research here, the relevance is stark when we see that Trump is already invoking executive privilege for current or former officials in order to prevent them from answering questions or testifying before Congress. As the investigations continue and unfold, it will be interesting to see not only if Trump will use executive privilege as a tool to deny information, but if he will follow Nixon in expanding the scope of its use to suit his needs in the context of the investigations. The potential already exists for Trump to claim privilege in order to deny a subpoena for testimony, or even to pardon himself. As we saw in this research, Congress or the courts remain the only ones able to properly check executive power, and they may be called upon again to do so.

Bibliography

Archibald, Sam (1993), "The Early Years of the Freedom of Information Act, 1955–1974," *PS: Political Science and Politics* 26(4): 726–31.

Bartels, Larry M. (2008), *Unequal Democracy*, Princeton: Princeton University Press.

Baumgartner, Frank R., and Bryan D. Jones (2009), *Agendas and Instability in American Politics*, Chicago; University of Chicago Press.

Beckmann, Matthew N. (2010), *Pushing the Agenda*, Cambridge: Cambridge University Press.

Berkes, Fikret (2009), "Evolution of Co-Management: Role of Knowledge Generation, Bridging Organizations and Social Learning," *Journal of Environmental Management* 90: 1692–1702.

Binder, Sarah A. (2003), *Stalemate*, Washington, DC: Brookings Institution Press.

Brass, Clinton T., and Wendy Ginsberg (2014), "Congress Evolving in the Face of Complexity: Legislative Efforts to Embed Transparency, Participation, and Representation in Agency Operations," in *The Evolving Congress*, Washington, DC: Congressional Research Service, Library of Congress.

Burke, John P. (2000), *The Institutional Presidency*, Baltimore: The Johns Hopkins University Press.

Carmines, Edward G., and James A. Stimson (1989), *Issue Evolution*, Princeton: Princeton University Press.

Cooper, Joseph, and David W. Brady (1981), "Toward a Diachronic Analysis of Congress," *American Political Science Review* 75(4): 988–1006.

Cross, Harold L. (1953), *The People's Right to Know*, New York: Columbia University Press.

Dodd, Lawrence C. (2012), *Thinking About Congress*, New York: Routledge.

Edwards, George C., III (1990), *At the Margins*, New Haven: Yale University Press.

Fenno, Richard F. (1973), *Congressmen in Committees*, Boston: Little, Brown and Company.

Fiorina, Morris P., and Kenneth A. Shepsle (1989), "Formal Theories of Leadership: Agents, Agenda Setters, and Entrepreneurs," in Bryan D. Jones (ed.), *Leadership and Politics*, Lawrence: University of Kansas Press.

Fisher, Louis (2004), *The Politics of Executive Privilege*, Durham, NC: Carolina Academic Press.

Foerstel, Herbert N. (1999), *Freedom of Information and the Right to Know*, Westport: Greenwood Press.

Fowler, Linda L. (1994), "Political Entrepreneurs, Governing Processes, and Political Change," in Lawrence C. Dodd and Calvin Jillson (eds.), *New Perspectives on American Politics*, Washington, DC: CQ Press.

Hall, Peter A. (1993), "Policy Paradigms, Social Learning, and the State: The Case of Economic Policymaking in Britian," *Comparative Politics* 25(3): 275–96.

Jones, Charles O. (1994), *The Presidency in a Separated System*, Washington, DC: The Brookings Institution.

Kingdon, John W. (1984), *Agendas, Alternatives, and Public Policies*, Boston: Little, Brown and Company.

Kuhn, Thomas S. (1970), *The Structure of Scientific Revolutions*, Chicago: University of Chicago Press.

Lemov, Michael R. (2011), *People's Warrior*, Madison: Fairleigh Dickinson University Press.

Mayhew, David R. (1974), *Congress: The Electoral Connection*, New Haven: Yale University Press.

Mayhew, David R. (2000), *America's Congress*, New Haven: Yale University Press.

Oleszek, Walter J. (1978), *Congressional Procedures and the Policy Process*, Washington, DC: CQ Press.

Orren, Karen, and Stephen Skowronek (2004), *The Search for American Political Development*, Cambridge: Cambridge University Press.

Pierson, Paul (2004), *Politics in Time*, Princeton: Princeton University Press.

Polsby, Nelson W. (1968), "The Institutionalization of the US House of Representatives," *American Political Science Review* 62(1): 144–68.

Polsby, Nelson W. (1984), *Political Innovation in America: The Politics of Policy Initiation*, New Haven: Yale University Press.

Polsby, Nelson W. (2004), *How Congress Evolves: Social Bases of Institutional Change*, Oxford: Oxford University Press.

Bibliography

Rozell, Mark J. (1999), "Executive Privilege and the Modern Presidents: In Nixon's Shadow," *Minnesota Law Review*, 83(5): 1069–126.

Rozell, Mark J. (2010), *Executive Privilege*, Lawrence: University Press of Kansas.

Schickler, Eric (2001), *Disjointed Pluralism*, Princeton: Princeton University Press.

Schickler, Eric (2007), "Entrepreneurial Defenses of Congressional Power," in Stephen Skowronek and Matthew Glassman (eds.), *Formative Acts*, Philadelphia: University of Pennsylvania Press.

Schrecker, Ellen (1994), *The Age of McCarthyism*, Boston: Bedford Books of St. Martin's Press.

Sheingate, Adam (2007), "The Terrain of the Political Entrepreneur," Stephen Skowronek and Matthew Glassman (eds.), *Formative Acts*, Philadelphia: University of Pennsylvania Press.

Storing, Herbert J. (1981), *The Complete Anti-Federalist*, Chicago, University of Chicago Press.

Storing, Herbert J. (1981), *What the Anti-Federalists Were For*, Chicago: University of Chicago Press.

Uslaner, Eric M. (1978), "Policy Entrepreneurs and Amateur Democrats in the House of Representatives: Toward a More Party-Oriented Congress?" in Leroy N. Rieselbach (ed.), *Legislative Reform*, Lexington: Lexington Books.

Wawro, Gregory (2000), *Legislative Entrepreneurship in the House of Representatives*, Ann Arbor: The University of Michigan Press.

Weingast, Barry R. (1979), "A Rational Choice Perspective on Congressional Norms," *American Journal of Political Science* 23(2): 245–62.

Zelizer, Julian E. (2004), *On Capitol Hill*, Cambridge: Cambridge University Press.

Index

Index